MOVING BEYOND DUALITY

ENOUGH FOR US ALL
VOLUME THREE

Dorothy I. Riddle

MOVING BEYOND DUALITY
ENOUGH FOR US ALL
VOLUME THREE

iUniverse books may be ordered through booksellers or by contacting:

iUniverse
1663 Liberty Drive
Bloomington, IN 47403
www.iuniverse.com
1-800-Authors (1-800-288-4677)

ISBN: 978-1-4917-8274-3 (sc)
ISBN: 978-1-4917-8275-0 (e)

Library of Congress Control Number: 2010902808

Print information available on the last page.

iUniverse rev. date: 12/11/2015

Enough for Us All is dedicated to my mother, Katharine (Kittu) Riddle, whose loving energy and inquiring spirit have brought joy to me and to hundreds of others all around the world.

It is from my mother that I first learned the meaning of abundance, as well as the worth and dignity of all beings, and began to see beyond the confines of our planetary life and to question the assumptions that seem to hold us captive.

Contents

Part Two

Recognizing Depersonalization in Action

Part Three

Moving Beyond the Dualistic Model

Preface

The three volumes of the *Enough for Us All* series are designed to help us expand our vision of what is possible. In 1980, the architect and futurist Buckminster Fuller asserted that we do now have the capacity to "take care of everybody at a higher standard of living than any have ever known"; however, that possibility is yet to be realized. Each volume explores both the personal and the societal aspects of shifting from a preoccupation with scarcity to participation in a collaborative process, from living in fear to embracing joy. In each volume, there are many practical exercises to help us apply the concepts in daily life.

This third volume, *Moving Beyond Duality*, focuses on the constraints of assuming outdated Newtonian scientific principles rather than embracing the new principles that flow from quantum physics. It exposes the illusion of duality—have/have not—that underlies our fear of scarcity and attachment to violence, and it helps us recognize opportunities for lasting change.

Those who have read the other two volumes will notice a change in language in this third volume. Previously I had used the term "objectification" to refer generically to what happens when we treat those around us as "other" or "them" However, "objectification" is most commonly used to mean treating others as objects or commodities to be used, and so I am limiting objectification to that subset of attitudes and behaviors in this volume. "Depersonalization" seems more appropriate because it refers to the broader concept of divesting others of their individuality or beingness.

Switching to "depersonalization" has the added advantage of capturing the dynamic underlying a propensity towards violence that applies equally to humans and nonhumans. In the interim since writing *Positive Harmlessness in Practice,* I have been focused on the issues of nonhuman personhood and moral standing, given the increasing scientific evidence of a range of other species as being highly intelligent, social, and self-aware.[1]

Moving Beyond Duality is without a doubt the most challenging, yet most important, book I have written to date. The complexity of the subject is reflected in the five-year hiatus between the first two volumes in the *Enough for Us All* series and this third volume.

You will find that many of the examples given have to do with sexism and misogyny. The World Health Organization has repeatedly declared that violence against women and girls is the number one human rights violation globally, yet there are very few community forums in which this issue is addressed. I believe that misogyny is the archetypical form of depersonalization—that all other social ills take their pattern from this most fundamental abuse of power. The United Nations' resource for speakers on "Ending Violence Against Women and Girls" indicates that up to 70 percent of women worldwide have experienced violence, usually by someone whom they know.[2] I have been preoccupied for years with how to address the "us"/"them" mentality that fuels violence, the dualism or distancing that is essential to justify harming another.

As with the other volumes in the series, *Moving Beyond Duality* draws on the seven principles that are explored in Volume One, *Principles of Abundance for the Cosmic Citizen* (listed below)—four that underlie how our reality operates, and three that govern our existence in the cosmos. Each discussion identifies and explores the limiting beliefs that we have acquired over the centuries. Until we are clear about who we actually are and our intended relationship with the rest of life, we are not in a position to actualize our potential and shift from fear to joy as our basic motivation. Accepting our actual reality, rather than the dualistic Newtonian model so familiar to us, is central to reversing the dualism that allows violence to occur.

Volume Two, *Positive Harmlessness in Practice*, explores what it means to "do no harm" and provides a Harmlessness Scale™ for self-evaluation. In it, we examine the concept of harmlessness and what it would mean for us to live respectfully with each other—i.e., recognizing our connectedness and celebrating our diversity. Harm is so embedded in our everyday lives that we do not yet have a common experience of living harmlessly. Abandoning dualism is fundamental to embracing harmlessness.

Principles That Underlie Our Reality	
Interconnectivity	We are all interconnected energy waves.
Participation	We create our own reality.
Nonlinearity	Our experience is fundamentally nonlinear.
Nonduality	Our reality is complex and non-dualistic.
Principles That Govern How We Coexist	
Interdependence	We are part of an interdependent community of life.
Adaptability	We survive because of our ability to adapt and collaborate.
Cooperation	We evolve through symbiosis and cooperation.

This third volume brings us to the tipping point of choice. Will we recognize that duality is an artificial construct that we impose on reality for the sake of convenience and self-glorification? If our answer is "yes," then we first need to understand why we have so thoroughly accepted our reality as being dualistic. In Part One of this volume, we examine the perceptual and cognitive patterns, including the use of dichotomies, that reinforce dualistic thinking. We then look at the types of distortions that sustain dualistic thinking and our legacies from patriarchy and Newtonian physics. We recognize the challenge posed by dualistic thinking being habitual so that its dynamics and implications operate at an unconscious level.

Part Two provides us with a framework for becoming aware of the different types of depersonalization that permeate our lives, bringing those dynamics into consciousness so that we can make choices about change. In order to explore nuances, Part Two uses a model of five types of depersonalization. For readers who are familiar with the work of philosophers Martha Nussbaum and Val Plumwood, a comparison of categories is presented below. If the philosophical comparisons do not matter to you, pay attention to the listing in the first column only. The specific dynamics of each type of depersonalization are illustrated primarily through analyses of sexism and misogyny, racism, homophobia and heterosexism, ageism, classism and anthropocentrism (the belief that humans are central) in order to help us recognize these dynamics in our everyday lives.

Model Types	Nussbaum[3]	Plumwood[4]
Hostile bigotry	Inertness (lacking agency)	Hyper-separation (radical exclusion)
Benevolent bigotry	Denial of autonomy Violability (no boundary integration)	Incorporation (defined as a lack)
Stereotyping	Fungibility (interchangeable)	Homogenization (stereotyping)
Invisibility	Denial of subjectivity	Backgrounding (not worth noticing)
Objectification	Instrumentality (a tool) Ownership (can be bought & sold)	Instrumentalism (means to an end)

Awareness brings with it responsibility. Part Three turns to how we can move beyond dualistic thinking and depersonalization. It examines strategies such as increasing our cognitive complexity so that we are no longer satisfied with either/or categorization, increasing our empathy so that we acknowledge the connections and commonalities that we share with others, and changing our behavior so that we no longer tolerate the harm to ourselves and others that comes from creating dualities and allowing the consequences of depersonalization to ourselves or others.

I would like to thank all who have helped me in my journey of exploration and questioning. That journey has included the privilege of living and working in over 85 countries, establishing the first degree-granting women's studies program in 1971 at City University of New York, undertaking the initial research on homophobia in the early 1970s, and studying and working over the years with the School for Esoteric Studies. In celebrating the finalization of these volumes, I would like to thank my various *Writer's Digest* instructors, particularly Carolyn Walker who has provided editing commentary and much valued encouragement. I would also like to thank my partner, Valerie Ward, for her continuing and invaluable support for my creative process, as well as Colleen Adair, Gail Gregg Jolley, and Miguel Malagreca for their critical input on this volume, and other friends who have read and commented on earlier volumes.

In the end, *Moving Beyond Duality* is about boundaries and relationships, about recognizing that nothing exists in discrete entities. It is relationship and connectedness that defines us—whether by their absence or their richness. May we learn together that joy is the keynote of our universe and that there is indeed enough for us all.

Part One

The Habit of Duality

ONE

Creating the Illusion of Duality

Must it all be either less or more?
Either plain or grand?
Is it always 'or'?
Is it never 'and'?

– Stephen Sondheim[1]

W hy move beyond duality, or the experience of our reality as a contrast of two parts or sides? Isn't duality a given in our universe? We talk about being right or wrong, being for or against an issue, being in or out of a group. It is easy to divide our lives into two categories. Dualistic thinking is familiar and takes little effort.

Actually, duality is *not* a given. It is a construct, a low-effort conceptual framework we use to make sense of our experience and of our complex universe. It is an assumption that we make, a habit of thinking or perceiving that we have collectively accepted as reality. It feels true because we create two-category distinctions (either/or) so frequently. We forget that *we* are the ones who create the categories. *We* are the ones who choose to limit those categories to two.

Managing Working Memory

Every minute we are bombarded by hundreds of stimuli—sensory input from visual cues, verbal chat, electronic messaging, various sounds, a range of odors, being touched, and so forth. We immediately capture many of these stimuli (known as "pre-attentive processing") before our brain has a chance to filter out what it will pay attention to.[1] It is not physically possible for us to pay attention to all stimuli at once, and besides they are not all equally important to us. So we have a reflexive way of managing this deluge of data so that we don't become overwhelmed.

As humans, we come equipped with two basic storage capacities for stimuli[2]: short-term or "working" memory and long-term memory. While our long-term memory can store an almost infinite amount of information once we place it there, our working memory is similar to the random access memory (RAM) in computers. It has a limited active focus capacity of around five to nine items[3] and a brief time frame of 10-15 seconds in which those items are first available.

We can think of the way we process stimuli as having two automatic sorting points in relation to our working memory: First we ask, "Do we need to process this at all?" We are continuously operating an initial "yes/no" decision-making program—"yes, I will process it" or "no, I will ignore it." If we choose "no," then we ignore it completely and have no memory of it at all (known as "inattentional blindness").[4] For example, if you walk into an unfamiliar room specifically to meet someone and are immediately engaged in conversation with them, you may fail to register details such as pictures on the wall or even other people in the room. In fact, there is recent evidence that being focused on a task that requires a lot of concentration can induce "inattentional blindness"—that is, we are so focused on remembering the task that we literally do not see what is right in front of us.[5]

Choosing "yes" (known as "attentional capture") leads to the second sorting point: "Do we need to pay active, mindful attention?" Again we sort into two categories—what we need to be conscious or mindful of and what can be stored passively as part of a habitual (mindless) response. So while we may remain mindful of certain details, we absorb all the rest of the data "mindlessly" and without critical evaluation. In other words, while we sort or filter data based on what is important to us — what we value — we don't examine the passively-processed data critically because they are not part of our immediate focus. This is important to remember when we examine why attitudes and beliefs become so difficult to change.

The difference in mindless and mindful processing explains, for example, how we can drive home along a familiar route and arrive safely without any conscious memory of the journey. While the data we observed were relevant to the drive ("yes, I will process it"), we were able to award it implicit or mindless attention. It also explains why experienced drivers can carry on an in-depth conversation while driving over familiar routes but need to stop the conversation in order to concentrate when following complex directions to a new destination.

Details do not have to be in our mindful awareness in order for us to be able to recall them later. The careful questioning of a witness often elicits data of which the witness was initially unaware. As early as the 1940s, there were public outcries over advertising with subliminal images below the level of our awareness because of not wanting to be unconsciously influenced — with good reason, as we are less able to resist subliminal messages.

This process of automatic either/or sorting becomes even more important as the amount of data increases. The rise in social media has had a potentially profound effect on how we manage our working memory. Not only has it dramatically increased the data flooding our senses every minute, but it has introduced new patterns of sensory engagement.

Many of us are finding it difficult to ignore social media input, even when we are engaged in an important conversation with a person who matters to us. That buzz or ding goes off signaling that we have a message and—oops—we look away to glance at it. In fact, there is now a growth industry in providing camps or retreats to help us go offline and interact with each other and the world of nature!

We experience "overload" if we try to hold and process too much information in our working memory. When that happens, we become confused, disoriented, overwhelmed, and irritable. It is in our best interest to process incoming data as quickly as possible to avoid overload and free up the "loading dock" of our working memory, so to speak, so quick methods work best.

What are the implications of this initial reflexive data processing? Unless we actively notice and save/store data, it disappears as though it had never existed. So if we notice only misbehaviors in a child, for instance, we will become convinced that the child is "bad" because we will not remember the times the child behaved exceptionally or moderately well. In other words, our choices about what we attend to affect what moves from working memory to long-term storage and so determine the options that we believe exist. We shape our own reality.

Exercise: Noticing

Pick someone you see or work with regularly but are not friends with. The next six times you interact with them notice only what you like about them or what they are doing well. Then check in with yourself—how do you feel about them?

We can see how time- and energy-consuming our processing of data would be if we did not have these two
"yes"/"no" sorting points—Pay attention? Be mindful? Since
we may do these automatic sorting activities thousands of
times a day, we gain a lot of practice in binary choices. It's no
wonder that we come to believe that the world is ultimately
dualistic!

One of the benefits of our initial yes/no sorting programs
is that they allow us to process an enormous amount of
information, but at the cost of overlooking a wide range of
details. Unfortunately, it is the overlooking of those details
that can get us in trouble because our world is not that simple.
If we confuse this cognitive sorting with "reality," we begin to
see the world in two dimensions, or dichotomies, like "for me
or against me."

Filtering Strategies

When we make initial choices in data sorting, we are filtering data based on rules that *we have created* about what de-
serves our attention. Those rules may have been absorbed
from our upbringing or developed through personal experience or adopted along with broader belief systems from
religion, politics, or structured study. No matter what their
origin, they become an integral part of how we act on our
values system.

Filtering rules help us make sense of our experience—
create a storyline for our lives. An important role of filtering
rules is determining what we consider to be "figure," or of
primary importance, and what we allow to fade into background insignificance.

Psychologists talk about two general filtering approaches:
exploration and exploitation, or drilling down.[6] When we
filter from an *exploration* perspective, we include as many
options as possible. This sounds like a benefit—at least we are

moving away from the restriction of only two categories. But the degree of benefit depends on how we select those options. If we are always looking for new data or new stimulation, we will begin to forget how to think deeply about a single concept.

With the increase in personal media technologies, more and more people are becoming what is known as chronic media multitaskers,[7] i.e., persons who routinely consume multiple media simultaneously. For example, they may Facebook while listening to music, respond to email, and text a friend while having the TV on the background. Chronic media multitaskers may perceive themselves as efficient, but research shows that they are more susceptible to becoming distracted by irrelevancies.[8] In fact, they are likely to seek out maximum, continuous stimulation with the consequence that they become less able to be selective and focused in their attention.

A drilling-down strategy, on the other hand, involves delving as deeply as possible into possible ramifications. It is what allows us to identify patterns, make new discoveries, and engage in creative thinking. But if we filter from a drilling-down perspective exclusively, we may focus so intensely in one area that we miss the richness of diverse input. So maintaining a balance between exploration and drilling down is critical.

Why does the type of filtering strategy we use matter? Remember that much of what we store in long-term memory is placed there without critical evaluation. Problems arise when we don't reflect on experience or periodically question the filters we are choosing. Because of the neuroplasticity of the brain—that is, its ability to change over time and adapt to our thoughts, emotions, and behaviors—whatever we do frequently gets engrained. Think of it as walking across an expanse of grass. The first time you do it, your footprints will be hardly noticeable. But after you walk the same way multiple times, a visible path or groove emerges. The same thing happens in our brain. Repetition creates "grooves" that then become our default experience. If we repeatedly adopt an exploration (going wide instead of deep) approach to perceptual filtering, after a while that is all that we do.

Multitasking is actually an illusion. Research shows that, in "multitasking," we don't really think or do two things at precisely the same time. Instead, we flip back and forth among multiple targets of focus very rapidly.[9] While media multitasking often gives us a sense that we are being more productive, in actuality that positive feeling comes from the multitasking itself—from being bathed in alternatives—rather than from actual improved performance.[10]

So while media multitasking can be emotionally rewarding, it can also be increasingly ineffective unless we are careful.[11] Psychologist Charles Nass warned, based on his research, that chronic media multitasking that seeks out rather than ignores irrelevant data can result in reinforcing exploration rather than drilling-down strategies to the extent that working memory develops poor category structures and task switching actually slows.[12] Those who multitask the most actually perform more poorly, underscoring the changes being made in the brain due to an excessive emphasis on exploration filtering. Instrumental music (particularly classical music) doesn't interfere with performance, but other media modalities definitely can. Nass commented in an NPR interview, "We train our brains to a new way of thinking. And then when we try to revert our brains back, our brains are plastic but they're not elastic. They don't just snap back into shape."[13]

In addition to reinforcing exploration filtering over drilling-down filtering, media multitasking has had another unintended consequence—addiction. When 200 students at the University of Maryland were asked to give up all forms of media use for 24 hours and then record their experience on a university blog, the results were surprising.[14] When no longer "plugged in," students reported a range of negative experiences:

> "miserable, anxious,…bored to distraction"
> "disconnected…just lost"
> "no idea how to occupy my time"
> "a deafening silence"
> "something I never want to do again"

Despite the clear symptoms of withdrawal, there were also positive experiences: "Studying was a million times more productive without the media distracting me" and "Classes went better…I took better notes and was more focused." Social media and handhelds are here to stay, so the question becomes how to help people take breaks—go off-line to engage in-person and to analyze and reflect on assumptions about, and the implication of, their experiences.

Media multitasking is not always inefficient. After all, being able to switch rapidly from task to task is critical to our interacting flexibly with our environment.[15] In some instances, being distracted by multitasking can actually improve routine, habit-based performance.[16] Ironically, recent research has shown that people who multitask the least are the best at multitasking precisely because they are more able to focus and screen out irrelevant data.

Categorization and Long-Term Memory

Not only is the storage capacity of our working memory limited, it is *time* limited. So if data are important to us, we need to move those data quickly into long-term memory. To make efficient use of our long-term memory, we store information in folders or categories. It is in creating and using these categories that we can learn to move beyond our initial reflexive dualistic choices.

The ability to make distinctions among stimuli or issues or groups is critical to our functioning. If we could not distinguish among different circumstances, we would always react in the same way and not be able to adapt to change. If, on the other hand, we treated every incident or interaction as unique, we would be unable to identify patterns and learn from experience. So we learn to group or categorize things very early in life. And this ability can serve us well when used appropriately.

Being able to distinguish and categorize our experience is important both in handling overload and deciding how we will act. As the psychologist Gordon Allport wrote in *The Nature of Prejudice*:

> The human mind must think with the aid of categories....Once formed, categories are the basis for normal prejudgment. We cannot possibly avoid this process. Orderly living depends on it.[17]

When we help young infants learn language, one of the first concepts that we teach is categorization.[18] We name objects and, in doing so, we introduce the infant to groupings. We pick up a red ball and say "ball." Then we pick up a blue ball and say "ball." So the infant learns that various round-shaped objects are balls, regardless of their color or size. Or, when we pick up the red ball, we say "red." Then we pick up a red block and say "red." And the infant begins learning that "red" refers to hue, not shape.

In essence, what we learn is to use implicit categories known as schemas,[19] "which are templates of knowledge that help us organize specific examples into broader categories. When we see, for example, something with a flat seat, a back, and some legs, we recognize it as a 'chair'....Without spending a lot of mental energy, we simply sit."[20] When we create schemas to categorize people by age or gender or ethnicity, we call those schemas *stereotypes.*

The details of our data categories or schemas depend on what is important in our lives — our values hierarchy. Let's explore an example to see how our mental filing system works. Take, for example, an accountant who plays violin in an informal quartet group as compared with a violin teacher who plays professionally in an orchestra and keeps her own accounts. The main categories for each one might look like this:

Accountant	Violinist
Accounting clients	Accounting
Accounting license	Insurance
Insurance	Music competitions
Referral sources	Orchestra
Tax law updates	Sheet music
Telecommunications	Students
Travel	Telecommunications
Violin quartet	Travel

The number of possible categories can become overwhelming so we create overarching categories. In the example above, the accountant might choose in essence "accounting" and "non-accounting" as the primary overarching categories while the violinist might choose "music" and "non-music." Then their file categories might change.

While the overarching categories might work well from a filing system perspective, there is a potential problem. When we place data in a particular category, we underscore the importance of the similarities to other data in the category and the unique differences begin to fade. For example, the accountant might have many kinds of clients — e.g., individual, corporate, nonprofit, estates, etc. — and differences in how to approach each type could get overlooked when they are all lumped together as "clients."

Accountant	Violinist
Accounting	Music
- Clients	- Music competitions
- License	- Orchestra
- Referral sources	- Sheet music
- Tax law updates	- Students
Insurance	Accounting
Music/Quartet	Insurance
Telecommunications	Telecommunications
Travel	Travel

Often when we talk about gaining a new perspective, what we are really describing is that our relevant categories have changed. Indeed it is important to remember that our long-term memory is not static and unchanging. In reality we continually reassess and reorganize what we remember, often while we sleep.[21]

Dichotomous Categories

When we create or choose a schema with only two categories, it is known as a dichotomy. A true dichotomy is composed of two categories that are *mutually exclusive* (no overlap) and *collectively exhaustive* (no options left out). The basic description of a true dichotomy in philosophical terms is "A" (or the *indication*) and "not A" (or the *complement*):

Indication ("A")	Complement ("not A")

The "indication" can be specific (e.g., blue) or more general (e.g., human). The complements would then be "not blue" and "not human." We might select a particular concept like "good" as an indication with a complement of "not good" or a characteristic like "black" with a complement of "not black."

In a dichotomy, the indication defines the issue or the basis for categorization. The complement is then defined *by* the indication or in relation to it—i.e., by the absence of "A" characteristics. For example, we could have an argument with a friend about whether or not to drive to the park together. So "drive to the park together" becomes the indication. The complement would include all other options—e.g., walking, taking the bus, driving separately, getting a ride from someone else, not going to the park at all. We might usefully reframe this dichotomy into "go to the park" (indication) or "don't go to the park" (complement). If we choose "don't go," the issue of driving becomes moot. Reframing options by changing the indication is at the heart of successful negotiating techniques, as first articulated by Fisher and Ury in *Getting to Yes*.[22]

While using dichotomies seems very sensible and straightforward, in reality they can create problems for us. We will explore some of these problems in the next chapter, but for now we can examine one illustration.

What happens if the categories of the accountant are transformed into a dichotomy as seen below? While the Accounting ("indication") category is coherent and makes sense, the Non-Accounting ("complement") category is a hodge-podge of unrelated characteristics whose only commonality is that they are not accounting.

Accountant	
Accounting	**Non-Accounting**
- Clients	- Insurance
- License	- Music/Quartet
- Referral sources	- Telecommunications
- Tax law updates	- Travel

Continuously creating two-option dichotomies, rather than seeing a range of options, reinforces our sense that the world is dualistic. Again, we tend to forget that we are the ones who have created the dichotomy in order to help us make sense of our experience.

In actuality, there are no given or absolute dichotomies — our world is more complex than that. You might respond that of course there are absolute dichotomies — what about gender? Either someone is male or female. Well, actually that is not the case. There has been increasing publicity focused on transgender or transsexual persons who feel as though they were "born into the wrong body" — that is, their internal sense of gendered self does not match their genital anatomy. They face a range of biases and barriers if they cross-dress or seek hormonal or surgical assistance to bring their internal and external selves into alignment.

Even more challenging to an assumption of clear-cut gender dichotomy are persons, known as intersex or androgynous, whose genital attributes are ambiguous at birth (approximately 1 in 1,000 people).[23] At its inaugural meeting in 2011, the International Intersex Forum articulated the core issue facing intersex persons because of social attachment to viewing the world in a dichotomous manner:

> Around the world intersex individuals are being subjected to inhumane and degrading altering surgical and hormonal procedures, without consent of the intersex person, at the discretion of doctors and outside legal regulation. This is done to "normalize" genitals and bodies in order to fit intersex people within the sex binary of men and women. Pathologization of intersex individuals results in gross human rights violations and abuse of bodily integrity and personal dignity.

The Third International Intersex Forum issued a public statement of rights and demands in December 2013 in order to ensure that intersex persons are accorded the dignity and respect promised in the United Nations Universal Declaration of Human Rights.[24] The issues raised in this public statement are an excellent alert to us all of the dangers of imposing dichotomies on the human experience.

From Stimuli to Perception

When we talk about what we will do with the stimuli that bombard us, we need to consider not only the choices we make about how we categorize that input, but also how we manipulate or process it. What ends up in our memory is not the precise equivalent of what we actually experience. For example, when we look at a "blue table" the sensory input is comprised of light waves of the vibrational frequency that we label "blue" and an awareness of a flat surface held up by vertical pieces. In other words, we create meaning through the process of perception.

It is precisely in this meaning-making process that we generate or reinforce a belief in dualism. We do not approach meaning making as a "blank slate" devoid of hypotheses. Instead, we impose a series of expectations based on our motivations, or past experiences, or emotional states. In large part the process of meaning making takes place outside of our awareness, using the schemas that we have created. If we are to move past a dualistic model of experience, we will need to become aware of the assumptions and choices we are making.

One of the factors that influences the meaning we create is known as "priming" — that is, once we are exposed to a concept or idea, we are more likely to use that concept to interpret what follows. This dynamic explains the dangers of gossip. Once a doubt is placed in our minds, it will color our experience.

For our discussion, priming plays an important role in reinforcing the assumptions that underlie stereotypes.[25] Once we have a belief about a certain category of people, we are predisposed to interpret subsequent behavior in terms of that belief — either confirmation or exception. For example, if someone believes you to be biased, then everything you do gets interpreted by them in that context. We have all had the experience of being caught in this kind of misperception.

Exercise: Priming

Try two experiments over the next 24 hours:

1. Notice a positive comment that someone makes to you (e.g., "you'll like this book") and then how the prediction affected your experience.

2. Notice a negative comment made to you by someone else (e.g., "she doesn't know what she's talking about") and then how the comment affected how you thought about the person mentioned.

If the comments influenced you, you've experienced "priming."

There is also a set of principles that our perceptual system uses to make sense of ambiguous data. These principles operate in our interpersonal relationships as well. Table 1 provides examples of some of these principles and how they affect our attachment to dualistic thinking.

Our interpretation of stimuli is also affected by emotional biases. We are usually more willing to give credence to data that has a positive emotional effect and less willing to accept facts that are unpleasant. So we may seek out data that confirms a negative bias about another group, while ignoring positive data.

Table 1: Examples of perceptual principles and their effects

Perceptual constancy	We identify someone correctly whether they are facing us or turned to one side or have their back to us
	Even if a person's behavior improves, we still assume they will perform poorly
Proximity	We consider people who are physically close together as a homogeneous or uniform group
	We generalize about those in the group
Similarity	We assume that people who are similar on one attitude are similar on other attitudes
	We view our in-group as more homogeneous or uniform than it is
Contrast	We perceive a person differently if the context if different
	We may dissociate ourselves from those in different economic circumstances

In situations of uncertainty, the emotion most likely to skew our perceptions is fear, particularly fear of the unknown. "The study of risk perception reveals that our responses to risk are not simply internal 'rational' risk analyses, but also intuitive 'affective' responses that apply our emotions, values and instincts as we try to judge danger."[26]

The Consequences of Dualistic Thinking

Dichotomies, by their nature, are constructs or ideas that we create. They are not absolutes of nature. Engaging in dualistic thinking is a choice that we make, consciously or unconsciously. It is like putting on a pair of sunglasses to dim the glare. Those sunglasses may change our experience of the light around us, but they don't change the actual strength of the sunlight. In the same way, we use dichotomies to organize our experience, but declaring that there are only two options doesn't change reality.

When we jump from creating and using dichotomies to help us make sense of our experience to assuming that those dichotomies represent reality, we lock ourselves into an assumption of a dualistic universe. We confuse the process we choose with external reality, overlooking the fact that, by shifting our perspective or assumptions, we can create a different sense of reality.

Once we have adopted the habit of thinking in dichotomies and overlooking the richness of multiple alternatives, it becomes reflexive to apply that approach to interpersonal relations. We begin to assume a "not-us" that becomes "them" or "the Other." Not only is such a separation a distortion of our reality, but it can have tragic consequences as is illustrated in the poem "First They Came" by Pastor Martin Niemöller regarding the apathy of German intellectuals during the Second World War:

> First they came for the communists,
> and I didn't speak out because I wasn't a communist.
>
> Then they came for the trade unionists,
> and I didn't speak out because I wasn't a trade unionist.
>
> Then they came for the Jews,
> and I didn't speak out because I wasn't a Jew.
>
> Then they came for me
> and there was no one left to speak out for me.

TWO

Perpetuating the Illusion of Duality

We continually frame our experience dualistically, even though our daily life bears witness to a much more nuanced and complex existence. And even though quantum physicists and molecular biologists and social psychologists have been trying to tell us otherwise.

The illusion of duality has to be nurtured and reinforced if it is to flourish—and that is precisely what we do! We exercise selective attention initially so that we purposely don't notice contradictory evidence. Then we rapidly accumulate a large body of unexamined attitudes because so much of what we experience is filed away in long-term memory without evaluation. Once filed, we have a range of ways that we distort information as it is being consolidated in long-term memory or recalled back into short-term memory. Our reflexive emotional judgments underscore the "rightness" of dichotomies. And we have a range of hierarchical social practices that underpin structural duality. No wonder we continue to believe that our reality is dualistic!

Our Common Distortions

We spend much of our mental and emotional energy ensuring that differences between individuals and groups are more memorable than the similarities. Test this for yourself. Pick two people you know and describe them, as if to a friend who doesn't know them. How many of the descriptors are similarities that they have and how many are differences?

Description by contrast—Janet's tall and thin, while Sushila's plumper—is like second nature to us. It is parallel to how we define the "complement" in a dichotomy—i.e., what the "indication" isn't. And it is what fuels in-group/out-group distinctions.

If we actually examine our cherished dualities, we will quickly discover that they reflect an abbreviated view of reality. To provide some perspective on issues in which we are often strongly vested, the following section continues to use the language of dichotomies to help us recognize the underlying distortions.

Remember that a *true* dichotomy contains an "indication" (which defines the issue) and a "complement" (which includes everything that is not the indication and is defined by *not* having the characteristics of the indication), and that neither the indication nor the complement is considered more important than the other. Appropriate indications and complements are mutually exclusive (no overlap), collectively exhaustive (include all possible options), and both are of equal value instead of one being more important than the other.

We can create false dichotomies in several ways: framing the complement so that it overlaps the indication, overlooking options that don't fit neatly into the complement, or manipulating the relationship between the indication and the complement so that they are not valued equally. We may create a false dichotomy intentionally ("do you agree or disagree?") or accidentally through the omission of other options ("do you want halibut or chicken?"). In the first instance, the false dichotomy purposely excludes the possibility that we might have no opinion or we might both agree and disagree or we might want to reframe the issue. In the second instance, there is a presupposition that we want to eat something (which might not be true) and that we are interested in a main dish rather than just salad or just dessert. In both examples, the dichotomy is false because it is not "collectively exhaustive."

There are at least five ways in which we use false dichotomies to rationalize a dualistic reality:[1]

Neglecting the middle. In this approach, we substitute *opposites* for *complements*. We choose two options that represent extremes, thereby forcing a false choice. For example, we may say, "If you are not with me (or us), you are against me (or us)." We ignore options like feeling neutral on the issue or feeling disengaged from the debate. We refer to this distortion as polarized or either/or thinking.

In this type of dichotomy where the "middle" of the continuum, or sequence, is ignored (or "undistributed"), what we have done is to choose two options that are not *collectively exhaustive.* In other words, we overlook the continuum that connects them. An example of a commonly voiced duality that actually represents the extreme ends of a continuum is "night and day." What we ignore is the transition from full light through dusk to full night, and then through dawn to full day.

day	dusk/dawn	night

In interpersonal relationships, neglecting the middle or focusing on extremes is known as "splitting" or all-or-nothing thinking. Here we talk about someone's behavior as being "good" (i.e., personifying virtue) or "bad" (i.e., personifying evil) when most of the time our behavior is not at either extreme. Each of us misbehaves at times, and each of us behaves with redeeming qualities.

One of the political issues in which "splitting" plays a leading role is the debate around abortion. The two extreme positions have become labeled "pro-life" and "pro-choice."

Regardless of one's political or religious views, it is important to recognize that naming these two positions as the only ones is an over-simplification of a complex issue. That over-simplification is achieved by ignoring the middle positions that include condoning abortion only in cases of rape or incest, condoning abortion only up to a certain time in the pregnancy term, and so on.

This type of false dichotomy has become popular in political rhetoric as a way to label anyone who questions a particular course of action as being unpatriotic. We can recognize neglecting-the-middle dichotomies by the use of "or" — the forced decision.

Probably the most strongly held belief based on this type of false dichotomy is the definition of gender as being either male or female, which we discussed in the previous chapter. Yet "complete maleness and complete femaleness represent the extreme ends of a spectrum of possible body types."[2]

Dismissing the context. An important variation on the neglected middle is an assumption that the extremes exist in a vacuum — i.e., that there is no contextual influence. Ursula LeGuin's 1969 novel, *The Lefthand of Darkness*, highlighted this error by describing a hermaphroditic society in which gender expressed as male or female depending on the social context. As one became emotionally drawn to an individual who was expressing as female, one's genitalia temporarily transformed into male genitalia. We find ourselves being viewed differently depending on the comparison point — in some groups our views may seem very liberal, while in other groups we may sound quite conservative.

Some of the ethical issues that are posed as dualities — for example, right/wrong or good/evil — represent this type of distortion. In each instance what is missing is the context. While we might frame an issue as right or wrong, we might also recognize that there may be extenuating circumstances—for example, it is wrong to kill another person and yet it is justified in self-defense or times of war. In the Ageless Wisdom, evil is sometimes defined not as an absolute but as "adherence to that which we should have outgrown, the grasping of that which we should have left behind."[3]

Time frame is a particularly important context that is often omitted, and the forced choice of "true" or "false" provides a good example. A true dichotomy would be "always-true"/"not-always-true." Then the not-always-true category could contain options like "not applicable right now" or "some of the time" or "that used to be true but not anymore."

Ignoring interconnections. The posing of two opposites as independent of each other when in fact they interact with each other is another false dichotomy. What is produced in that interaction is as important, or sometimes more important, than the two opposites. An example of ignored interaction is the distinction some make between mind and body as separate entities. Not only is the mind energetically part of the body, but psychosomatic medicine has made it clear that our bodies change based on what we are thinking. As the psychologist William James observed, "The greatest revolution of our generation is the discovery that human beings, by changing the inner attitudes of their minds, can change the outer aspects of their lives." Similarly, the state of our physical body affects the clarity with which we think. So we see a third component—the field of interaction between mind and body.

If we take an example from biology, we may have been taught that the nucleus of the cell is the vital component. But the cell biologist Bruce Lipton has shown that it is the membrane, not the nucleus, that is the "brain" of a cell.[4] In other words, it is the portion of the organism that mediates interaction with the external environment that is critical to our survival. We become aware of what is happening around us via the Integral Membrane Proteins (IMPs) and then respond.[5]

All living creatures are interconnected rather than existing in isolation, and we create problems when we overlook those interconnections. Examples include our introduction of nonnative plant species that then crowd out other needed vegetation—as has happened with the introduction in North America of kudzu to contain soil erosion—or our destruction of primary carnivorous predators (like wolves), opening the way for an explosion in the omnivorous "mesopredator" population (like coyotes) that create many more problems.

Oversimplifying the complement. Another way that we create false dichotomies is by assuming that the complement is more homogenous or uniform than it actually is. Let's go back to a true dichotomy for a moment and look at the complement:

While the "black" category may seem clear to us, the "not-black" category is a real hodgepodge. It contains at least 255 colors, all with the defining characteristic of not being black. So the complement is actually much more diverse than the standard "black" category—just as we saw in the last chapter in the example of the accountant.

What is interesting is that we don't think that way when it comes to people in groups. Research shows that we assume that the defining group--"us"—is quite diverse, and we assume that the "them" group is quite homogeneous. This makes it easy for us to develop stereotypic beliefs: "All Blacks have rhythm" or "All Asians are good at math" or "All women are emotional."

Glorifying the indication. Possibly the most socially danger-ous type of distortion is to make the indication superior in value to the complement so that there are no longer two equivalent options. Not only is the complement defined by being what the indication is *not*, but it is also framed as being less valuable, less important, less mature. Various forms of prejudice represent this type of false dichotomy. We may assume, for example, that traits associated with male — of being rational, logical, physically strong — are desirable, and then devalue nurturing or emotional traits typically associated with female. This type of distortion is fundamental to the process of stereotyping.

Many social activist movements have emerged based around explicitly valuing the complement in order to level the playing field, so to speak. And so we have slogans such as "Black is beautiful" or "Sisterhood is powerful" or "We're here. We're queer. Get used to it."

Exercise: Identifying False Dichotomies

Select two of the five types of false dichotomies and identify an example for each from your own life:

1.

2.

How could you reframe each one so that it is no longer a false dichotomy?

Emotions Mediate Dualistic Habits

In the previous chapter, we focused on how we think and how we process sensory data. Research shows that, in certain situations, we actually make judgments faster and with greater confidence based on our feelings than based on a mental assessment.[6] In fact, there is growing evidence that decisions based on thought and decisions based on emotions come from two separate and partially independent internal systems.[7]

"Emotional energy works at a faster speed than the speed of thought. This is because the feeling world operates at a higher speed than the mind. Scientists have repeatedly confirmed that our emotional reactions show up in brain activity before we even have time to think. We evaluate everything emotionally *as* we perceive it. We think about it *afterward*."[8]

What does this mean in practical terms? It means that our first response is a reflexive, chemically based emotion, which colors what that response will be and how long we will remember it. Research also shows that there is an interactive relationship between emotion and reason, rather than those processes being separate and distinct.[9] How we feel influences our decisions, and our decisions in turn influence how we feel.

Psychologist Elizabeth Phelps has demonstrated that we are more likely to remember details related to time and place than interpersonal details.[10] Within one year of an event, 50 percent of the details that we recall will have changed. How we felt at the time gets modified each time we recall the memory based on how we feel in the present.

To be retained, memories need to be replayed and consolidated; otherwise, they fade away. One way that we replay them is by telling others about the event. However, that process of telling changes the memory from a visual one to a verbal one, and the words we choose can affect the memory itself. For example, if we say "I was shocked to find out..." we will have a different recall than if we say simply "I was interested to find out..."

The science of psychoneuroimmunology (the interaction between psychological and immune system processes), which has developed from the work of molecular biologist Candace Pert, is underscoring the critical role played by the hormones that circulate through our bodies and share information that affects all of our bodily systems.[11] Her research shows that only two percent of communications in the body occurs electrically, with the rest being mediated by hormones throughout the body. Many of our memories are stored throughout the body, not just in the brain.

Recent neuropsychological research suggests that we are primitively hardwired to react negatively to those who are different or unfamiliar, and we can identify such differences in milliseconds.[12] Using fMRI technology the social psychologist Susan Fiske and her team have shown that the portion of the brain associated with a feeling of disgust (the insula) will light up in research subjects when shown pictures of people who appear homeless, while the portions of the brain associated with thinking about other people or ourselves showed no activity.[13]

Amplifying Dualistic Habits

There are other practices that we assume are "natural" that serve to reinforce dualistic thinking and amplify its negative consequences. Below are four of the most common:

Simplification. All else being equal, we look for the simplest solution. This practice is related to a principle known as Ockham's Razor, which states that among competing hypotheses the explanation that requires the fewest assumptions should be adopted. So when our brain processes new data, it chooses the pattern that provides the briefest representation of those data.[14]

We need to remember that our long-term memory is not like a physical filing cabinet or even the hard drive of a computer. When data arrive in long-term memory, they are broken down into their component parts, which may then be stored in different parts of the body. One of the reasons why sleep is important is that, during sleep, our brain spends time consolidating memories—combining certain sets of data, modifying older data to conform to new data sets, and generally putting our mental house in order.[15]

One of the goals of our cognitive system is compressing data—i.e., coding it so that it can be easily recovered when we want to remember it and deleting what appear to be redundancies.[16] Now reflect on the fact that much of what has gone into long-term memory did so implicitly, without evaluation. So we take in data that may appear to support duality, then we impose a compression pattern that simplifies the data set by removing redundancy, and finally we eliminate nonconforming bits that could contradict our present beliefs and attitudes. Is it any wonder that we are over one hundred years from when quantum physicists first started telling us that the world was not dualistic and still we have not internalized that information?

Fear of the unknown. Concern about the future and even phobias about the unknown are common dynamics that can reinforce a dualistic division of "safe" and "not safe" or "similar" and "not similar." Repeatedly research has shown that we have an initial fear of those not like us, however we define "like."[17] The most common form that this fear takes is xenophobia, or an intense dislike of those from other countries, with a resulting vigilance when around those who appear different. So we see the benefit of expanding our circle of inclusion—actively looking for commonalities with others.

Vigilance does not have to be fear-based. Research has shown that infants raised in a bilingual environment develop a perceptual vigilance for language variations—that is, an almost-continuous alertness to different language sounds. This stems from an early ability to distinguish different language sounds, which is fully present by the age of four months but disappears by eight months if the capability is not utilized.[18]

Bias-free language. We may think of language as what we use to express concepts and ideas. But in addition the language we use shapes our thoughts. For example, before the use of "Ms." became common practice, females were labelled as "Miss" (not married) or "Mrs. (married), underscoring marital status as a critical factor in all settings. Early research by Benjamin Lee Whorf and Edward Sapir, which was formalized as the Sapir-Whorf hypothesis, demonstrated that the language we use shapes how we view the world.[19]

In the 1970s and 1980s extensive research was conducted on the impact of sexist language since English is a "gendered" language. It is not possible to use English, unmodified, without having to express gender unless one speaks about others always in the plural ("we," "our") or the impersonal ("one," "one's"). As a result of that body of work, both the American Psychological Association and the American Philosophical Association have issued guidelines on bias-free language in scholarly publications.

Despite evidence that sexist and racist language has negative psychological effects, the use of gendered language continues—particularly the use of "girl" to refer to mature women. We also continue to use "generic" terms that imply a distinction, as when we use "man" to mean "everyone" while the underlying dichotomy of "man" and "woman" still exists. To test this, you can try using "woman" and "she" to mean "everyone" and see what reaction you get.

In 1986 Douglas Hofstadter, a philosopher, wrote a satire intended to highlight why language matters. He used the analogy of race to underscore his points. Here is an excerpt:

Most of the clamor, as you certainly know by now, revolves around the age-old usage of the noun "white" and words built from it, such as *chairwhite, mailwhite, repairwhite, clergywhite, middlewhite, Frenchwhite, forewhite, whitepower, whiteslaughter, oneupuwhiteship, straw white, whitehandle,* and so on. The negrists claim that using the word "white," either on its own or as a component, to talk about *all* the members of the human species is somehow degrading to blacks and reinforces racism. Therefore the libbers propose that we substitute "person" everywhere where "white" now occurs. Sensitive speakers of our secretary tongue of course find this preposterous. There is great beauty to a phrase such as "All whites are created equal."…

There is nothing denigrating to black people in being subsumed under the rubric "white" — no more than under the rubric "person." After all, white is a mixture of all the colors of the rainbow, including black. Used inclusively, the word "white" has no connotations whatsoever of race. Yet many people are hung up on this point.…

Nrs. Delilah Buford has urged that we drop the useful distinction between "Niss" and "Nrs."… Bler's argument is that there is no need for the public to know whether a black is employed or not. *Need* is, of course, not the point. Ble conveniently sidesteps the fact that there is a *tradition* in our society of calling unemployed blacks "Niss" and employed blacks "Nrs." Most blacks — in fact, the vast majority — prefer it that way. They *want* the world to know what their employment status is.…

The parallels of the above with current gendered language are obvious and hopefully revealing, and Appendix A provides an overview of the research on the negative effects of gendered language. There are other contextual issues involved in removing bias from language, but recognizing that terminology itself matters would be a great start.

Exercise: Correcting Sexist Language

Over the next three days, identify three instances when you read, heard, or used sexist language and write down a gender-neutral alternative:

1.

2.

3.

Once you have identified the alternatives, say them out loud and reflect on your experience. How did it feel to make these changes to more inclusive language?

Deifying competition. We hold a belief that competition and domination are the natural order, overlooking massive amounts of evidence that our universe has not evolved primarily through competition but rather through cooperation. As biologist Lynn Margulis has pointed out, "Life did not take over the globe by combat, but by networking."[20] and then later, "Competition in which the strong wins has been given a good deal more press than cooperation. But certain superficially weak organisms have survived in the long run by being part of collectives, while the so-called strong ones, never learning the trick of cooperation, have been dumped onto the scrap heap of evolutionary extinction....If symbiosis is as prevalent and important in the history of life as it seems to be, we must rethink biology from the beginning."[21]

It is our commitment to competition as the benchmark for a dynamic society that helps to hold structural depersonalization—divesting others of individuality—in place. However, we have only to look at the early experiences of our own human species to see that we are not originally "wired" for competition. Research has shown that 18-month-old babies will notice the preferences of those around them and then try to meet that desire rather than their own.[22] And infants as young as six months show a marked preference for adults who help others rather than those who remain neutral or actively hinder.[23]

Sustaining Structural Duality

We have seen that an assumption of duality influences how we categorize and evaluate our experience and how we relate to others. It is important also to look beyond the personal dynamic to the social structures and rules that hold duality and its consequences in place. While it sounds nice to say, "Everyone's the same to me" or "I don't make any distinctions" or "Race [religion, sexual orientation, gender] doesn't matter," our reality is that difference *does* matter. If we refuse to see that, we will be unable to make choices for sustainable change.

Hate crimes, which we will explore in more detail in Chapter Four, are frequently based on differentiating between individuals or groups based on physical characteristics or ideological doctrine. For example, even when the bias is implicit rather than explicit, research shows that racial discrimination occurs despite there being a financial cost for the discriminator.[24]

While all of the world's major religions espouse some form of the Golden Rule ("treat others as you would wish to be treated"), religious differences have been a major motivation for many of the world's wars. Singer/songwriter Holly Near gives voice to this dynamic in "I Ain't Afraid" when she sings:

> I ain't afraid of your Yahweh.
> I ain't afraid of your Allah.
> I ain't afraid of your Jesus.
> I'm afraid of what you do in the name of your God.

By far the most damaging and far-reaching of the social structures that underpins the illusion of duality, though, is that of patriarchy. This structure is the system in which males hold primary power and dominate in roles of political leadership, moral authority, social privilege and control of property. In the domain of the family, fathers or father-figures hold authority over women and children. We see, as a consequence, young males having authority over their mother's behavior and women losing the ability to determine the use of their financial resources (if any), their educational pursuits, or even their bodies.

It is this engrained belief that men should be deferred to by women that has led to a wide range of inequities. After fifty years of focus in North America on "equal pay for equal work" the gap in wages between women and men with the same qualifications performing equal work is unfortunately alive and well.[25] It is true that in the U.S. a woman now earns 79 percent of what a man earns, as compared with 59 percent in 1974, but that gap is still significant and tends to increase over a woman's work life. Pay is just one of the many arenas in which we see gender-based power differences, but it is a straightforward inequity that we can keep in mind as we reflect on the dynamics of patriarchy.

Anthropologists, sociologists, and historians have documented for us that a shift occurred across most cultures in prehistory, moving from matrilocal societies (where married couples remain near the wife's parents), in which women were respected and cooperation and collaboration were the norm, to patriarchal societies in which women and their fertility were controlled by men and domination became accepted as the way of life.[26] This shift took place in both religious and secular contexts as the role of the male in reproduction became clear and men sought to ensure their own biological offspring.

Notice the use of the term "matrilocal." Evidence from archeological excavations shows that civilizations that preceded patriarchy were not societies in which women, rather than men, were dominant. Rather those societies had a completely different and more egalitarian structure, which has been called the "partnership model".[27] Diversity was not equated with domination and submission as is the case in patriarchy.

As reverence for the male grew — fueled by male philosophers and male religious institutions — an odd contradiction began to emerge. The feminine continued to be revered in a spiritual context (Virgin Mary, female goddesses) but the human women were viewed increasingly as childlike chattel, wombs to be safeguarded. While men enjoyed sexual freedom, women were to preserve their monogamous virtue through practices like being locked into chastity belts or, in modern times, having their labia sewn shut (as part of female genital mutilation). In China, we can trace parallel practices to control women through foot binding to current female infanticide.

In present times, we can identify a range of blatantly patriarchal societies around the world, each with the theme of male domination and institutionalized, socially acceptable violence. At the extremes we see rape used as a weapon of war in the Democratic Republic of the Congo with sons forced to publicly rape their mothers and fathers their daughters, ISIL/ISIS abducting and raping women in order to enlarge their nation, young girls being murdered by the Taliban for going to school, and over 300,000 American girls being sex trafficked in the U.S. each year in a rapidly growing industry (an illustration that this is not just a problem in developing economies).

We may believe that we have moved past this violent patriarchal heritage, but the daily news says otherwise. Practices such as honor killings of rape victims (not the perpetrators) by male family members, the throwing of acid in the faces of females not cooperating with forced sex, and the selling of girls as young as eight by their fathers to older men in marriage continue today.

In Chapter Four, we will explore the misogyny — the intense hatred of women — that underpins patriarchy. Then, in Chapter Five, we will examine patriarchy's covert enshrining of male superiority and its companion dynamic, domination or feeling good at the expense of another, as benevolent bigotry. Any form of depersonalization, of "us" and "them," is problematic and ultimately unacceptable. But the fundamental essence of the domination that flows from depersonalization is most clear in patriarchy. The author Ursula LeGuin described the dynamic succinctly when she wrote about the duality of patriarchy as represented by "civilized man":

> Civilized Man says: "I am Self, I am Master, all the rest is other — outside, below, underneath, subservient. I own, I use, I explore, I exploit, I control. What I do is what matters. What I want is what matter is for. I am that I am, and the rest is women and wilderness, to be used as I see fit."[28]

Is this the model that we wish to perpetuate? Are we not ready to unmask the illusion?

THREE

Avoiding Disconfirmation of Duality

We are stubborn! Once we have a worldview that feels accurate and manageable, we avoid disconfirming evidence whenever possible — which is not as hard as it might seem. We may unwittingly picture the brain as a group of computer-like processing centers (vision, hearing, language, and so forth), but in fact it is a sophisticated, self-modifying organ. It adapts itself in use-dependent ways — learning from practice and experience, consolidating data to modify memories, discarding input that doesn't fit with our original assumptions, and creating shortcuts for common actions.[1]

The rise of neuroscience and the ability to directly monitor brain functioning[2] has provided us with new insights about what actually happens in our mental processing. Remember that most of what we perceive and decide to keep goes directly into long-term memory without a lot of reflection. Once there, the brain manipulates it to provide a coherent storyline. While we may know a lot about how data gets into memory and how it is retrieved for our use, we still know relatively little about how it is processed or consolidated, especially during sleep.[3] What we do know is that to hold on to memories we need to mentally rehearse or give energy to them; otherwise, they gradually fade away.[4]

Our Mechanistic Heritage

The non-dualistic nature of our reality has been apparent to quantum physicists for over 120 years, but we have been a reluctant audience. Our entire cosmos is a vast energy field, a surging sea of potentiality. Indeed, some physicists speculate that we actually exist within a multiverse, with our cosmos being only one of multiple universes.[5] Components of the cosmic energy field appear to us as physical particles from time to time, but our predominant mode of being is energy.[6] Still we cling to the familiar but outmoded mechanistic model of Newtonian physics — a "matter"/"not matter" dichotomy.

How did we get so attached to this mechanistic model in the first place? In the last chapter we reviewed our transition in prehistory to our current competition-based patriarchal model. That heritage got unexpected reinforcement when authority passed from religion to science in the 1800s. The laws of motion, developed by Isaac Newton, became the new "religion" and the foundation of what is even now equated with "scientific thinking." The Newtonian model has remained firmly embedded in popular culture and continues to shape how we view life and its possibilities. So what are the assumptions of Newtonian physics that influence us so profoundly even now?

Materialism. The central principle states that only what we can see and measure is important, or "what matters is *matter.*" Actually what matters in our cosmos is *energy* — waves, or energy oscillations.[7] We are comprised of energetic waveforms and are interconnected through the sea of cosmic energy. We think of our world as comprised of solid particles, but in fact it is comprised of waves "collapsing" at given points in time to create our perception of the material universe. The defining characteristic of our universe is possibility or process, not measured results.

In describing our universe, mathematical cosmologist Brian Swimme has said:

> The universe emerges out of all-nourishing abyss ["space-time foam"] not only fifteen billion years ago

but in every moment. Each instance protons and an-
tiprotons are flashing out of, and are as suddenly absorbed back into, all-nourishing abyss. All-
nourishing abyss then is not a thing, nor a collection
of things, nor even, strictly speaking, a physical
place, but rather a power that gives birth and that ab-
sorbs existence at a thing's annihilation. The foundational reality of the universe is this unseen ocean of
potentiality. If all the individual things of the universe were to evaporate, one would be left with an
infinity of pure generative power.[8]

Doesn't sound much like the mechanistic images of Newtonian physics, does it? But even knowing that we are energy
and that the wave function is primary, scientists continue to
search for *the* particle, that bit of matter that is the ultimate
building block—assuming that the answer to "What is the
universe made of?" is "What is the smallest subatomic particle?"

Unfortunately, this focus on the concrete has led to society
over-valuing visible physical production and dismissing the
wide range of invisible service activities that comprise over
two-thirds of the world's economy.[9] In economist Marilyn
Waring's book, *If Women Counted*, she details the essential
services provided primarily by women that are not included
in economists' calculations of the world's economic activity,
determining that the overall value is vastly underestimated
because of these omissions.[10]

There have been some attempts to counterbalance this
over-emphasis on the physical, which has been accompanied
by an assumption that "more is better." Bhutan's Gross Domestic Happiness Index is one, as is the OECD initiative to
develop a well-being index. One of the latest initiatives is the
World Happiness Report, begun as an annual report in 2012
by the Sustainable Development Solutions Network.[11]

At the same time, there has been increasing pressure to exploit natural resources, including legal pressure from multinational corporations charging that environmental protection regulations restrict competition. Monsanto, for example, has been pressuring Mexican authorities to allow in genetically modified corn, which could decimate 8,000 years of corn cultivation and eliminate dozens of native strains of corn.[12] Environmentally destructive practices can be traced to valuing physical exploitation at the expense of quality of life and viewing our Earth as nothing more than "a combined park, zoo, and kitchen garden."[13] Examples include pollution in our air or water and the expansion of drilling in the Alberta tar sands (the third largest crude oil reserve in the world) in a manner that has led to environmental contamination and destruction that can be seen from outer space.

Reductionism. Materialism has led, in turn, to the principle that any complex system can be understood by examining its static, material component parts. In other words, reductionism says that what we see is an adding together of a series of micro-mechanic interactions. Scientific focus on finding the smallest particle of matter—originally thought to be the atom, which was then replaced by protons and neutrons and most recently by quarks—is grounded in the belief that studying them will tell us all we need to know. What makes material objects different from each other, it is assumed, is only the configuration of those elementary particles in space, with the space between particles considered empty "dead" space.

What scientists are learning instead is that, even if we could identify the component parts, they are not static. Indeed, the cosmos itself is not static—galaxies can change in structure.[14] Instead those parts are interconnected in quirky ways, with particles potentially in more than one location.[15] Particles do not operate independently; rather they are entangled or intertwined and they seem to communicate with each other across vast distances in a manner known as "non-local connection."[16] So we are left with the question of what component parts would we be examining to explain this phenomenon.

The belief in reductionism has been offset to some extent by systems such as Gestalt psychology that focus on the interaction between component parts and demonstrate that, in fact, the whole is greater and different than a simple sum of component parts. You can witness this dynamic in action if you consider a melody. Simply hearing the notes one by one, regardless of order (the reductionist theory), provides no real music. It is when we combine the notes in particular relationships that the beauty of music emerges.

There are circumstances in which it works well for us to reduce a set of complex facts to a simpler concept.[17] We can glance briefly at a group of objects or data and draw conclusions. This is extremely useful in many circumstances where we want a quick decision—such as determining today's weather or whether there are enough leftovers for a decent supper.

What we miss out on when we jump to quick conclusions is learning about relationships. In an alternate approach, we focus instead on finding patterns in the world. We consider not only the data but also the dynamic context in which they exist. This approach allows us to learn language and understand changes over time.

Determinism. A third central principle in the Newtonian model is that if the causal conditions are known, the effect will be predictable and always the same. Human characteristics such as choice, purpose, ethics, or free will become irrelevant. Newton assumed that we could learn about the physical aspects of nature, but that we would be unable to affect them. We see the influence of this principle in some aspects of law regarding whether or not individuals should be held responsible for the consequences of their actions.

Determinism leads to a belief in a static, predefined universe — in complete contradiction to our actual reality. Our universe and we ourselves are dynamic beings, constantly changing, or capable of change, as we are learning through research on neuroplasticity.

The belief in cause and effect is so deeply engrained that it has withstood repeated scientific evidence that "reality" is "potential" not "actual."[18] Physicists have demonstrated that "entangled" particles can become "disentangled" or separated if a researcher *in the future* measures them as separate rather than entangled.[19] A mind bender? In other words, measurement in the future can influence what happened in the past. This is not what we usually think of as cause and effect!

Looking at the issue from the perspective of biology rather than physics, biologist Lynn Margulis has pointed out that continual bacterial genetic recombination and transfer is actually what is responsible for most evolutionary change, in a manner not necessarily predictable by humans:

> As a result of [the ability to routinely and rapidly transfer bits of genetic material], all the world's bacteria essentially have access to a single gene pool and hence to adaptive mechanisms of the entire bacterial kingdom. The speed of recombination over that of mutation is superior: it could take eukaryotic organisms [such as humans] a million years to adjust to a change on a worldwide scale that bacteria can accommodate in a few years.... The result is a planet made fertile and inhabitable for larger forms of life by a communicating and cooperating worldwide superorganism of bacteria.[20]

Objectivity. Finally, we have the principle of objectivity — a belief that the state and activities of various forms of matter are absolute and experienced in the same way by all observers. There is no place for novelty or creativity as everything already exists in its molecular structure. Thus, the scientist has only to observe carefully.

For centuries the "scientific method" has been founded on this belief in objectivity. Only reluctantly are we admitting the role of observation. As long ago as 1988, researchers began demonstrating that our mental activity affects—even determines—the reality we experience. For example, researchers at the international Weizmann Institute of Science in Israel reported in 1998 that, at the quantum level, quanta (very *very* small particles) could behave as waves and could in essence be in more than one place at once—as long as they were not being observed. But once they were observed, they began behaving as particles rather than waves—they restricted themselves to a single option.[21]

Scientists are repeatedly demonstrating that it is the act of observation, or expectation, that determines the outcome.[22] Until they are observed, subatomic particles exist as probability waves. What may seem more outlandish is the discovery—for which Takaaki Kajita and Arthur McDonald won the 2015 Nobel Prize in Physics—that the tiniest bits of reality imagined (the abundant subatomic particles called neutrinos) begin life as rippling waves from the sun and then transform, when observed, into one of three particle "flavors."[23]

Now this may sound very esoteric and not make much sense, but we do actually live in the type of universe described, only we don't talk about it that way. Here's an almost parallel example to illustrate the point. Suppose your extended family liked to have a family reunion every five years, with the location rotating at random among family members. As you prepare for next year's reunion, each part of the family lobbies for their location: Seattle, Chicago, Toronto, Boston, or Montreal. So you have five simultaneous "probability waves" or possibilities. Finally a decision is reached—Chicago—and so the other four possibilities "collapse" in on Chicago as the singular reunion site.

Exercise: Correcting False Beliefs

Give an example of when you acted as if you believed each of the following Newtonian assumptions:

1. Determinism:

2. Objectivity:

How would your actions have changed if you understood that the assumption was incorrect?

Duality and Moral Exclusion

Reducing our experiences and choices to static options and predictable sequences does make life simpler. It also removes or glosses over the richness of our lives, the array of opportunities that confront us, and the need to make more complex ethical choices. If the consequences of such simplification were limiting but benign, it wouldn't matter. But the consequences are anything but benign.

When we accept only two options and, in contrast to ourselves, create an "other" category of beings (the second component in a dichotomy, the complement), we usually assign a value to that category. Remember "glorifying the indication," which we discussed in the last chapter? Recent research has verified what we would suspect—that the value we assign in comparison to ourselves or our group is "lesser than," a diminishing of moral status.[24] In other words, we begin to experience the "other" as less deserving of moral consideration and ethical treatment.

Moral exclusion involves placing individuals or groups outside the boundary of where we need to behave ethically and fairly towards them. In other words, we decide that we have no obligation to treat them with respect. Once outside that boundary, once morally excluded, anything goes — violence, injustice, loss of rights and privileges, a diminished sense of safety. We can feel free to be as violent as we wish.

The process of at least temporary moral exclusion is one that occurs with disturbing frequency and often outside of our awareness. In essence what we do is to deny personhood to the "other." We ignore them or consider them as less than ourselves, meaning also being less of a "real" person. We even depersonalize ourselves — dismissing premonitions, deferring to authority, and not valuing our own perspective or experience. This denial of personhood, to self or others, is known as *depersonalization*.

What is the "personhood" that we deny when we depersonalize an entity or group? Consolidating a range of research, personhood's attributes can be summarized as:[25]

   a. *Agency*, including competence, intelligence, ability to think abstractly, self-control, and being able to reflect on and choose one's actions.
   b. *Warmth*, including trustworthiness, empathy, prosocial values, complex social relations, and able to work cooperatively.
   c. *Identity*, or self-awareness and a sense of individuality and autonomy, with a rich inner life.
   d. *Inclusion*, or being viewed as within one's circle of care or moral community and seen as having congruent values.

e. *Rights*, or having the moral standing to be "beyond use" as an object.

Once personhood is acknowledged, an entity becomes entitled to certain moral or inherent rights:

a. "Negative" rights, which include freedom from:
   o The threat of unnatural death.
   o Slavery or being owned by another.
   o Kidnapping or trafficking.
   o Torture or experimentation.
   o Servitude or inhumane treatment.
   o Inability to live in one's natural habitat.

b. "Positive" rights, or assurance of being:
   o Treated with respect and dignity.
   o Allowed to develop one's own personality, within one's own community.
   o Given just and favorable remuneration for work, as well as periods of rest and holidays.

The above focus shifts us from the primarily psychological and social manifestations of duality to the moral and legal dimensions because they are what govern what we find acceptable. The degree of moral censure that we apply to our own behavior relates directly to whether or not we believe we are relating to an entity with moral standing.

Let's take an example to illustrate this dynamic. Assume that you are enraged about something that happened and, as a result, you slam your door. Would anyone think there was a problem, other than that you had an extremely noisy way of showing that you were furious? After all, we assume the door experiences no pain and is yours to do with what you wish. Now suppose that instead you slam your spouse's head into the wall and then begin beating her. Is there a problem? Absolutely, because we assume that your spouse is a person with moral standing—i.e., a right not to be battered just because you are angry.

As we proceed in our analysis, language becomes an issue as each social context and each type of depersonalization has its own common terminology. To be consistent, we will be using "perpetrator" to refer to the individual or group that is creating the depersonalization and "target" to refer to the individual or group being depersonalized.

In order to justify behaving disrespectfully or harmfully, we have to somehow diminish the target's personhood. The dynamic applies both ways. If we perceive the target to already be depersonalized (lacking in individuality and personhood), we will usually treat that target as having no moral standing and behave however we feel at the time.[26] If we perceive the target as having no moral standing, we will assume that the target lacks personhood and proceed to act in accordance with our own self-interest. Either way the target loses.

When we talk about a target (human or nonhuman) being morally excluded, we are referring to a belief that we can make moral decisions about them based solely on the benefit to ourselves rather than on any benefit to the target in question. For example, in an intimate adult-adult partnership, we typically behave in a morally inclusive manner—i.e., we consider the needs and desires of the other person as well as our own. When we order a subordinate to work on a holiday so that we don't have to, we are behaving in a morally *exclusive* way—i.e., we are taking only our own needs and desires into consideration. Moral exclusion is the first step towards violence and injustice being considered acceptable, expected, and indeed normal.

Historically we have viewed nonhumans—such as plants and animals—as "things," resources for our own use. Our position has been one of ownership and exploitation. We may have been benevolently protective, but we have not necessarily thought of them as having moral standing in their own right — or as being "beyond use" by us.

Where is the boundary of care that we should maintain intact? What entities may we exclude morally? The answer may surprise you. Research is showing that depersonalization of a whole range of plants and animals, and even of the Earth itself, is not morally justifiable. See Appendix B for a summary of some of that research as many are still unfamiliar with it. The right of humans to deny moral standing to non-human entities is being challenged both scientifically and legally.[27] These include the Center for Earth Jurisprudence,[28] the Nonhuman Rights Project,[29] and Wild Law UK,[30] as well as community action groups such as the Global Alliance for the Rights of Nature.[31]

Through a range of initiatives, various jurisdictions are now moving beyond the rights of natural persons (i.e., human beings) and juridical persons (e.g., corporations) to also recognize the legal personhood and accompanying rights of other nonhuman entities. The Nonhuman Rights Project is shifting the focus from animal welfare to legal personhood and the right to bodily liberty and bodily integrity for various chimpanzees through the courts of New York State. In May 2013 the Indian government moved to forbid the use of captive dolphins for entertainment, emphasizing that they should be seen as non-human persons with their own specific rights.[32]

To illustrate specific initiatives underway, a proposed Universal Declaration on the Rights of Mother Earth has been presented to the United Nations by Bolivia.[33] There is also an online Declaration of Rights for Cetaceans: Whales and Dolphins already signed by over 100 scientists (and available for public signature) in light of the fact that current conventions regard cetaceans as sources of food rather than as highly intelligent beings with moral and legal rights.

Exercise: Identifying Moral Exclusion

Try two experiments:

1. Identify a human group that you feel distant from. What would you need to change in order to identify with members of that group?

2. Identify a nonhuman species that you would be willing to include morally (i.e., treat as a person). What would change if you stopped thinking of them as things (non-persons)?

Depersonalization and Violence

Violence is a learned behavior, one that is modeled to young people as an appropriate way to resolve conflict or feel good about oneself. The U.S. National Academy of Sciences, in a review of hundreds of studies on the relationship between biology and violence, stated: "No patterns precise enough to be considered reliable biological markers for violent behavior have yet been identified."[35] This is good news in terms of the potential for social change.

Examining statistics on violence highlights an underlying gender imbalance. While there are many factors that influence the rate of violence, close to 90 percent of perpetrators of violence outside of armed conflict are males and the vast majority of victims are girls and women. The World Health Organization estimates that at least 30 percent of women in relationships have experienced physical or sexual violence by their partner.[36] UN Secretary-General Ban Ki-moon has been explicit about the need to recognize violence against women as a leading human rights violation:

> We must unite. Violence against women cannot be tolerated, in any form, in any context, in any circumstance, by any political leader or by any government.

> There is one universal truth, applicable to all countries, cultures and communities: violence against women is never acceptable, never excusable, never tolerable.

> Men must teach each other that real men do not violate or oppress women—and that a woman's place is not just in the home or the field, but in schools and offices and boardrooms.

Violence based on the gender dichotomy of us=male and them=female, held in place by our patriarchal heritage, is so all-pervasive that we often overlook it; therefore, many of the examples provided in Part Two will relate to misogyny in its various expressions.

Research has shown that, in order to be intentionally violent, the perpetrator needs to view the target as a depersonalized "other," a target available for whatever atrocities the perpetrator desires to inflict.[37] This depersonalization may include, in extreme cases, removing the physical cues of being a free agent so that potential empathy is decreased. Thus, in media coverage of torture or rape or genocide, we often see people who have been stripped naked, bound or chained, and reduced to a barely human state. In domestic violence, a similar effect is frequently achieved by preceding physical or sexual violence with verbal abuse (yelling, criticizing, name calling) to strip the target of her humanity and thus provide "justification."

Once we create the dichotomy (the duality) and depersonalize an "other," we no longer have to be concerned about moral treatment because "they don't deserve it." It is just a small further step to violence.

Most people do not wish to be violent. They view themselves as productive and caring members of society. So why do we have these problems? We will see in Part Two that the very people who do not wish to be violent, including ourselves, have absorbed some implicit or unconscious biases and have learned a range of harmful behaviors that they do not yet understand to be violent.

As we saw in *Positive Harmlessness in Practice*, harm can take many forms, some of which are so widely accepted (e.g., dismissiveness) that we don't even recognize them as harmful. In order to identify the nuances of depersonalization (the distancing of self from "other") and the harm it generates, we will examine five of its manifestations in Part Two:[38]

Hostile bigotry, or the outward expression of hatred towards another group and its members

Benevolent bigotry, or the outward expression of positive beliefs while behaving in a manner that disempowers the other group or its members

Stereotyping, or beliefs about a group that can vary from contemptuous to envious and that view persons only as group members, with all the characteristics attributed to that group, rather than as individuals

Invisibility, or the dismissal of a group or its members as being "beneath notice" or whose feelings and experiences need not be taken into account

Objectification, or viewing a group or its members as commodities to be used or bought and sold without regard for personal dignity

We can link these five forms of depersonalization to the four types of harm or violence outlined in *Positive Harmlessness in Practice*, as follows:

Form of Depersonalization	Type of Harm
Hostile bigotry	Brutality
Benevolent bigotry	Harassment
Stereotyping	
Invisibility	Dismissiveness
Objectification	Defensiveness

As we explore the five primary ways in which depersonalization occurs in Part Two, we need to recognize that each of these is harmful, either overtly or covertly — there are not "better" or "worse" ways to be depersonalized or deprived of the dignity of being "seen" as a whole person. Also, each operates based on, or intensified by, the following general dynamics:

o *Interpersonal data is automatically categorized in schemas*
In Chapter One, we reviewed the process by which we place data that we have about people and groups into schemas — or patterns of thought that organize relationships among data — which then generate prejudgments. The most common categorization is into in-group and out-group along whatever dimension we are interested in. So if we meet a series of new people, we immediately begin automatically placing them into categories — like me (in-group), not like me (out-group) and then assigning characteristics to each category.

Data related to a particular person or group are not all stored together — i.e., we don't have a photo album of people or groups. Instead, the schemas we develop are like a set of instructions that says, "To see Jane's face, put the shape of her face together with the color of her eyes, the color and texture of her skin and hair, the sound of her voice, all the things I have heard her say, [and so on]." You get the picture—remembering or recognizing someone is a complex process.

The content of schemas literally influences what we experience. We are more likely to notice things that fit into our existing schema (confirmation bias),[39] while reinterpreting contradictions as exceptions or distorting them to fit (disconfirmation bias).[40] Only if the new contradictory information cannot be ignored do we typically make a change.[41]

o *Memories are constantly reworked to become more coherent and consistent*
Memories are not stored in a static manner—that is, we don't tuck them away in long-term memory intact. Instead, we store portions of the memory in different parts of our brain (the emotional experience, the tactile component, etc.), ready to be reassembled when needed.

But then we whittle away at those pieces, compressing them to remove redundancies and increase consistency among our memories based on the principle of simplicity or choosing options that provide the simplest explanation.[42] We go for consistency and may "see" or "remember" something that hasn't happened because it is more believable to us. Much of what we "remember" is actually confabulated (adjusted and rationalized) narrative that allows us to think of our past as a continuous and coherent string of events.[43]

In the same way, we fail to see things that don't fit. A famous perceptual bias study had someone in a monkey suit walk through the visual field and none of the participants noticed anything unusual.[44] All of this whittling and ignoring eventually results in memory distortion.[45] Because we want to see ourselves as impartial, we then forget that we have tinkered with the memory and believe that the memory is accurate.[46]

To be more specific, the brain extracts structure and patterns in order to form coherent, stable impressions in long-term memory.[47] We are thus able to view people as being consistent when in fact we are all quite variable in our behavior across time and situations — how we act at forty will be different than how we acted in the same circumstance when we were ten, and how we act when we are discussing a hypothetical threat and how we respond if someone is actually threatening us with a gun will be different.

What our brains do to achieve consistency in our memories is to:

a.   Discount what is inconsistent so that we are able to detect and learn from a pattern. This works well if we are not directly affected by the outcome.

b.   Integrate what is inconsistent by expanding nuances until everything fits, which takes effort. That effort is worth exerting only if the outcome matters to us.

o   *Working memory's capacity limitations affect performance*
We have already seen in Chapter One that our working memory processes a tremendous amount of data each minute and can only consciously focus on five to nine items at a time.[48] We may become preoccupied with tracking nonverbal cues, worrying over the motivation of the perpetrator, or rehearsing our response — all of

which involve working memory — and thus have little capacity left over to learn new things or modify our behavior.[49]

o *Inferred intention affects evaluation*
Research shows that, when people believe that harm is inflicted intentionally, they will judge the magnitude of harm as greater — there is a kind of "harm-magnification" dynamic at play.[50] In addition, people are more likely to see harmful actions as intentional.[51] So if we see someone behaving in a harmful way, we are predisposed to assume they are doing so on purpose and to believe that the action is very harmful.

Conversely, if we believe that the action, even though harmful, was not intentional, then we give people the benefit of the doubt ("they didn't really mean it") and will see the target as exaggerating the extent of harm caused (just a step away from blaming the victim). This reworking is possible because of the "illusion of objectivity" that we have around our memories.[52]

Becoming Sensitized to Depersonalization

Simply naming the forms of depersonalization is not enough to precipitate change, or a "moving beyond." Psychologists Julia Becker and Janet Swim have demonstrated, for example, that subtle sexism (a form of benevolent bigotry) is so pervasive in our everyday lives that it goes unnoticed by most of us.[53] The same can be said for most discriminatory and objectifying behavior that underlies the dynamic of depersonalization, such as racism, ageism, classism, homophobia, xenophobia (an irrational fear of people from other countries), anthropocentrism (the belief that humans are morally superior to other species) and so on.

Our challenge, then, is twofold: First to become aware of the dynamic of depersonalization, and second to choose to change the dynamic. Part Two will deal with that critical awareness, leaving options for change to Part Three.

In the chapters of Part Two, we will examine the five forms of depersonalization in detail — the various methods of creating an "us" and a "them" — and how they manifest so that we can be alert to their appearance. To understand how widespread and insidious depersonalization is, we will explore it not only as expressed in misogyny and sexism, but also in racism and immigrant rage, heterosexism and homophobia, ageism, attitudes towards the homeless and differently abled, and anthropocentrism.

Linking back to our discussion of personhood, we see below the various personhood attributes that are withheld or denied in each form of depersonalization.

Form of Depersonalization	Personhood Attributes Withheld
Hostile bigotry	All
Benevolent bigotry	Agency; Identity; Inclusion
Stereotyping	Agency; Warmth; Identity; Inclusion
Invisibility	Agency; Identity; Inclusion; Rights
Objectification	Warmth; Identity; Inclusion; Rights

The analyses in Part Two will provide us with an opportunity to learn in detail the various faces of depersonalization — the dynamics created by dualistic thinking — rather than remain ignorant. However, the content of Part Two will be challenging to read. It will force us to confront the aspects of our behavior that are problematic, that we usually ignore. Part

Two reveals the underbelly of ways that we act to entitle ourselves and our in-groups and discount others.

We have a number of national initiatives around the world focused on healing past wounds. What we know from that truth and reconciliation process is that we must start by facing squarely what we have done and are doing before we can move forward. We must remember so that we can change.

Do we have the courage to face our shortcomings, to understand the wide range of ways in which we depersonalize others, and even ourselves, in everyday life? If we do, we will reap the benefits of more complex, emotionally-nuanced ways of experiencing our world and each other.

Part Two

Recognizing Depersonalization in Action

FOUR

"They're Not Like Us": Hostile Bigotry

Hostile bigotry is the overt expression of hatred towards persons or groups labeled "other" simply because they have features or traits we consider to be different from those of "normal people." Differences are typically based on race or ethnicity, gender, religion, political ideology, sexual orientation, age, ability, or socio-economic group. The defining characteristic of this type of depersonalization is purposeful action to subdue or humiliate the target, whether by public ridicule or beating or murder.

Aggressive acts of brutality and violence are being tolerated less and less (outside of the context of armed conflict), so hostile bigotry is becoming a less common version of depersonalization. It occurs primarily in contexts where perpetrators have determined either that they are morally justified ("any thinking person would have done the same thing") or that they are morally compelled (by a deeply-held belief) or that any punishment that ensues is worth having acted.

The Roots of Hostile Bigotry

To understand this form of depersonalization, we need first to define what we mean by "hatred." Within the psychological literature, hatred is used in a number of different ways.[1] For our purposes, the following components are relevant:

o Distancing—denying any commonality with the target

o Blame—viewing the target as the cause of our having been thwarted or mistreated

o Fear—believing there is a future threat from the target

o Revulsion—feeling disgust and loathing regarding the target

o Contempt—feeling that the target is beneath consideration, worthless, or deserving of scorn

Hatred always includes distancing, as well as a kind of negative intimacy or entanglement that accounts for the intensity of the feeling. In addition, hatred includes at least one of the other components in order to provide internal justification for the distancing—sort of like a restaurant menu ("I'll have one Distancing plus one Blame and one Revulsion"). The intensity with which hostile bigotry is expressed and the deadliness of the form it takes (from intimidation to bloodshed) can be linked to how many of the five components we have chosen to engage.

In the dynamic of hostile bigotry, we see a fundamental denial of the universal relevance of two of the articles of the UN Universal Declaration of Human Rights:

Article 1: All human beings are born free and equal in dignity and rights.

Article 3: Everyone has the right to life, liberty and security of person.

Since the 1950 publication of *The Authoritarian Personality*,[2] social psychologists have been researching various aspects of the belief in the superiority of one's own group coupled with a contempt for all others. The research most relevant to hostile bigotry is that on "social dominance orientation," which is a strong preference for inequality among social groups coupled with a desire for one's group to be superior to others, all supported by a series of legitimizing myths.[3] From a cognitive perspective, hostile bigotry is directly related to a need for structure, a preference for predictability and order, and discomfort with ambiguity.[4] Translated into how we process incoming data, hostile bigotry is nurtured by a strong preference for clear, unchanging, and simplistic categories.

Val Plumwood, an Australian ecofeminist, has referred to the dynamic of hostile bigotry as "hyperseparation" and has commented, "The function of hyperseparation is to mark out the other for separate and inferior treatment through a radical form of exclusion."[5] In other words, differences are magnified to create an extreme polarization, and any possible similarities are denied. This polarization happens because we (a) minimize differences within categories or our in-group (assimilation), and (b) exaggerate differences between categories or between in-group and out-group (contrast). If the differences are consistent with well-known stereotypes, the distortion may be highly resistant to change.[6]

Investigations into the neurodevelopment of children have shed some important light on the link between childhood violence and violent behavior as an adult. Researchers have found that being exposed to violence in the home, either as a target or as an observer, changes the child's brain.[7] The neuroplasticity of the brain facilitate changes related not only to use — i.e., supporting our routine activities — but also as a consequence of our emotional state. Children who are in a constant state of low-level fear and hypervigilance are less likely to learn easily and more likely to over-respond to relatively neutral stimuli. What happens is that part of their brain is constantly scanning the environment and evaluating non-verbal cues regarding their safety. So they have less working memory available to learn, they become extremely adept at reading nonverbal cues ("streetsmarts"), and they are strung tight, apt to overact.

There has been considerable controversy around the effect of *viewing violence* in movies or video games or music videos.

In 1998 researchers at Harvard Medical School analyzed the content of hundreds of music videos and found a disturbing amount of violence, as well as racism and misogyny, which creates the perception of the world as a dangerous place where you have to protect yourself physically.[8] The researchers went on to establish that exposure to sexual violence "desensitizes male viewers to violence against women and heightens a sense of disempowerment among female viewers." The effects were all the more powerful because the violence was usually committed by "heroes" without showing negative consequences or ethical ramifications.

Since then the body of research has grown, as has the controversy. While direct links between viewing and committing violence have not been consistently substantiated, research does support the fact that youth act more aggressively in real-world relationships when they spend time immersed in violent video games.[9] Their reckless behavior increases as well, including being willing to drink and drive.[10] In addition, those playing violent video games report feeling not only more aggressive but also less "human" and thus more likely to depersonalize themselves and others.[11] By contrast, those playing prosocial video games behave in a more helpful manner and perceive themselves as more "human."

In August 2015 the American Psychological Association released the report of its Task Force on Violent Media, which stated that while a direct link to criminal activity had not been established, "the research demonstrates a consistent relation between violent video game use and increases in aggressive behavior, aggressive cognitions and aggressive affect, and decreases in prosocial behavior, empathy and sensitivity to aggression."[12] For our purposes, what is particularly troubling is the documented decrease in empathy and helping behavior and an increase in the tendency to depersonalize others.

There have been similar findings regarding disparaging sexist humor, showing that it sends the message that acting sexist is "fine".[13] Unfortunately, not only is it made to seem "fine" but men already high on hostile sexism are then more likely to rape after being exposed to sexist jokes.[14] The dynamic seems to be that humor loosens moral constraints on behavior and helps the perpetrator feel that depersonalization and violence are acceptable.

Hostile Bigotry Expressed as Hate Crimes

One subset of hostile bigotry is legally known as hate crimes. These are criminal actions that are intended to harm or intimidate individuals or groups because they belong to a target group. The U.S. Southern Poverty Law Center[15] tracks and reports on over 1,600 extremist groups whose focus is anti-immigrant, anti-LGBT, anti-government, Black separatism, Christian identity, Holocaust denial, Ku Klux Klan, neo-confederates, neo-Nazi, racist skinheads, or white nationalism.

Legally hate crimes can be of several kinds. Crimes against humanity focus on the killing of large numbers of individuals during armed conflict.[16] Genocide, by contrast, focuses on the annihilation of groups.[17] Genocide is the deliberate and intentional eradication of an ethnic, religious or social group through one or more of the following:

- o Killing members of the group
- o Causing serious bodily or mental harm to members of the group
- o Deliberately inflicting living conditions calculated to bring about the group's physical destruction
- o Imposing measures intended to prevent births within the group
- o Forcibly transferring children of the group to another group

We can see that the motivation for the two can be different. In crimes against humanity, the intention is to win by terror and elimination. In genocide, the intention is to completely eliminate a particular group so that there are no remnants left.

The most extensive research in relation to hate crimes and related aggression has been on racism, which constitutes the motivation for approximately half of reported hate crimes in the U.S. At least eight Black people and one Latino person become hate crime victims in the U.S. each day, with a hate crime committed every hour and at least one cross burned a day.[18]

Racism in the U.S. was aggravated by adoption of the "one-drop rule" (you could not be classified as Caucasian if you had any non-Caucasian parentage), which gave birth to laws against mixed-race marriages starting after the Civil War. The concept of frowning on mixed parentage was not restricted to the U.S. British colonists left behind them a trail of shunned mixed heritage children, and the same has happened in other parts of the world. In an effort to help people understand that "race" is a social (invented) construct, not a biological fact, the American Anthropology Association issued a public statement in 1998 (see Appendix C).[19] It is clear that this message has not yet permeated our collective awareness.

The next extensively-researched demonstration of hostile bigotry is anti-Semitism, or hatred towards Jews as an ethnic, religious or racial group. Organized persecution of Jews has been documented as far back as the pogroms of 1096, the expulsion of Jews from England in 1290, the massacres of Spanish Jews in 1391 and expulsion in 1492, the Cossack massacres in Ukraine in 1647-1657, pogroms in Imperial Russia between 1821 and 1906…and the list goes on.

The most horrifying of these initiatives, though, was the planned genocide of the Holocaust by the Nazis during World

War Two, billed as the "Final Solution." It saw the systematic annihilation of six million Jews (or two out of three European Jews) as well as a substantial number of Gypsies, homosexuals, disabled persons, Jehovah's Witnesses, Communists, intellectuals, and trade unionists with the rationale of ensuring the purity and strength of the German "master race." While some were executed or starved in ghettos, the majority were gassed in the six death camps established by the Nazis in occupied Poland.

Given the long history of violence towards Jews, it is not surprising that a large collection of myths, folklore, and imagery has accumulated about the "bad nature" or "cosmic evil" of Jews to justify their displacement or destruction. A 2014 global survey by the Anti-Defamation League[20] has found that 26 percent of the global population (polled in every geographic region) harbor anti-Semitic attitudes, with the lowest rate being in Oceania (14%) and the highest being in the Middle East and North Africa (74%).[21]

Even more disturbing, Holocaust denial continues to be alive and well, with only 54 percent of the current global population having heard about the Holocaust and 32 percent of those believing that it was either a myth or greatly exaggerated. Denial is highest in the Middle East, with 54% in Iran and 46% in Turkey acknowledging that it happened but believing that accounts have been greatly exaggerated.

The Holocaust is not the only recent example of genocide, now classified as a crime against humanity. Three examples serve as reminders of the inhuman treatment we can visit on each other. When the Khmer Rouge gained power in Cambodia in 1975, it began a killing spree, over a period of four years, of ideologically suspect groups, resulting in at least 1.7 million Cambodians dead, including Vietnamese and Cham minorities. In 1994 Rwanda witnessed a well-organized massacre over a period of three months of up to 900,000 Tutsis and politically moderate Hutus by Hutu militia groups. This genocide also displaced at least two million refugees into surrounding countries. In the Bosnian Genocide of 1995, the Serb armed forces engaged in "ethnic cleansing" of over 8,000 Bosnian Muslims and the expulsion of up to 30,000 more from the town of Srebrenica.

There is also the matter of "cultural genocide," or destruction of a culture by eliminating their cultural integrity, removing them from their lands, population transfer or forced assimilation. While the systematic eradication of Tibetan culture by the Chinese stands as a particularly visible example, there are clear parallels in the "cultural genocide" practiced against indigenous peoples over hundreds of years.

In Canada that cultural genocide was obscured through the system of more than 130 residential schools across the country in which more than 150,000 First Nation, Metis and Inuit youth were stripped of their identity, starved, beaten, and sexually abused—under the auspices of the government and the Catholic church. The Canadian Truth and Reconciliation Report, issued in June 2015, details the horrors and proposes recommendations for a way forward.[22]

Some historians have stated that the reduction of the U.S. North American Indian population from approximately 12 million in 1500 to barely 237,000 in 1900 was the worst and longest lasting human holocaust anywhere in human history.[23] It was carried out through slavery, theft, starvation, introduced disease, beatings, torture, murder, and forced relocation (the Trail of Tears of the Cherokee Nation being one of the best known instances).

Xenophobic violence, or immigrant rage, has been an issue in a number of countries. The U.S., for example, has continued to be concerned about illegal immigrants crossing its southern border.[24] Meanwhile, various parts of Europe have struggled with integrating immigrants from very different cultural and linguistic backgrounds. Periodic demonstrations have blamed immigrants for economic woes and called for their wholesale expulsion—rhetoric that often leads to physical violence.[25]

A new wave of xenophobic violence swept South Africa in 2015 at the height of unemployment for which foreigners were blamed. Goodwill Zwelithini, king of the Zulus, called for all foreigners to "pack their belongings and go back to their countries" and is quoted as saying, "They dirty our streets...there are foreigners everywhere."[26]

These concerns were submerged in 2015, though, under the stresses created by the millions of Syrian refugees fleeing from civil war in Syria.[27] The first four million to flee were absorbed into neighboring countries—Turkey, Lebanon, Jordan, Iraq, and Egypt. While 7.6 million remained internally displaced within Syria, millions more were pouring out of the country, trying to reach northern Europe or any place where they could begin their lives again. Hungary expressed xenophobia most publicly, battering arriving refugees and constructing a fence along its border with Serbia. Anti-refugee sentiments and a desire to prevent refugee entrance warred with humanitarian efforts across Europe and North America.

One of the manifestations of hostile bigotry now receiving hate crime publicity has been anti-LGBT activity, which is gaining in numbers and geographic spread. The crimes include beatings, forced conversion therapy, "corrective rape" (mainly of lesbians), imprisonment, or incitement to murder.[28]

Touting that homosexuality is sinful and unnatural, a range of practitioners continue to pressure LGBT people to have conversion therapy (sometimes known as "reparative" or "sexual reorientation" therapy) in order to "convert" them from gay to straight. The practice can include violent role play, reenactment of past abuses, and exercises involving nudity and intimate touching; it results not in "conversion" but in increased anxiety, depression, and sometimes thoughts of suicide. Not only is the premise that gay people are "broken" incorrect, but the practice has been discredited by virtually all major American medical, psychiatric, psychological and professional counseling organizations.

As a first step in ending this shameful practice, in June 2015 a New Jersey jury delivered a unanimous verdict that promoting so-called conversion therapy violated the state's consumer fraud laws. Superior Court Judge Bariso Jr. wrote that "the theory that homosexuality is a disorder is not novel but—like the notion that the earth is flat and the sun revolves around it—instead is outdated and refuted."[29]

The hate crime of "corrective rape" has not yet had that type of legal advocacy. In this practice, lesbians are raped (sometimes gang raped, or held captive and raped repeatedly for days) by men in order to convert them to heterosexuality. While it occurs in a number of countries, it was first noticed and reported in South Africa in the early 2000s where it is currently rampant and accelerating, often accompanied by murder.[30] The perpetrators are typically known to the victims and are often family members or males recruited by mothers. It is estimated that only four percent of perpetrators are ever tried and convicted. One man is quoted as saying, "After everything we're going to do to you, you're going to be a real woman, and you're never going to act like this again."

In June 2015 the *Times of India* reported that the practice of "corrective rape" had spread to India, with a twist—the rapist is virtually always a family member. On instruction from the gay child's parents, brothers and cousins rape lesbian relatives, while mothers rape gay sons.[31]

It is still illegal to be gay in 76 countries, five of which impose the death penalty for same-sex intimacy: Iran, Mauritania, Saudi Arabia, Sudan, Yemen. U.S. Christian evangelical groups have been instrumental in promoting homophobia and anti-gay legislation abroad, with the most publicized case being Uganda. Scott Lively and his Abiding Truth Ministries (listed as a hate group by the Southern Poverty Law Center) have been actively campaigning against homosexuality in Uganda since at least 2007, reportedly trying to get a death penalty for gays passed.[32]

In an unexpected turn, the U.S. Center for Constitutional Rights filed a federal lawsuit against Lively on behalf of Sexual Minorities Uganda (SMUG) under the Aliens Tort Statute (ATS) in March 2012.[33] The case seeks accountability for persecution ("the intentional and severe deprivation of fundamental rights contrary to international law by reason of the identity of the group") on the basis of sexual orientation and gender identity as a crime against humanity. The summary judgment briefing is set for Fall 2015.

Transgender violence has begun to escalate, particularly in the U.S. where the issue is most visible, with transgender women and people of color most at risk.[34] The National Coalition of Anti-Violence Programs reported in June 2015 that attempts to report violence to the police were met with hostility and excessive force, and only a small percentage were correctly classified as hate crimes.

Exercise: Noticing Hate Crimes

Over the next week, as you read or watch the news, identify at least one example of a hate crime (even if it is not labelled as such) and reflect on:

1. What were the key components of the hatred being expressed—i.e., Distancing + what?

2. What could or should be done to provide restitution for the victim and reduce the chances of it happening again?

Hostile Bigotry and Misogyny

Misogyny, or the hatred of females, is unfortunately so ubiquitous that it is often not even listed as an issue. The Southern Poverty Law Center, for example, has published several Intelligence reports on misogyny and its March 2012 *Intelligence* report contains a list of misogynistic websites[35]; however, it does not list these sites among those monitored regularly. There's just too much!

Social media has accelerated the spread of misogynistic beliefs and calls to action, particularly through the portion of the internet known as the "manosphere." The most common of these hundreds of websites are those advocating "corrective rape" of girls and women, with the rationale that women are "stupid and disgusting and promiscuous, and need to be put back in their place."

Violence against women and girls because of their gender has been called by the United Nations (UN) a "pandemic in diverse forms."[36] The range of brutality and murder that stems from misogyny is so horrifying that many of us try not to be aware of it. While research shows that such violence is vastly underreported (estimated at one in seven attacks), UN estimates show that up to 70 percent of women have experienced physical and/or sexual violence.[37] Here are some sobering statistics from 2012:

- o 1 in 2 women killed were killed by their partners or family (compared with 1 in 20 men).

- o At least 4.4 million women and girls are being trafficked by being forced into sexual exploitation.

- o At least 11.5 million women and girls are being trafficked as slaves (forced labor).

- o More than 133 million girls and women alive have undergone female genital mutilation (FGM).[38]

o 700 million married girls were married before they were 18 years old, 250 million before they were 15.

o Every minute a bride is burned in a dowry death in India.

o Worldwide every two minutes a woman is raped.

o In the U.S., 83% of girls in grades 8-11 have experienced sexual harassment.

A particularly brutal form of violence is that known as honor killing, which includes not only murder but acid attacks, mutilation, and severe beating. Here the woman or girl is killed by family members (usually planned for as a group, with the actual attack led by a young boy) based on the perpetrators' belief that the victim has brought shame or dishonor on the family or violated the code of honor of the community. Note that proof is neither necessary nor sought; a rumor is enough to trigger murder. The most common forms of "dishonor" are refusal to enter into an arranged marriage, dressing inappropriately, being in an unsanctioned relationship, having sex outside of marriage, being gay, or being the victim of rape.

Controversies over a woman's right to control her body reflect another face of misogyny—that of viewing women as wombs designed to produce offspring for men. While many countries have anti-abortion laws to ensure that pregnancies are carried to term, El Salvador has a particularly brutal set of laws that make it illegal to terminate a pregnancy for any reason, including rape, incest, severe fetal abnormalities, or a threat to the woman's life.[39] Women can be jailed for up to 40 years for having unintentionally miscarried or experienced a still birth. Such laws stand in stark contrast to the recent UN declaration that access to contraception is "an essential human right."[40]

The World Health Organization (WHO), in a ground-breaking 2013 report, differentiated for the first time between intimate and stranger violence. The findings? The vast majority of women and girls are attacked or abused by family members, people with whom they should be safe. And this is happening every day, in every country, to women of every socio-economic class.

Unfortunately it takes high-profile cases to remind us of what is happening to some woman or girl every minute. One such case was the December 2012 brutal gang rape of Jyoti Singh, an Indian medical student returning home from a movie with her boyfriend. Immediate global outcry forced the Indian government, which has exhibited complacency in the face of almost unimaginable nation-wide violence against women (rape, acid attacks, dowry murders to name a few), to both place the offenders on trial and enact long-overdue laws against voyeurism, stalking, and trafficking of women. But the underlying, widely-shared misogyny is clear in comments made by one of Jyoti Singh's attackers, Mukesh Singh:[41] "A girl is far more responsible for rape than a boy. A decent girl won't roam around at 9 o'clock at night....Housework and housekeeping is for girls, not roaming in discos and bars at night doing wrong things, wearing wrong clothes....She should just be silent and allow the rape." A documentary on the case, "India's Daughter" by British filmmaker Lesslee Udwin, has been banned in India.

South Africa has become known as the rape capital of the world, with a woman raped every 17 seconds. Twenty percent of men say, "She asked for it." In a survey of men in the Eastern Cape Provinces by the Medical Research Council, 25 percent said they had raped at least once, 20 percent said their victim was underage (often under 10 years old), and 25 percent of school boys in Soweto described gang rape as "fun."[42]

We may fantasize that rape only occurs "elsewhere," in poorer countries. But the reality is that in a wealthy country like the U.S. a sexual assault occurs every 107 seconds—less frequently than in South Africa but much too frequently all the same. Again the most frequent perpetrators are intimate partners or family members.

Even on college and university campuses in North America, among the most highly educated, sexual assault is rampant. More focus is finally being placed on the post-secondary rape culture (date rape, inciting hate rape, rape chants for newly arriving students), with the practice of "rape chants" performed for newly arriving students in colleges throughout Canada and the U.S. finally being classified as a hate crime. But very little has yet been done to offset administrations' "boys will be boys" mindset. Survivors are encouraged to keep quiet in order to let the rapist graduate.[43] One of the highly publicized cases was the "Class of DDS 2015 Gentlemen," a Facebook group of 13 Dalhousie University dental school students, which advocated for hate-raping female classmates. While some intervention was provided, the dental students were allowed to graduate, over the protests of faculty, female classmates, and dental licensing authorities in several provinces.[44]

Hostile sexism includes the all too familiar domination, degradation and hostility expressed as offensive jokes, harassment, and physical violence.[45] It consists of a belief that men should and need to control women (dominative paternalism), a feeling of increased self-confidence and a boost to the male ego ("men are better"), and a view of women as sex objects to be used but feared. The Southern Poverty Law Center has posted an *Intelligence* report on an online site run by PhilosophyofRape that moralizes, "For the good of society, these women need to be raped....[and] put back in their place by violent sexual assault."[46] Lest we think that all misogynists are ignorant bigots, reflect on the experience of a 17-year-old U.K. student who started a feminist society at her all-girls high school to help empower other students. Male peers at other schools reacted online with a massive backlash of degrading and abusive sexual remarks.[47]

Psychologist Susan Fiske and her colleagues have demonstrated that, when males high on hostile sexism were shown pictures of women in bikinis, their brains showed no activity that would indicate that they viewed the women as human beings with thoughts and intentions.[48] It was clear that the women were being viewed as objects.

Exercise: Addressing Hostile Bigotry

Reflect on the following questions:

1. How do you feel when you hear or see hostile bigotry?

2. What do you do if you hear derogatory remarks or jokes made about an individual or group?

3. Has this approach been successful in raising awareness? If not, how else could you respond?

Why are we surprised? Early philosophers, whose writings still influence Western culture, were uniformly misogynistic. Here are some quotes that we don't hear often but that resound through modern culture:

> We should look upon the female state as being as it were a deformity, though one which occurs in the ordinary course of nature.
>
> — Aristotle, *Generation of Animals*

Woman has been made for man.
—St. Augustine, *Confessions*

The male sex is more noble than the female.
—St. Thomas Aquinas, *Summa Theologica*

Hostile Bigotry Expressed in Armed Conflict

Each year since 1992 the Heidelberg Institute for International Conflict Research publishes a Conflict Barometer, which includes a Global Conflict Panorama.[49] In 2014, the Institute reported on 223 violent conflicts of which 46 were highly violent wars and 25 limited wars. The primary rationale for the armed conflicts was ideological differences, followed by struggles for national power or for control of natural resources.

Not all of these conflicts spring from hostile bigotry; however, the most obvious ones that do involve extremist non-State perpetrators, where primary alliance is to a religious identity rather than to a nationality. The most visible has been the Islamic State of Iraq and the Levant (ISIL), which has been accused of ethnic cleansing on an historic scale. It has used social media to display beheadings as a terror tactic.

While violence in armed conflict typically focuses on military actions, the oldest and least condemned crime in relation to armed conflict is the use of sexual violence as a weapon of war, including the public forced rape of mothers by their sons and daughters by their fathers and infants as young as six months by the military. In April 2013 the G8 leaders finally addressed this issue by shifting from the age-old belief that "sexual violence in conflict is inevitable" to the following position:[50]

> Sexual violence in conflict will not be tolerated, and the full force of international order will be brought to bear to ensure accountability for such crimes. For the perpetrators, there can be no hiding place; no amnes-

ty; no safe harbour. They will be pursued by any and all means at our collective disposal. In the process, we will begin to transfer the stigma of this crime from the victims, to the perpetrators.

On 24 June 2013 the UN Security Council passed Resolution 2016 (2013) condemning sexual violence as a war tactic and classifying it, in Article 2, as a "crime against humanity or a constitutive act with respect to genocide." On 2 September 2015 the International Criminal Court trial of Congolese rebel leader Bosco Ntaganda began; he stood accused of 13 counts of war crimes and five counts of crimes against humanity, including ordering the use of sexual violence.

Other Targets of Hostile Bigotry

As populations age, the issue of *elder abuse* is beginning to surface.[51] Elder abuse includes, but is not limited to, physically restraining elders, depriving them of dignity (e.g., leaving them in soiled clothes) and choice over daily affairs, intentionally providing insufficient care (e.g., allowing them to develop pressure sores), over- and under-medicating and withholding medication, and emotional neglect and abuse. Few data are available, especially from developing countries, as the targets are often fearful that reporting it will escalate the abuse.

The World Health Organization has reported that both *children and adults with disabilities* are at much higher risk of violence than their non-disabled peers in high income countries due both to social stigma and a lack of support for those who care for them.[52] If placed in an institution, their vulnerability to violence increases. While data are not yet available, one can only speculate that the situation may be worse in low- and middle-income countries.

What we do know is that children with disabilities are 3.7 times more likely to experience any sort of violence than non-disabled children, 3.6 times more likely to be victims of physical violence, and 2.9 times more likely to be victims of sexual violence.[53] The most vulnerable are children with mental or intellectual impairments; they are 4.6 times more likely to experience sexual violence. Adults with disabilities are 1.5 times more likely to be a victim of violence than those without a disability, while those with mental health conditions are at nearly four times the risk of experiencing violence. There is a United Nations Convention on the Rights of Persons with Disabilities that reinforces the need to ensure their full and equal participation in society without the threat of violence.

Another arena with little research to date is hostile bigotry directed towards the *homeless*. In many communities those sleeping rough or in emergency shelters not only lack secure financial means but also have mental health issues and are unable to function effectively. That we would force those least able to cope into unsafe sleeping situations where they need strong coping skills to survive is an obvious contradiction.

An unfortunately common approach to engaging with the homeless is to treat them like animals or public health risks and ensure that they are restricted geographically (much like ghettoization). The conflict that erupted in London, UK when building residents placed spikes in the ground around doorways and partially protected areas to prevent the homeless from being able to lie down is one example.[54] Over 50 U.S. cities have adopted some kind of anti-camping or anti-food-sharing law, which some say suggests a kind of "compassion fatigue."[55] The result of such laws has been to criminalize homelessness.

The National Law Center on Homelessness and Poverty estimates that up to 3.5 million Americans are sleeping rough or in emergency shelters, while an additional 7.4 million are in unstable housing.[56] Further, there are homeless living on the street or in tent cities in at least 41 of the 50 states, 34 percent of cities have citywide laws banning camping in public, 43 percent prohibit sleeping in vehicles, and 53 percent ban sitting or lying down in certain public places.

In August 2015, the U.S. Department of Justice intervened to say that such laws violate the Eighth Amendment protections against cruel and unusual punishment:

> When adequate shelter space exists, individuals have a choice about whether or not to sleep in public. However, when adequate shelter space does not exist, there is no meaningful distinction between the status of being homeless and the conduct of sleeping in public. Sleeping is a life-sustaining activity — i.e., it must occur at some time in some place. If a person literally has nowhere else to go, then enforcement of the anti-camping ordinance against that person criminalizes her for being homeless.[57]

Finally, we have the violence committed against nonhuman persons, including the Earth itself. As long as we feel justified in morally excluding nonhumans, we can condone actions like Japan's killing of minke whales under the guise of research though the meat is sold as food, or dolphin drives where dolphins are slaughtered by the dozens, or murdering elephants for their tusks, or caging chimpanzees and subjecting them to experiments that can be fatal or create lifelong health problems.

British lawyer Polly Higgins has helped to uncover official documents indicating that the UN was planning to accept "ecocide" as a fifth crime[58] against peace, which could be tried at the International Criminal Court. She has asked the UN Law Commission to recognize ecocide, which is defined as "the extensive destruction, damage to or loss of ecosystem(s) of a given territory, whether by human agency or by other causes, to such an extent that peaceful enjoyment by the inhabitants of that territory has been severely diminished."[59] A mock trial in the U.K. Supreme Court found the CEOs of two major oil and gas companies guilty of ecocide for their role in extracting crude oil from Alberta's tar sands.[60]

Affirming Hostile Bigotry's Presence

Because it involves overt violence, hostile bigotry can be easy to identify. In contrast to other forms of depersonalization, the issue is not so much identification as a willingness to take it seriously. If we do pay attention, we are appalled by the enormity of the pain and anguish visited on those around us. By its nature, hostile bigotry is distressing and disgusting—almost unbearable to contemplate. We want to turn aside and damp down our awareness. It is soothing to say to ourselves, "It can't be that bad. Surely they are exaggerating." We may even find ourselves indulging in blaming the victim (a form of hostile bigotry itself!)—"They probably asked for it"—to ease the pain.

But the worst thing we can do is to overlook or discount these actions. That will only allow them to continue unabated. Research tells us that, while it can be dangerous to act, bystander intervention can halt the violence.[61] Even if we cannot intervene, at least we can have the fortitude to endure hearing or reading about the atrocities that others are suffering, "lest we forget." We can bear witness so that there comes a time of "never again."

FIVE

"They Need Protection": Benevolent Bigotry

A strange thing has happened to bigotry—it has become more covert, at least in North America and Europe. Overt bigotry has decreased, and so it would appear that we are less prejudiced.[1] But at the same time, the willingness to reverse the effects of centuries-long bigotry has not increased.

People have learned not to say certain derogatory words like chink, homo, nigger, wop even though they are thinking them and the underlying hostility is still there. Bigotry, and its milder cousin prejudice, have simply gone underground so that there is an increasing disparity between what people say and how they behave. More importantly, when bigotry and prejudice are suppressed, it becomes almost impossible to address and eliminate them because they appear to be absent. That is the focus of this chapter—to make the invisible visible.

The Nature of Prejudice

Much of social psychological research now focuses on the dynamics of two related but different faces of prejudice: (a) explicit—overt, consciously accessible, modifiable, and (b) implicit—covert, subtle, aversive, ambivalent, stable.[2] Explicit prejudice manifests as hostile bigotry, the topic of Chapter Four. In this chapter, we look at what has variously been called implicit prejudice or subtle prejudice or benevolent bigotry, as well as the contrasts between the two.

Prejudice refers to a feeling—a "pre-judging"—that we develop separate from any knowledge of facts. While we can be positively prejudiced in favor of an individual or group, we generally reserve the term "prejudice" for negative or hostile feelings that are unfounded and highly resistant to rational influence. If we reflect on our categorization process, we can see that all of us have prejudices.[3]

In his book, *The Nature of Prejudice*, psychologist Gordon Allport was the first to describe prejudice as a normal human characteristic that has its roots in our perceptual process of categorization. When we create schemas related to social groups, we combine a number of points along a continuum of traits and assign them to a particular category. For example, one person's schema of "elderly" might be defined as everyone with grey or white hair (which could include people who are in their fifties, or even younger) while another person's schema of "elderly" might focus on degree of physical fragility and include only those who have become physically dependent on others, regardless of hair color. So how we each make the distinction between elderly and not elderly is a matter of personal definition. We are not born with schemas; we create them.

Prejudice becomes resistant to change because of a double standard in how we decide cause and effect (known as "causal attribution") for different schemas or categories in our schemas. We often explain away the successes of out-group members as being due to luck or a special advantage, while viewing their failures as due to a lack of ability or sheer laziness. We may go further and actually blame out-group members for causing the failure ("blaming the victim"[4]) when we say things like, "Well, she was asking for it—dressing that way and being out alone at night." Then we may do the reverse for our in-group—attribute successes to personal talent and failures to external, situational factors, particularly the actions of target groups. So we say, "The deck was stacked" or "They're out to get us" or "I'd have a job if it weren't for those [minorities] horning in."

While the above description of causal attribution is generally accurate, researchers have found intriguing gender differences in the *self*-attribution process. Men follow the in-group pattern, attributing their own success to personal talent and hard work and their failures to external factors. Women, on the other hand, tend to follow the *out-group* pattern, treating themselves as if they were *not* part of the in-group. They attribute their successes to luck and their failures to a lack of talent or application.[5] One of the practical implications in the workplace is that men are more likely to promote themselves and their successes than women are, which in turn helps men advance in their careers.

We can think of the generic term "prejudice" as having three components: the opinion or belief, expressed as a stereotype; the feeling, expressed as a positive or negative prejudice; and the behavior or action, expressed as harassment or discrimination or violent physical behavior. While the dynamics of prejudice are generic, its expression varies along a number of dimensions. It may be overt or subtle, unambiguous or ambivalent, conscious (explicit) or unconscious (implicit).

Implicit Bias

Before we go further, we need to understand an unconscious dynamic that occurs for us all—implicit bias, or prejudices that develop outside of our awareness. We accumulate these implicit associations over a long period of time, starting as young as six months old based both on our experiences and on exposure to media.[6] Although they can be unlearned, it is challenging to do so because we first have to bring them into our awareness.

As prejudice has become less overtly expressed, researchers have documented a surge in implicit or covert prejudice (whether racism, sexism, etc.). It is as though, if you suppress explicit expressions of prejudice, it has to pop up somewhere. Prejudice doesn't just fade away.

People who consider themselves free of prejudice are now often being shown to be quite prejudiced, only it is implicit. Recognizing this can be very unnerving! How can you know what implicit attitudes or stereotypes you are harboring if you are not aware of them?

Researchers have developed the Implicit Association Test (IAT) for just that purpose.[7] Its design is based on the fact that we can respond more quickly if we are drawing on concepts already linked in our minds—i.e., implicit bias—instead of ones that seem unrelated. If you want to test yourself for hidden biases, you can take the test at Project Implicit's website.[8] Organizations like the Kirwan Institute for the Study of Race and Ethnicity are developing strategies for people to "de-bias" themselves.[9]

Implicit and explicit biases are related but distinct. Researchers have found, for example, that while explicit bias may predict racist slurs, implicit bias predicts the nonverbal behavior that can convey racism.[10] Unfortunately, "nonverbal signals can be especially effective in transmitting social attitudes because they can be spontaneously understood with minimal effort and are perceived as a source of valid information....Nonverbal messages influence relatively sophisticated participants who are especially motivated to appear unbiased."[11] We all know the power of the raised eyebrow or the head position.

Most people have some implicit biases that do not align with their expressed beliefs. Indeed, research estimates are that between 75 and 93 percent of all North Americans have some level of unconscious bias.[12] These can get activated by the process of priming or prior sensitization (which we discussed in Chapter One).[13] They can be offset by a sense of shared identity.

Law professor Jerry Kang has done an excellent job of summarizing the implicit bias that results from our use of schemas to organize data in long-term memory and then analyzing implications for everyday transactions in the court room.[14] Research shows that, generally speaking, we have implicit biases that match up well with general social hierarchies, consistently giving preference to groups with higher social status. We also have an implicit, or unconscious, positive preference for schemas that include ourselves and negative biases towards schemas that are not similar to us. These tendencies interact so that, if we are from a lower-status group, our preferences may be divided between our own group and the higher status group, depending on the circumstances.

The dynamics of implicit bias have specific ramifications when it comes to a range of discriminatory actions, such as:[15]

- o The rate of callback interviews
- o Perception of whether one is being treated fairly or courteously
- o Perceptions of friendliness
- o Assessment of ambiguous actions by Blacks
- o Severity of criminal sentencing
- o Negative evaluations of confident, assertive women
- o Racial disproportionality in school discipline[16]
- o Frequency of prescribing pain medication for four pediatric conditions[17]
- o Murder of unarmed Blacks by police officers[18]

Our usual implicit bias is to favor and identify with our own in-group and distance ourselves from those that we consider the out-group. In fact, wanting to maintain social distance from another has been a reliable measure of the strength of prejudice.[19] But it is not uncommon for members of stigmatized groups to internalize the prejudice expressed towards them by others and therefore to want to distance themselves from their own group. The psychological costs of this internalization of prejudice are high—including depression, self-loathing, and even suicide.

Accepting the myth that the dominant group (the perpetrator) is indeed superior is foundational to the internalization process. This aspect of internalization is reminiscent of the Stockholm Syndrome, where victims of kidnapping or abuse bond emotionally with the perpetrator as part of an often unconscious dynamic of keeping the perpetrator happy so that the victim remains alive. Internalization can be activated by feeling rejected or bullied or even by feeling shame at how others treat the stigmatized group.

When racism is internalized, one of the consequences is that the person can develop a dislike of visual traits that are associated with the stigmatized group, which can result in attempts to "normalize" their appearance. So we see Asians getting double eyelid surgery or Jews getting rhinoplasty or Blacks chemically straightening their hair. The person may also try to "pass" or refuse to associate with others in the stigmatized group.

When sexist myths and stereotypes are internalized, the process is slightly different. Women, too, experience a psychological sense of inferiority—that they are less competent, less valuable—that results in a lack of self-confidence and a sense of powerlessness. But women and girls are in the unique position of being bombarded continuously with sexist messages and misogynistic images, which they then have to accept or reject repeatedly (absorbing some working memory energy). Documented consequences for women and girls include self-surveillance and body shame[20] (which can lead to eating disorders), competing with other women for men's attention, and self-objectification (which we will return to in Chapter 8).

Social worker Janet Thomas, who created BreakFree in 1993 to help women identify and eliminate implicit bias constraints, described the dynamic articulately in her August 1997 blog:

> The message of sexism comes at us in two ways: external and internal oppression. The *external sexism* is messages and behavior coming to us from outside, through institutions and individuals, e.g. "Women are too emotional to be in positions of authority." *Internalized sexism* is taking in and believing the stereotypes and misinformation that our sexist culture tells us about being female and what it means to be a woman, resulting in e.g. "What do I know…", "Who am I to speak…" Both external and internal avenues of oppression are painful and limiting for women as individuals and as a group, and deprive the world of our best thoughts, decisions, and actions.[21]

The other arena in which internalization of negative stereotypes and prejudices has been extensively researched is the internalization of homophobia (or heterosexism) by lesbians and gay men. There continues to be strong social pressure to be heterosexual (including the threat of death) and to devalue any other lifestyle. What results is an internal conflict between that social pressure and one's actual identity, often being resolved by a rigid adoption of the belief that only heterosexuality is "normal." The resulting self-hatred and rejection of gay positive beliefs makes it difficult not only to value oneself but also to be present in a quality intimate relationship.[22]

Because of the stress of functioning in an inhospitable social environment, the self-hatred often continues to grow in intensity. It is not a simple matter of self-acceptance, as with racial minorities or females; rather, there can be real-world costs to "coming out" that need to be considered—e.g., loss of family and friends, job, professional license, child custody, physical freedom, etc.

The strength of disapproval gays face, even in legally-sanctioned contexts, is illustrated by the uproar caused in Kentucky by a county clerk who refused to issue marriage licenses to gay couples after the U.S. Supreme Court had ruled that it was illegal to deny gays the right to marry—and who was then feted by the Family Research Council for flaunting the law. Unfortunately, "coming out" does not automatically dissolve internalized homophobia, which can continue to affect gays for years after.[23]

The Dynamics of Benevolent Bigotry

Benevolent bigotry is the expression of positive feelings toward the target but in the form of chivalry—e.g., "character-izing women as pure creatures who ought to be protected, supported, and adored."[24] It is the result of an attempt to appear unprejudiced while still harboring negative stereo-types. The depersonalization strategy underlying benevolent bigotry is that of viewing the target as an immature version of the perpetrator. It is motivated in general by paternalism, or the belief that the limits being placed are for the target's own good.

Benevolent bigotry is a particularly seductive form of de-personalization. It feels good to have someone else want to look after and cherish us. But the consequences are damaging if that "looking after" comes with a disempowering implica-tion that we are not capable of looking after ourselves, that we are somehow inferior. The underlying paternalism occurs in all social contexts, displayed by all types of people. The problem with paternalism is that the limitation on the target's freedom or autonomy occurs whether or not the target desires it.[25]

The lurking negative prejudice gets expressed in discrimination when the situation is one where prejudice can be denied.[26] For example, if White experimental participants high on benevolent prejudice are presented with Black job applicants who are clearly qualified for the position, they will approve the hiring. But if the qualifications are ambiguous, they will not.[27] And they will not approve hiring the better qualified Black candidate if they feel they can demonstrate that an authority figure has instructed them to prefer the less qualified White candidate.[28] If asked, though, the participants would be certain that they were not prejudiced.

What about for the perpetrator? What is the consequence of being benevolently prejudiced? Any prejudicial attitudes or discriminatory behaviors are justified as complying with social norms—"women are such good caregivers"—and any problem is not in the perpetrator's awareness.[29] So we have a situation where perpetrators believe they are behaving in an unprejudiced and kindly manner and yet the impact on women is negative because of the implied incompetence or weakness.[30] The more subtle the expression of benevolent bigotry—for example, with no accompanying offer of assistance that could be identified as sexist—the more unpleasant women found the encounter though they had difficulty saying why.

Part of what holds benevolent bigotry in place is the dynamic that we have referred to before (in Chapter One) as that of mindfulness and its companion, mindlessness. We have become so used to the "small" slights, the innuendos that comprise benevolent prejudice that we are literally unaware of them, or mindless. When researchers asked targets to keep diaries over a two-week period (i.e., to become mindful), they found that the following previously ignored sexist behaviors were noticed: 36% gender role stereotyping remarks, 31% demeaning comments, and 25% sexual objectification (staring at breasts, unwanted touches). For those observing racist behavior, the breakdown was: 36% hostile stares or being watched closely, 24% racial slurs and jokes, 18% preferential treatment to Whites, and 15% rude behavior and avoiding contact.[31]

Benevolent and hostile bigotry are two faces of the general dynamic now known as ambivalent prejudice, or the holding of both positive and negative stereotypes simultaneously. Of course "positive" is not *that* positive when it refers to being incompetent or in need of protection. We may accept the notion of equality in general but not as applied to specific groups. We may accept intellectually that groups we grew up thinking of as social inferiors or even as unclean are actually entitled to the same respect as we are, but that doesn't mean that we want to sit down to dinner with them or have them as neighbors or invite them to marry into our family.

Research shows, for example, that those with hostile sexist attitudes rated women lower when applying for a male-dominant position. Additionally, high hostile sexist individuals recommend males to fill this position more often than women — an example of the "glass ceiling" effect (the unseen yet unbreakable barrier to corporate advancement for women and minorities).[32]

In untangling the dynamic of benevolent bigotry, researchers have found two primary dimensions in operation: warmth (friendliness, trustworthiness) and competence (intelligence, skills).[33] Others first form an impression of warmth,[34] which takes precedence in impression management. Then they evaluate competence. The unfortunate double bind is that, if an individual (particularly a female) is judged high on warmth, they are then assumed to be low on competence. If they are assessed as high on competence, they are assumed to be low on warmth.[35]

Subtle or benevolent prejudice is particularly pernicious because it reflects current social norms that support inequality — women are warm and caring, women are more nurturing, etc.[36] As social pressure builds to be less overtly racist or sexist or chauvinistic, people have learned to suppress or keep quiet about negative feelings — but that doesn't mean that those feelings have gone away.[37] Research methods and advances in technologies like fMRI allow researchers to look beyond verbal report or role playing to actual physiological responses and actual brain activity. So we find that people may report low levels of prejudice and yet have physiological responses associated with negative emotions.

Exercise: Combating Benevolent Bigotry

Reflect on your own intimate relationship or a close friendship and decide:

1. Are there any ways that benevolent bigotry is expressed between the two of you?

2. If so, what could you change so that you are more empowering of each other?

While benevolent bigotry has been explored in a number of human contexts, we have yet to formally recognize it when applied to nonhumans — that is, ways in which we assume that particular nonhumans are not mature enough to manage their own lives. There are three dynamics to consider. The first dynamic is that we evaluate nonhumans against humans as the norm — much as we evaluate females against a male norm. As an example, news coverage of Koshik, the Korean-speaking elephant held captive at the Republic of Korea's

Everland zoo, focused on the astounding fact that he could speak Korean.[38] What was not even mentioned is that highly-social Koshik, isolated from other elephants, had filled his social needs by becoming bilingual.

Further, we express astonishment and disbelief when we find shared characteristics that would suggest a need to treat the nonhuman with the same respect that we accord another human. One example is our inability to credit rituals and mourning expressed around death. When Lawrence Anthony died in South Africa in March 2013, members of elephant herds with whom he had worked travelled for 12 hours through the bush to his home, stood in silence for two days, and then left—a tribute to the "elephant whisperer."[39]

A similar question could be raised in relation to a report that NOC, a beluga whale held captive for 30 years at the National Marine Mammal Foundation in San Diego, was overheard (starting in 1984) carrying on conversations in a human-like voice, several octaves below the frequency of whales' usual speech.[40] After four years, NOC stopped speaking English and the hypothesis of scientists was that he had matured out of it. What if he stopped using his second language because no one talked back to him?

The second dynamic is that we have a paternalistic relationship with animals that we have domesticated. We have invited a wide range of animals into our homes, but generally speaking we expect them to behave the way we want them to rather than in a manner consistent with their behavior in the wild. We also expect them to be grateful to us for caring for them, though what we have actually done is to remove them from their extended family and natural social context. Indeed, their survival depends on their adapting to our needs and expectations. Sound familiar in terms of other stigmatized groups needing to adapt to the higher status group?

The third dynamic is that our view of good stewardship of the environment, or of animals living in their natural habitat, is tainted by our own self-interest rather than being focused on their best interest. In some ways we have already moved from viewing all nonhumans as resources to be exploited to the paternalistic feeling that we have a responsibility to treat natural resources (including the animal kingdom) humanely.

But we fall short of considering that a wide range of non-humans have moral rights and are entitled to have their needs be as important as ours. This is challenging because inevitably there are conflicting needs. But that is also true within our human family. Our focus needs to be on boundary management so that all living beings can flourish.

Benevolent Sexism in Operation

While there is a "benevolent" version of prejudice operating in all social domains, it is in the realm of gender relations where psychologists Peter Glick and Susan Fiske first identified the dynamic and developed the Ambivalent Sexism Inventory (ASI).[41] Sexism represents a specialized version of depersonalization because the vast majority of women's lives are intertwined with men—as daughters, sisters, wives, mothers, aunts, grandmothers—in a manner that is not true for other stigmatized groups.

As research with the ASI progressed, the complexities of sexism became clearer, with both hostile and benevolent sexism being identified and measured.[42] Hostile sexism, a form of hostile bigotry, refers to attitudes of power, dominance, and a desire to punish women for violating traditional passive, subordinate sex roles—the precursors of violence against women. Benevolent sexism, on the other hand, refers to a set of anti-egalitarian, gender-traditional attitudes, expressed as paternalistic affection—"women are wonderful."[43] And so we see the common contradiction in attitudes towards women—the "Madonna" or woman in her traditional nurturing role on which men depend,[44] and the "whore" or woman as sexualized being that needs to be controlled and intimidated in order to keep her serving men's needs.[45]

On the surface perpetrators are complimentary, gallant, and respectful; so is benevolent sexism really a problem? Oh, yes! A challenge for women is that benevolent sexism can seem like simple friendly behavior, but it isn't. Its expression seems positive and complimentary—hence the term "benevolent"—and yet that expression will leave thoughtful women queasy. Why? The psychologist and science blogger Melanie Tannenbaum captured the dynamic like this:[46]

> There are plenty of seemingly positive portrayals of women that nonetheless perpetuate harmful stereotypes, such as the omnipresent depiction of the "how-does-she-do-it-all" housewife. Although a woman might feel complimented by this stereotype and the way in which it paints women as the kind of people who can "magically" get so much done, it is also quite possible for a woman to feel like this stereotype creates an unfair standard of comparison, or, alternatively, like it depicts women as weak, frazzled creatures who should be receiving more help from men in order to manage their lives without suffering a nervous breakdown. In social psychology, we refer to this phenomenon as *benevolent sexism*. Although it is tempting to brush this experience off as an overreaction to compliments or a misunderstanding of the communicator's benign intent, benevolent sexism is a phenomenon that is both real and insidiously dangerous.

Researchers have also verified that both hostile and benevolent sexism are alive and well in a range of countries.[47] Benevolently sexist men frequently, but not always, hold hostile sexist attitudes. More importantly, the research shows that benevolent sexism (independent of hostile sexism) is a significant predictor of widespread gender inequality—e.g., lower female participation in politics and the economy, lower literacy rates, less education, and shorter life expectancy for females. Benevolently sexist men classify ideal women into traditional roles, while hostilely sexist men classify those same women as worthless and servile.[48]

The dynamic of benevolent sexism places women in a bind when offered chivalrous help from a man. If she accepts help courteously, she is viewed as warm but incompetent; while if she refuses the offer (even if she has no need of it), she is viewed as cold and unwomanly.[49] In situations where a woman is reporting harassment, men high in hostile sexism find less evidence of harassment if the woman is assertive in her behavior.[50] Women who are primed by exposure to a submissive complainant find less evidence of harassment if the target reports harassment in a neutral manner—in other words, they blame the victim.

Speaking of priming, when men play video games high in sexist content, they then show higher levels of benevolent sexism.[51] When exposed to advertising content that shows women either in traditional or nontraditional roles, men high in benevolent sexism are more likely to evaluate women positively if they are in traditional roles; men high in hostile sexism were more likely to evaluate women negatively if they are in nontraditional roles.[52]

In examining the dynamic further, we find that authoritarianism predicts both benevolent and hostile sexism, but only hostile sexism predicts overt sexual harassment.[53] Benevolent sexism is lauded in religious circles as reinforcing behaviors that maintain social stability.[54] While benevolently sexist men are generally more supportive of women, if the woman violates gender role norms, all bets are off—the men will downgrade her job performance.[55]

When both hostile and benevolent sexism are present (as in ambivalent sexism), both men and women justify the status quo of male dominance; these research results provide unique verification that ambivalent sexism provides support for, and faith in, our legacy patriarchal system.[56] Hostile sexism leads to negative evaluations of men or women who step out of traditional gender roles, while benevolent sexism results in positive evaluations of women who adhere to traditional gender roles.[57] Table 2 compares the dynamics of hostile sexism and benevolent sexism, depending on whether the female is in a traditional or non-traditional role.

Table 2: Comparing Hostile and Benevolent Behaviors

Male Attitude	Female in Traditional Role	Female in Non-Traditional Role
Hostile Sexism	Tolerant Treat as servile Evaluate negatively	Punitive Discriminate; harass Evaluate negatively
Benevolent Sexism	Supportive Assume warm, not competent Evaluate positively	Chivalrous Assume competent, not warm Evaluate negatively Discriminate if deniable

Researchers have shown that there are many individuals, men and women alike, who still do not believe that benevolent sexism merits concern, believing instead that it is harmless.[58] This is problematic because, while the consequences of hostile sexism are widely known and accepted, research has shown that benevolent sexism may in fact have a more severe impact on a women's cognitive abilities.[59] The anger and frustration triggered by *hostile* sexism can increase the target's motivation to perform well and "show them;" as well, hostile sexism is blatant, easy to identify, and equally easy to ignore.

Benevolent sexism, by contrast, is subtle and ambiguous. While hostile sexism is antagonistic, benevolent sexism is chivalrous. Targets need to use working memory capacity trying to figure out what is going on, with the result that they perform poorly, thus undermining their self-confidence and precipitating even worse performance. It is a vicious circle. Glick and Fiske themselves write:

> We do not consider benevolent sexism a good thing, for despite the positive feelings it may indicate for the perceiver, its underpinnings lie in traditional stereotyping and masculine dominance (e.g., the man as the provider and woman as his dependent), and its consequences are often damaging. Benevolent sexism is not necessarily experienced as benevolent by the recipient. For example, a man's comment to a female coworker on how 'cute' she looks, however well-intentioned, may undermine her feelings of being taken seriously as a professional.[60]

Paradoxically, women themselves may develop benevolent sexist attitudes after experiencing hostile sexism.[61] Unfortunately, when exposed to covert benevolent sexism or internalizing it themselves, women begin focusing on the advantages of the status quo (system justification). Women report being significantly less likely to engage in anti-sexist collective action unless they are exposed to overt hostile sexism that triggers anger.[62] Since benevolent sexism is replacing hostile sexism, there is an increased likelihood that benevolent sexism will continue unchallenged.

There are several psychological costs involved.[63] First, benevolent sexism assumes traditional gender roles. If the target is a traditional housewife and mother, all is well; after all, "women are naturally more nurturing than men." But if the target steps out of role—gets an advanced degree, holds a position of administrative authority, excels at a sport—watch out! Hostile sexism will quickly emerge. So in order to get the "benefit" of those compliments, the target has to be willing to constrain herself to fit the role—to "act the way a woman is supposed to act"—regardless of her personal inclinations.

Second, the traditional role or standard to which women are held is highly idealized. Women are supposed to be pure and chaste (a moral example), a ready support and companion for their spouse while invisibly cleaning house, caring for children, doing laundry, acting as chauffeur, shopping, cooking, and all the other activities that come with maintaining a household—in other words, a super-mom. In the midst of all this, women are to maintain a physical appearance worthy of a Playboy centerfold and be continuously available to their partner for sexual gratification. If she also has paid work outside the home ("two shifts"), she will be even more challenged for time and energy. Regardless of the woman, she will inevitably fall short and then be patted on the head with condescending understanding.

Third, and probably more damaging, benevolent sexism reinforces the view that men are strong and competent while women are weak and fragile. It creates a confusing dynamic for any woman with aspirations other than that of homemaker as the hidden message is that it is men's responsibility to take care of women, thus justifying lower pay because "the man has to provide." It lures a woman into believing that the ideal is to have a male protector (parallel to children having an adult protector) rather than being potent in her own right. And it sets the stage for the yo-yo we see in domestic violence where the man, feeling that his authority has been challenged, first beats the woman and then tearfully begs forgiveness— only to repeat the cycle over and over until the woman leaves or is hospitalized or is murdered.

In work settings, researchers have shown that women frequently face covert barriers to achieving upper levels of management known as a "glass ceiling."[64] The unequal treatment represents a gender difference that:

o Cannot be explained by job-relevant characteristics.
o Is greater at higher levels than at lower levels.
o Affects the chances of advancement.
o Increases over the course of a career.

In other words, the closer the woman gets to upper management positions, the more unlikely advancement becomes. Professors at the University of Exeter have added the concept of the "glass cliff," pointing out that women tend to be put into leadership roles during periods of crisis or downturn when the risk of failure is highest.[65]

So what does all this research look like in real life? Let's look at Tara (a half-time kindergarten assistant) and Josephine (a public prosecutor), both with young children, and Mark (a traditional "man's man," high on hostile sexism) and Edward (gentle, high on benevolent sexism). Tara will be treated courteously by both men, though she may be nervous of Mark's violence, if she slips up, and be wary of Edward's gallantry. The situation will shift to negative if she decides to go to law school. Josephine can expect hostility from Mark and condescending remarks from Edward, though he will not actively undermine her unless he can blame someone else. Generally speaking, the only "positive" position for women is in traditional caretaking roles with an acceptance that they will be viewed as incompetent.

We have been focusing primarily on individuals. What about in intimate relations? Research has shown that the higher heterosexual men score on hostile sexism, the less open they are to dialogue, the more hostile both partners are and the less successful they are at resolving conflict.[66] However, if the man adopts a benevolent sexist attitude, the result is more openness to partner influence, with less hostility and a high likelihood of successfully resolving conflict. If only the heterosexual woman shifts to benevolent sexism, the woman then behaves like her male partner, with no successful resolution.

So success in heterosexual couples' conflict resolution appears to rest with the man's motivation.

While not the dynamic that we traditionally associate with prejudice, benevolent sexism has the clear consequence of gender inequality. Underneath the veneer of gallantry, women are viewed as being of lower status, as less than fully human just as Aristotle said!

Exercise: Identifying Benevolent Sexism

Pick a situation where someone you know is subject to benevolent sexism and answer the following:

1. What is the impact of the benevolent sexism on that individual?

2. How does or could that individual empower themselves?

3. Who could they enlist as allies to offset the benevolent sexism?

Contending with Benevolent Bigotry

In order to recognize benevolent bigotry, we have to be willing to examine our own motivations more closely than we might be used to doing. Dissipating benevolent bigotry requires a commitment to mutually respectful, non-patronizing relationships. If we want the benefits of self-acceptance and being accepted by others as ourselves, we have to be willing to relinquish burdening others with our care when we are capable of caring for ourselves. If we want to stop resentment or being triggered into violence, we need to look for validation within ourselves instead of from controlling others.

SIX

"They're All the Same": Stereotyping

All Blacks have rhythm. All Asians are good at math. All blondes are dumb. Really? Are we that naïve that we believe *all* people in a group share a particular trait?

One of the most commonly-recognized forms of depersonalization is stereotyping. Here, for efficiency's sake, we categorize the almost infinite variety of human beings into a few, more manageable groupings or schemas. Then we focus on differences between our in-group ("us") and the out-group ("them"), assuming a uniformity or homogeneity in each group that robs the members of their individuality, or individual identity.

As the late journalist Walter Lippmann wrote, "For the most part we do not first see, and then define; we define first and then see." Until we have a framework for interpreting what we are looking at, we literally can't see it. This is the experience that people blind from birth have when they first gain their sight. The stereotypes we develop form a filter through which we experience and understand the world around us.

Prejudice and Stereotypes

Until now our focus has been on prejudices, the positive and negative evaluative attitudes or feelings that we have regarding ourselves and others. We know that our first response in any new situation is emotional — there is an immediate hormonal reaction (e.g., adrenalin) before the mind has a chance to swing into gear.[1] So we have an initial gut feeling…and then what?

Along with developing prejudices about social groups (starting around two years old), we also compile supporting beliefs from what we observe or are taught. Stereotypes provide us with a rationale for our emotional response. When we are busy or distracted, they provide a quick and easy way to process social data.[2] They provide depth and content and answer the question, "Why do I feel this way?" In a sense, we retrofit stereotypes, or our rationales, onto prejudices, after which the two operate in tandem. To change a prejudice, we must change the underlying stereotypes, the foundation or building blocks upon which the prejudice rests.

In Chapter Five, we looked at the dimensions of warmth and competence that comprise benevolent sexism. Researchers have developed that initial dichotomy (known as the Stereotype Content Model) into a more complete model that can help us see the roles played by stereotypes and prejudices.[3] In Table 3 below, we can see the initial dichotomy of warmth/competence supplemented by designations of status and cooperation/competition.[4]

Table 3: Stereotype Content Model

Warmth	**High (cooperative)**	***Paternalistic*** *Pity* Housewives, disabled, elderly	***Admiring*** *Pride* In-group, close allies
	Low (competitive)	***Contemptuous*** *Disgust* Homeless, poor	***Envious*** *Resentment* Jews, rich people
		Low status	**High status**
		Competence	

Key: ***Stereotypic thought***
       Prejudiced feeling

The other four forms of depersonalization all draw on ste-reotypes to determine how we treat others. We can think of the combination of prejudice and stereotypes as follows:

Table 4: Depersonalization, Attitudes, and Beliefs

Form of Deper-sonalization	Attitude (Prejudice)	Belief (Stereotype)
Hostile bigotry	vilify, demonize	unnatural, not human
Benevolent bigotry	patronize, condescend	immature, can't care for self
Invisibility	dismiss, overlook	of no account
Objectification	possess	for our use

Social Identity and Group Membership

Feeling part of a group (or groups) forms an important part of our self-concept, our social identity. To develop a sense of group membership, we first categorize people, including ourselves, in order to make sense of our social context (known as "social categorization"). We use the group as a reference point for learning about ourselves and how we are similar to, or different from, others in the groups to which we might belong. At this point, we begin to recognize the *descriptive* stereotypes (typical traits and behaviors) of various groups.

Next we select and identify with what we define as our in-group (known as "social identification"). Indeed, this is often how we introduce ourselves to other group members — for example, "I am your neighbor / classmate / coworker." We adopt the associated traits and behaviors, and begin to absorb the *prescriptive* stereotypes that tell us how we *should* act as a member of that group. That identification brings with it an increase in "social" self-esteem.

Finally, in order to maintain self-esteem, we typically compare our group favorably with other groups—"we are better than you" (known as "social comparison")—to ensure that our group is indeed *the* best. In this process, we exaggerate differences between groups and also exaggerate the similarity of persons in our in-group. This comparison process can lead to competition and hostility between groups. Of course, "better than" is not the only model. We could also say, "We're great and you're great, too."

While this process of group categorization, identification, and comparison sounds straightforward, several questions arise. First, what group will we choose as our primary in-group? We belong to multiple groups, some given (like gender or ethnicity or parenthood) and some chosen (like an interest group). British social psychologist Henri Tajfel pioneered the work we know today as in-group bias.[5] When he and his colleagues placed strangers in groups randomly and assigned each group an unfamiliar task, they found that quite quickly the participants reported liking members of their own group more than members of other groups and feeling their group was superior.

His work demonstrates that we identify with an in-group even when the division into groups is artificial. He called this dynamic "minimal groups." For example, Jane Elliott, a third grade teacher, divided her class into those with brown eyes and those with blue and then gave privileges to those with brown eyes.[6] Within hours, the two groups were at odds with each other. Similarly Ron Jones, a high school teacher, recruited students into an imaginary new cultural program, "the Wave" (since memorialized in a short story, TV movie, and novel), and the same dynamic occurred as with the third graders.

What is important from the perspective of depersonalization is that the students immediately identified as members of the assigned groups, thereby giving up a sense of personal uniqueness and in turn depersonalizing others. So not only do we stereotype and depersonalize others, but we do the same to ourselves.

Second, since we belong to multiple in-groups, which one is salient, or most important, and when? To answer this, we need to recognize that different groups have different social status, and we tend to gravitate to high-status in order to reinforce our self-image and self-esteem. Take, for example, a parent who coaches Little League softball and is the CEO of a major company. Now assume that this parent is male. If he is feeling at all insecure he might draw on his highest-status identity, CEO, and act like a CEO even around the house or when coaching. Now assume that this parent is female. Prescriptive stereotypes would say that her best chance of acceptance is as a parent (lower status than CEO) — but what does that mean for her perceived effectiveness at work as a CEO?

Third, what happens when the descriptive or prescriptive stereotypes of our different in-groups conflict with each other, or the actual group norms conflict with the prescriptive stereotype? Let's say you identify as a member of a seniors advocacy group. The group itself is clear that its purpose is to press for changes to the quality of life for seniors in the community through workshops, publications, and appearances at municipal council meetings. However, the prevailing prescriptive stereotype of "seniors" is as fragile community members to be pitied, not as dynamic, articulate advocates. You may well have difficulty getting council members to listen and take you seriously, if your view of seniors is different, because they will be viewing you through that prescriptive stereotype.

Being part of a high-status group usually makes us feel good. Most of us like to be on the winning team, to be seated at the head table, to have special status on airlines or at hotels. And as long as others are not being hurt, what's the problem? Social identity theory[7] tells us that group membership, while an important mechanism for maintaining and reinforcing our self-esteem or sense of self-worth, can come with some negative consequences in terms of how we treat others.

Exercise: Boundaries of In-Groups

List at least three groups that you consider in-groups for yourself and then reflect on:

1. When or under what circumstances does each group become your primary or number one in-group, or stop being your primary in-group?

2. Which, or how many, characteristics do you need to share with other members of the in-group in order for you to feel you are in the same group?

3. What could change about you or the group so that you no longer identified with it as an in-group?

We feel good about ourselves when we belong to a group with "positive distinctiveness," which helps reinforce a positive self-concept. We call this a positive social identity, and it can be as important as our individually-developed self-esteem. If we are already a high-status individual in a high-status group, no problem. But if we are otherwise low status (e.g., from a stigmatized group) or in a group whose social status is not guaranteed, we are likely to adopt one of the following strategies, all of which increase depersonalization:

o Denigrate other groups and their members—i.e., enhance our group at the expense of others ("we've won more games").

o Assert the superiority of our group over other groups by changing the context of comparison ("we have a better coach").

o Try to move into a higher status group at the expense of others in our current in-group, thereby implicitly putting down those in-group members.

Bottom line, we are socialized to feel good about ourselves as part of an in-group by identifying and depersonalizing an out-group.

The flip side of group identification is that we cease to have a strong sense of individual identity. We can begin to feel as though we are nothing without the group, and so we feel personally threatened if we think the group is being criticized. As an extreme, we can become so strongly vested in seeing our group as more important or more powerful than other groups that we actually experience a diminished moral sense of responsibility (known as "herd mentality" or "mob mentality").

The Dynamics of Stereotyping

The stereotypes we develop about different social groups are a consequence of categorizing data in long-term memory into schemas. A stereotype allows us to respond quickly when interacting with someone new. For example, suppose you are at a social event, sponsored by a group of importance to a friend of yours, with lots of people you don't know. You need to be sociable, but you are at a loss to find common conversational ground. You are introduced to an Asian male and, with relief, you plunge into a discussion of the funding of education. Why would you choose that topic from among a dozen others? Probably because of a stereotype that Asians are concerned about academic performance.

Stereotypes serve as mental shortcuts if you will. They are the reverse of the saying, "I can't see the forest for the trees." When we stereotype others, we stop being able to see the trees and can only see the forest, the group. But not all trees — and not all people — are the same. So stereotypes are generalizations and oversimplifications of real world dynamics. They have the potential to be harmful because so often they treat others as part of a category, not as individuals.

We have already mentioned two general types of stereotypes when we talked about group creation — descriptive (what are typical traits or behaviors), and prescriptive (what the group member should do).[8] These can operate together in generating discrimination. The key, though, is prescriptive stereotyping — the "should." Research has shown that descriptive stereotypes do not predict gender bias or prejudice, but prescriptive stereotypes do. Further, prescriptive stereotypes can lead to males not only favoring male applicants, but also penalizing equally-qualified female applicants. Objective data about qualifications are able to diminish descriptive stereotyping but have no discernable impact on prescriptive stereotyping.[9] In other words, not only do we depersonalize others directly by treating them stereotypically, but the set of "shoulds" we create makes it virtually impossible for them to be seen and related to as persons.

For women in upper management, for example, gender role stereotypes are likely to prevent further progress because not only are women supposed to be subordinates, but their performance will be devalued, they will not be credited for their successes, and they will actually be penalized for being competent.[10] A similar dynamic occurs when a prescriptive stereotype appears to have been violated by an East Asian who behaves in a dominant manner that is appropriate and allowed for Whites but not for East Asians.[11]

These findings are in keeping with research showing that, while we may feel only a minimal amount of explicit social bias (the descriptive element), we could still have implicit social bias (the prescriptive element) with regard to whether or not members of other racial groups can be trusted, and that implicit social bias could affect how we deal with strangers who are members of those out-groups.[12] This subtle and unexpected discrimination can actually be more damaging to the target than overt prejudice because the target will use valuable working memory resources trying to understand why the bias happened and how they could have prevented it—just as we saw in the Chapter Five with regard to benevolent sexism.[13]

When we feel included in a particular group, we are likely to act in accordance with the stereotypes about that group. What happens if those stereotypes are negative, as can be the case for female math ability? When calculus students were informed that math skill was a fixed trait in which females were deficient, female students' sense of belonging in that calculus class and the math profession in general decreased; however, the sense of belonging returned when math was described as a skill that could be acquired.[14]

In general, stereotypes, like prejudice, have become more complex and ambiguous, and triggers of depersonalization have become more diverse.[15] Fortunately, they have also become more malleable or open to change.[16] As an example, in previous years (particularly prior to the two world wars), forming groups along socioeconomic class lines was virtually automatic, and people talked about those of a different socioeconomic class as being "not our type." But, especially since the wider availability of post-secondary education, group characteristics have become more nuanced. Now people can identify with a group based on the common love of a sport (like basketball or golf), with financial status and education not necessarily being similar.

We are also finding that the stereotyping process is not unidirectional—i.e., you belong to that group so you have that trait. We also place people in particular groups because of certain traits—i.e., we can notice the trait first and then make the group identification.[17] So instead of only saying, "She goes to the senior center so she must be at least 65," we can also say, "She is over 65 and so she must be part of the senior center." In actuality, neither stereotyping might be accurate. The person might be in her fifties and volunteering at the senior center, or the person might be over 65 and have never gone to the senior center.

We learn stereotypes not only from those around us but also from mass media, which is saturated with racial and gender stereotypes. Unfortunately, even when heterosexual males simply watch sexist ads, they are then more likely to judge female job applicants as less competent, remember less about their actual qualifications, and pay attention primarily to their physical attributes.[18]

We don't have to be driven by learned stereotypes. While we do have multiple mechanisms to keep us from considering data that do not support prescriptive stereotypes (the "shoulds"), we can also choose to question and modify those stereotypes.

The Dangers of Stereotyping

Stereotypes also get us into trouble. They are generalized descriptions of a group of people and do not necessarily apply to individuals in the group, though we assume that they do.

Let's look back at that social event described earlier. What are some reasons why your conversational gambit might not have worked? Perhaps the Asian male came from an upper class family, educated in private schools, and didn't believe in educating "the masses." Perhaps he came from an immigrant family and felt embarrassed to talk about education because he himself had very little. Perhaps he had refugee relatives and felt that the plight of refugees was much more important than how schools were funded. Perhaps he was a hockey fan and would much rather talk about sports.

Relying on stereotypes means that we fail to pay attention to the nuances of actual interactions and ask questions. Stereotypes create problems because they can influence our thoughts, feelings, and actions without our awareness. Research has shown that "implicit bias" — that is, bias that occurs outside of our awareness — can activate prescriptive stereotypes with the following results:

o Assuming that boys prefer math and science while girls prefer arts and language (robust across 34 countries)[19]

o Associating males with strength and females with weakness[20]

o Associating Blacks with traits like athletic, musical, poor, promiscuous[21]

o Labeling professions by gender — females as elementary school teachers, males as scientists[22]

o Associating "lazy" and "incompetent" with obese persons[23]

o Evaluating employees with later starting times as less conscientious and lower performers compared with those with early start times[24]

o Evaluating Blacks as being ape-like and more deserving of violent treatment[25]

Can we resist a prescriptive stereotype automatically taking over and influencing our thoughts and actions? Yes, but it takes conscious effort and the availability of cognitive resources (i.e., working memory capacity).[26]

Exercise: Changing Prescriptive Stereotypes

Notice a time when you say, "They should…" and then list at least five alternate ways "they" could behave that would be just fine.

1.

2.

3.

4.

5.

What would help you modify/expand other prescriptive stereotypes?

Stereotype Activation

Over time we form a number of stereotype schemas that can be activated under different circumstances. They may compete with non-stereotypic perceptions or with each other for expression. For example, let's say that you have been raised to believe that only Christians are truly spiritual and that persons from all other faiths are immoral in some way. Then you are helped by a wonderful, very spiritual Moslem. What happens to your stereotype of non-Christians? You could misconstrue her motives, deciding that she wasn't actually trying to be helpful. You could classify her as an exception and continue to hold the stereotype. Or you could modify your stereotype by including Moslems in your in-group, making Christians and Moslems the truly spiritual.

So how and when are stereotypes activated? Stereotype activation is assumed to be an automatic process, happening mindlessly and with little effort.[27] It happens most commonly by priming. The example earlier of men being more likely to behave in sexist ways after viewing a sexist ad is a good illustration of the dynamic of priming. What disrupts stereotyping is conscious attention or mindfulness—a good hint if we want to be less driven by stereotyping.

Research shows that stereotypes of Blacks can be activated within 15 seconds of beginning to watch a taped interview, but can dissipate as we continue to watch. But a disagreement—an emotionally-charged interaction—will reactivate the implicit stereotype.[28] A range of studies have shown how easy it is to stimulate intergroup bias—that is, viewing one's own group more favorably than the out-group—even when people have no knowledge or exposure to the out-group.[29] When stereotypic representations of behavior are activated, the relevant emotion or behavior is also activated.[30] So when we watch movies or play video games that present a particular ethnic group as violent or dangerous, for example, we are then more likely to react fearfully when we meet a member of that group.

Another way that stereotypes are activated is through repetition. Research shows that the more stereotyping messaging we receive, the more likely we will be to internalize the stereotype. Each activation of a stereotype reinforces it. While a single activation may be harmless, the cumulative effects of repeated activations can be substantial.[31]

Once we ourselves become stereotyped as a target, it is very difficult to change how others perceive us. The concept of self-fulfilling prophecy is that an initial false assumption becomes true because of the behavior it evokes. For example, if we are very skilled at playing pool and find ourselves in a situation where an onlooker keeps saying, "You're going to miss...you're going to miss...you're going to miss," we might very well miss and then be told that we are not that good after all. Our tense behavior creates the foretold conclusion.

Stereotype Threat

One of the dynamics affecting how we feel and behave is known as "stereotype threat," or a fear that we are about to confirm a negative stereotype about our in-group.[32] As a result we under-perform on stereotype-related tasks. For example, if we are female and we have been "primed" with a reminder that females are not supposed to do well in math, we are likely to perform more poorly than if we had not been primed. Research has confirmed this dynamic in a variety of circumstances—such as Black students underperforming on the Scholastic Aptitude Test (SAT).[33] To understand this dynamic, recall the limited capacity of our working memory. If we have been triggered or primed to worry about our performance, that worrying takes up part of our working memory, so we have less available for the performance task.

But the effects go beyond academic test performance to include a reduced sense of belonging, a reduced desire to pursue non-stereotypic occupations, poor sports performance, and even poor driving ability. Identifying strongly with a particular group leaves us open to stereotype threat as we don't want to let the group down[34]—"I am elderly. Elderly folks are supposed to have trouble remembering, and I've got a lot that I have to remember in order to organize this event." Indeed research has shown that, when reminded of negative ageist stereotypes or even spoken to in a slow patronizing manner, older adults underperform.[35]

Stereotype threat interferes with our performance not because of our belief in the stereotype but because of the anxiety that we will not perform well and so will confirm the negative stereotype.[36] Asian women, when primed to focus on their ethnicity, improved in math, while when they were primed to focus on their gender their math performance declined.[37]

Another reason for interference is similar to what we found in regard to benevolent bigotry — the limited capacity of our working memory.[38] Being alert to screen out stereotypic messages takes up some of our working memory capacity, leaving less to process the actual task. Since many of us have at least one social identity that is negatively stereotyped (gender, ethnicity, social class, age, sexual orientation, religious affiliation, etc.), we are at risk when we encounter a situation in which that stereotype seems to become relevant. The stronger our attachment to the social identity in question and to not confirming a negative stereotype, the more likely that we will perform poorly.[39]

It is easy to see how a downward spiral can develop if we lose working memory capacity, perform less well as a result, become fearful that we will continue to perform less well and confirm the group negative stereotype, and so forth. In a revealing but discouraging study, researchers found that the math-gender stereotype was already alive and well in nine-year-old girls who saw themselves as less competent than boys in math, performed more poorly on math tests, and were less likely to want to pursue math-intensive careers.[40]

Of course, social comparison can work the other way. We can get "stereotype lift," or enhanced performance, when we learn negative stereotypes about an out-group and so can affirm that our group is better. Our self-esteem goes up and our self-doubt goes down. Or we can get "stereotype boost" when we remember that a positive stereotype of our own in-group is highly relevant. But while the performance outcome may be better, we are still relating in group terms instead of as people.

Assuming Out-Group Homogeneity

One of the oddities of stereotyping, which we encountered in Chapter One, is that we develop a stereotype and then apply it unthinkingly to all members of an out-group. As a result, we start to believe that all members of the out-group are the same—that is, that the out-group is homogeneous.[41] But remember the structure of a dichotomy, where the whole is divided into two parts? There is the "indication" or standard of measurement—in this case, the in-group. Then there is the "complement," or the out-group that is defined most basically as *not* being the indication. People lumped together into that "not" category may be quite different from each other—not homogeneous at all! So how did we get from very different (heterogeneous) to all being the same (homogeneous)?

Part of the answer is, "Due to intergroup anxiety." Intergroup anxiety refers to the ambiguous feelings of discomfort or anxiety when we contemplate interacting with members of an out-group. Some of the reasons for this discomfort include a fear of negative evaluation from:

o The out-group if we are not aware of its social norms (including the possibility of being mocked)
o Our in-group for associating with members of the out-group (including the possibility of being socially ostracized)
o Ourselves if we fear we will be deemed prejudiced
o Ourselves if we believe there may be a threat from the out-group

Not surprisingly, if we are anxious about contact with an out-group, we will tend to avoid members of that group and thus have to rely even more on stereotypes, which themselves reinforce a sense of out-group homogeneity.

As our anxiety goes up, our negative feelings about the group intensify even though the content of the stereotype itself may not change.[42] Unfortunately, our over-simplification in perception can cause us to miss opportunities to avoid conflict and engage in collaboration.

Our tendency to perceive out-group members as being more similar to each other than are in-group members is known as "out-group homogeneity bias." This bias is unrelated to the number of people known and allows us to see people in the out-group as interchangeable or expendable "non-persons."[43]

We apply this same dynamic of assumed homogeneity to nonhumans as well. For example, how many of us are aware that there are at least four different personality types among female elephants — i.e., not all elephants are alike?[44] First there are the Leaders, the ones who are able to influence (rather than dominate!) others and problem solve effectively. Then there are the Playful ones, displaying curiosity. Next the Gentle ones, who provide physical caressing and comfort. And finally the Reliable ones, who provide consistent decision-making. When combined with personal characteristics, each member of the herd stands out as an individual.

Resisting Stereotyping

We can see that using stereotypes unthinkingly, though efficient, reinforces precisely the "us"/"them", in-group/out-group distinction we are trying to move beyond. As well, individuals cease to exist for us, blending into the group mix. When we become more aware of the stereotypes in use by ourselves and others, we become able to act in a more nuanced and reality-based way.

Excessive stereotyping is limiting of ourselves, not just of others. Our sense of identity evolves over time as we have different life experiences. Not only does an in-group/out-group system enforce rigid role expectations but it does not support our own maturation process. We need to encourage ourselves to develop our own sense of distinctiveness and individuality rather than worrying about what others will think. As we become able to relate to ourselves as unique and intriguing individuals, we are likely to relate to others in the same manner.

SEVEN

"They Can Be Ignored": Invisibility

Richard Gere, a well-known and frequently photographed actor, begged for change with a coffee cup on a New York East Village street for 40 minutes, posing as a homeless man (as they filmed the movie, "Time Out of Mind"), and no one recognized him. How could that be? It is an excellent illustration of what happens when we decide that someone is beneath our notice, not part of our community. Gere himself commented, "It was really freaky. No one paid any attention. No one made eye contact. It was worse than being invisible. It's like [being] a black hole that people are afraid to get sucked into."[1]

Invisibility as a form of depersonalization can happen to anyone. But there are groups to which it is more likely to occur. The homeless, or the persistently poor, is one of those groups. Not only do we ignore the person, we also ignore how soul-crushing the experience of homelessness can be — the continuous assault of noise, the constant vigilance needed if "sleeping rough" or the indignities of shelters, the experience of immediate rejection as people walk by with averted eyes, and the devastating impact of being treated as though you simply don't exist.

The Dynamic of Dismissiveness

Each of us has a sense of self that is comprised of our self-concept, or set of beliefs about ourselves. When that is strong, we talk about having high self-esteem or believing in ourselves. When it is weak, we talk about lacking confidence or not believing in ourselves. That belief in self, however, does not happen in a vacuum. There is a social component, part of which is the social identity that we discussed in Chapter Six. We experience ourselves in a context, in relation to others. As the late theologian Nelle Morton has said, "We hear each other into existence."[2]

What happens when that context and connection disappear, when we are left socially isolated? We can look within ourselves for validation, but it is extremely difficult to maintain self-confidence when external messages convey that you simply don't matter. The dynamic of dismissiveness describes situations of depersonalization where the target is assumed to be linked to (or dependent on) the perpetrator, while the perpetrator displays no need for, or identification with, the target.

Imagine yourself sitting on a park bench on a warm sunny day, in a community where you know lots of people. You're in a good mood, feeling happy and relaxed. People stroll by and call out greetings. You smile and answer back. Now imagine the same scene—the beautiful outdoor location, the sun, people you know strolling by—only now no one talks to you or responds to your greetings. They don't act like they are avoiding you. Instead they act as though they literally don't see or hear you, even when you call out repeatedly. How would you feel?

Generally speaking, we don't function well unless we have some feedback that acknowledges our existence. In the example above, some of us might close our eyes so that we don't have to notice the indifference. Some of us might get up and leave so that the experience ends. Some of us might continue to try to get a reaction and end up sounding like we are talking to ourselves. If we were to transfer this experience to a sensory deprivation tank where there was absolutely no external feedback, most of us would create sensations through delusions or hallucinations. Bottom line—we don't like being treated as though we are invisible. We want and expect some social interaction.

As humans, one of the complicating features of the scenes just described is that we engage in virtually continuous self-talk. Whether we are aware of it or not, our mind runs an ongoing soliloquy, much like a news commentator or sports-caster: "That was silly—you know better." "Wonder what he's thinking?" "Nicely done—now you need to match that." When we are overlooked, it is only natural for that self-talk to zero in on, "What's wrong with me?" "Why don't they like me?" and similar self-deprecating comments.

The extent to which we rely on feedback from others de-pends in part on our personality (e.g., how introverted, how internally controlled) and on our cultural context. Some non-Western cultures place particular emphasis on interdepend-ence and feeling part of a group, while Western cultures tend to place more emphasis on defining ourselves independently. Regardless of context, though, we all need to feel "seen" and "heard" by someone else who matters to us.

When we are the perpetrator, what is happening? Some-times the overlooking is an engrained bias, such as the ones we've already discussed—inattentional blindness, change bias, or confirmation bias. But more often it is intentional. And we may, as perpetrators, feel that we are doing nothing wrong (similar to the perpetrators of benevolent bigotry). We are simply living our lives. If they feel left out (we reason), it's their fault. They should do something about it.

Becoming Disempowered

That uncomfortable feeling of invisibility comes from be-ing routinely dismissed as unimportant. It is a core dynamic in what we refer to as being disenfranchised, or literally losing the right to vote and make our view or our needs known. We become marginalized, without power or privilege. When someone in a position of authority (or with the power of the in-group behind them) refuses to recognize us or talks over the top of us, there is often little that we or any out-group member can do.

This is particularly true of stigmatized individuals and groups that face barriers to effective social participation. We have already mentioned the poor and homeless. The U.S. National Alliance to End Homelessness has reported that, in 2014, 14.7 million Americans were homeless, with an additional 4.8 million living in poverty, at risk of homelessness.[3] While we may think of poverty as being relegated to developing economies, these statistics show 6.1 percent of the U.S. population being, or verging on being, homeless in one of the richest countries in the world! And more than one in every four children under the age of five live in poverty.[4] While there are governmental and nongovernmental organizations responsible for the welfare of these poorest of the poor, individually they are likely to be ignored or considered not worth bothering about. All too often they face dismissive attitudes such as that any monetary difficulties are their own fault, that they must be lazy, that they are a health hazard.

The elderly in Western societies are frequently another disenfranchised group. Whereas traditionally elders have been revered as sources of wisdom, in today's rapidly-changing world they are often assumed to be irrelevant or out of touch. Remaining within a multigenerational family group has been replaced by two-generation family units, with older relatives consigned to nursing homes or, at best, seniors communities. The World Health Organization has estimated that the population of people aged 60 or older will have grown to 1.2 billion by 2025, exacerbating already challenging problems.[5] From an invisibility perspective, the elderly are often overlooked because physical fragility gets interpreted as a loss of mental acuity. While physical abuse is certainly an issue, 40 percent of nursing-home staff in the U.S. admitted to psychologically abusing the elderly, primarily by ignoring them and their needs.[6]

People with disabilities also frequently end up marginalized. If you do not have a disability, imagine for purposes of illustration that you have fallen and broken both your wrists and your ankle. Now imagine needing to travel to a conference, using a wheelchair that requires that someone push you. Picture being parked facing a wall or left without the brakes on or having a customer service representative and your "helper" talk about you over your head. These are unfortunately frequent occurrences when being the "invisible" target in a helpless position.

One of the important reasons why the disempowered need to come together in support groups is to recognize that the dynamic is not personal—there is actually nothing wrong with them. By acting together they can begin to exercise a more powerful voice than if they were to act individually.

We have mentioned repeatedly the need to feel "seen" and "heard" as human beings, rather than be depersonalized. Ironically, a frequent target of this type of depersonalization is ourselves. How many times have you dismissed an intuitive urging or failed to speak up (advocate) for yourself or put yourself down or assumed that your viewpoint didn't matter? These are all common ways in which we disempower, and ultimately dismiss and dehumanize, ourselves.

Purposeful Backgrounding

We have been talking about invisibility that occurs by virtue of being part of a particular ignored out-group, where there is a possibility of being noticed and respected through group action. Now we turn to what happens when we (as perpetrators) make ourselves or our in-group feel good by moving "center stage," into the "foreground," while relegating members of the out-group to the "background." Gestalt psychology describes this as viewing ourselves and our in-group as the "figure" — what we focus on and value. Everything else fades into the background and gets discounted — becoming "ground."

So, in this case, the invisibility is intentional and purposeful and directed at specific individuals or groups. We commit micro-instances of "purposeful backgrounding" when we actively avoid another person. Perhaps we are momentarily annoyed with them, or we are too busy to pay attention, or we are embarrassed because we have not kept a promise, or any one of a number of reasons. Each time we allow ourselves to treat the other as invisible we lose a bit of our own humanity.

Exercise: Recognizing Backgrounding

Notice someone you see periodically and would be inclined to overlook:

1. Is this someone you are aware of but choose to ignore? If so, why?

2. Were you aware of the person only when you chose to focus on them? If so, why do you think you hadn't noticed them before?

The most common example of purposeful backgrounding is shunning. Here the motivation is different in that the target, who has been an in-group member, is treated as invisible as a tool to pressure the target into conforming with group norms. So the target loses his or her usual group support and sense of community and inclusion as well as being ignored and dismissed. The resulting invisibility generates a sense of "I've done something wrong" or "Something's wrong with me."

Groups approach shunning differently. In cases of social shunning by classmates, the purpose is typically for the group leader to feel powerful, and it lasts as long as the group leader decrees. There may be hidden individual contact—e.g., if a group member needs academic help from the target—but the public invisibility is maintained. The target typically has no control over either its beginning or its end. The shunning may be complete or may be accompanied by active bullying, usually in the form of taunts and ridicule.

When the issue is marrying someone outside the faith, some ultraorthodox Jewish congregations will actually hold a funeral for the target, signaling that the breach is permanent. In some cultures and religions, violators of doctrine are not just shunned but put to death.

Shunning, in some religious circles, means that there should be no contact at all with the target. In Scientology, the practice is called "disconnection," and no interaction of any sort is allowed. Among Jehovah's Witnesses the person is "disfellowshipped" and all contact stops, including with immediate family.

While shunning in Scientology and the Jehovah's Witnesses is truly an act of depersonalization, Amish shunning is a sanction designed to convince the wayward ex-member to return to Amish values and practices. Amish shunning entails members not being able to eat at the same table, ride in the same vehicle, receive anything or do business with the target. So there is an ejection from the familiar support system, but not total loss of contact or complete depersonalization.

The experience of being shunned can be quite traumatic. Imagine walking down the street in your neighborhood and having people that you know well look right through you or cross to the other side of the street to avoid you. Having someone ignore you consistently leads to a loss of self-confidence, a lowering of one's sense of self-worth, and an increased distrust of others. After all, if those close to you can suddenly turn against you, how can you trust any interpersonal relationship?

One method of disenfranchisement that falls short of shunning is the practice of "separate but equal," or creating a separate space for the "other" group and pretending that it is not inferior in any way. Whether we are referring to racially segregated schools in the United States or apartheid in South Africa, we have plenty of evidence that the designation of different groups carries with it an evaluation that one group is superior to the other. This evidence of in-group bias should not surprise us given our exploration in Chapter Six.

One of the more subtle dynamics in purposeful backgrounding is to discount the contribution of individuals or groups through what we described in Chapter Five as causal attribution. When an out-group member has failure attributed to a lack of ability and success attributed to luck, the actual achievements of the out-group member become invisible.[7]

Purposeful Backgrounding of Women

There are dynamics involved in gender backgrounding that deserve specific focus. For example, traditional economics places value only on activities outside the home that generate "income." The activities of caregiving in the home or the community are taken for granted and treated as "anyone can do that" or "unskilled" (though they may actually require considerable skill). This relationship between external paid work and home/family maintenance assumes that housework and child care, and increasingly senior care, activities are not "real" work; they occur in the background. But it is not only work in the home that is invisible, it is also the volunteer community activities that contribute to our quality of life.

Marilyn Waring and others have estimated that the "non-work" that is considered "women's work" is actually worth at least fifty percent of what is currently measured as economic activity. In other words, if economists place a nation's gross national product at $1 million, the real value of economic activities (including those in the home) is $1.5 million.

In developing economies, the invisibility of rural women's work has been taken to an extreme. Projects to improve agricultural productivity, run by development agencies, focus primarily on males, although up to eighty percent of non-mechanized agricultural work is performed by women.[8]

Another form of backgrounding targets girls, again particularly in developing countries. Often their births are considered to be of so little importance that they are not even officially registered, which limits options later in life. When food is scarce, girls (and women) are expected to go without in order to leave more for the males in the family.

The education of girls has become a particularly hot topic with the rise of the Taliban and their ban on female education. High profile cases of schoolgirls being abducted and murdered have brought this issue, however briefly, to world attention. For example, in Nigeria we have the April 2014 Boko Haram abduction of 276 schoolgirls, most still not found a year later. In Pakistan alone, we have the October 2012 near-murder of 12-year-old Malala Yousafzai (a girls' education activist and now the youngest winner of the Nobel Peace Prize), the slaughter of 150 school children in Peshawar in December 2014,[9] and perhaps most distressingly three young girls strangled to death by their father to "avoid wasting money" on their education in June 2015.[10]

A 2012 survey of high potential business school graduates in Asia, Canada, Europe, and the United States identified visibility on large, mission-critical projects as a key factor for success. Not only were female graduates offered lower salaries and positions initially, but they were then placed in charge of smaller budgets and lower-profile projects and were overlooked for international postings.[11]

Differential treatment of world class athletes in preparation for the London 2012 Summer Olympics made headlines when it was revealed that Australian women's basketball, soccer, and cricket teams flew economy class on the 26-hour flight to London while their male counterparts were seated in the more comfortable business class.[12] To add insult to injury, the women's basketball team (the Opals) had won Silver at the past three Olympics while the men's basketball team (the Boomers) had not yet won an Olympic medal. In the London Olympics, the Opals went on to win a Bronze medal while again the Boomers did not medal.

Gender-based differences in causal attribution are strikingly noticeable in the reporting of sporting events, such as the Olympics. A study of the NBC coverage of the Vancouver 2010 Winter Olympics showed the following:[13]

- o When female athletes succeeded, commentators focused on luck rather than on physical ability.
- o When female athletes failed, the focus was on a lack of physical ability and commitment.
- o When male athletes succeeded, commentators applauded their skill and commitment to the sport.
- o When male athletes failed, commentators focused on how their competitors succeeded rather than on failure.
- o 75 percent of Canada's most mentioned athletes were male, though 60 percent of gold medalists were male.

So the picture that is presented by the commentators is that female athletes never really win on merit and, in addition, their physical appearance is more important than their talent and hard work. Similarly, male athletes can never really lose as any failure is attributed to the bad luck of having a more skilled opponent. At this event, as in many international competitions, the attribution differences were strengthened by a lack of parallel language on the part of the commentators — e.g., referring to the "men" competing in the "men's slalom" and then to "girls" competing in the "ladies' slalom." A similar pattern was reported by the same researchers based on race, with African-American athletes described in terms of physical ability and strength, Asian athletes described in terms of intelligence, and White athletes described in terms of commitment and composure.[14]

A variation on this theme occurs when we create a self-fulfilling prophecy. For example, the Australian Olympic swimming champion and most decorated Olympic athlete, Leisel Jones, was harassed repeatedly in the press for putting on weight.[15] Her actual 2012 performance in the 100-metre breaststroke ranked her fifth in the finals; however, the winner from Lithuania did not best Leisel's 2008 performance time of 1:05:17. The question of what accounted for Leisel's "slower" (by just over one second!) 2012 performance of 1:06:36 remains open. Was it her refusal to starve herself down to her 2008 weight, the sports announcer mused? Or was it the undermining effect of being expected to fail?

Purposeful Backgrounding of Nonhumans

If women's contributions are downplayed, environmental supports are usually completely invisible to us. Unless there is a problem, we take completely for granted the fact that there is oxygen available for us to breathe in and that the carbon dioxide we exhale is recycled for us by surrounding vegetation. We also overlook a range of natural assets and ignore their well-being—for example, forests, wetlands, grasslands, rivers, and marine environments that act like giant utilities, providing a plethora of eco-services including the storage of flood waters, water capture and filtration, air pollution absorption, waste decomposition and detoxification, pest and disease control, erosion prevention, and climate regulation due to carbon storage. You might argue that these natural assets are not "persons," but look at the science in Appendix B before you do. You'll find that plant life, for example, is intelligent, self-aware, and highly social—and Switzerland already recognizes the rights of plants while New Zealand has recognized the legal standing of a river.

European "pioneers" in Australia, New Zealand, and North America ignored aboriginals who had been settled for centuries on land that the Europeans claimed was "unoccupied." We see here a twofold invisibility issue: One has to do with not respecting aboriginal culture and values as a legitimate alternative to an industrialized way of life. The other has to do with not respecting the land itself, in its own right—not recognizing that it is valuable in and of itself, not simply as space for industrial development.

We typically remain blind to nonhuman indigenous life, not just indigenous peoples. Virtually every space on and within our planet is already occupied by life forms, including deep in the Earth and in locations with extreme temperature variations.[16] But we have not developed either the methodology or the commitment to determine "win-win" solutions that acknowledge the life forms surrounding us. Rather than pursuing models of planetary cohabitation, we frequently simply ignore or choose to exploit other life forms.

We routinely treat our oceans as bodies of water for our convenience rather than as home to hundreds of nonhuman species. As one of hundreds of examples, on 11 September

2015 a news article on trash in the St. Lawrence River (in Canada) carried the quote: "You've got kids swimming in here, people fishing....people need to remember that's source water...we drink that water."[17] Nowhere is there a mention that it is also source water, and living environment, for wildlife.

The Natural Resources Defense Council has posted warnings about plastic pollution that is clogging every waterway, sea and ocean in the world, saying: "Plastic that pollutes our oceans and waterways has severe impacts on our environment and our economy. Seabirds, whales, sea turtles and other marine life are eating marine plastic pollution and dying from choking, intestinal blockage and starvation."[18] The takeaway message is about the harmful effects on the marine life we *consume*, rather than on the marine life itself, but at least the marine life was mentioned.

A new study has shown that eight million tons of plastic are dumped in the ocean each year,[19] to comingle with at least 245 million tons already there. Research shows that ocean plastic is turning up everywhere, including buried in Arctic ice, and that it is being ingested with unhealthy consequences by over 700 species of marine life. In addition, our Earth's waters now contain large quantities of other consumer products such as metals, rubber, paper, textiles, fishing gear and so on.

While all of the world's oceans are affected, scientists have identified particularly large garbage patches in the Pacific Ocean composed of concentrations of plastics, chemical sludge, and other debris, and covering an area that varies from the size of Texas to the size of the United States itself. In other words, we are treating the world's oceans as if they were garbage cans, forgetting about the impact on inhabitants.

Ocean Conservancy has released a report titled *Stemming the Tide: Land-Based Strategies for a Plastic-Free Ocean*, which outlines steps that can be taken by various nations (particularly China, Indonesia, Philippines, Vietnam, and Thailand).[20] What is particularly interesting about this report, from our perspective, is that nothing is said about cleaning up the oceans — i.e., our responsibility to restore the habitat of marine life to an unpolluted state. One would think that, with the proper commitment, it would be possible to "skim" the trash from the garbage patches, much as one separates fine coffee grounds from coffee. But who is willing? Who recognizes the right of marine life to a healthy environment?

When there are oil spills in our oceans or waterways, reports focus typically on the clean-up results for humans. However, the impact on both wildlife and habitat typically goes far beyond that focus. Some scientists estimate that the spilled oil can remain absorbed in the soil or sediment for up to 30 years,[21] with dire consequences for marine life, and also that the methods used for clean-up can be 52 times as toxic to marine life.[22]

Similar issues arise in relation to the use of wind power and its effects on birds and bats, when wind farms are land-based. There are an increasing number of initiatives to site wind farms and wave farms in offshore areas, each with their own risks to other forms of intelligent life.[23] While risks to marine mammals include collision with machinery or the effects of underwater noise on echolocation capabilities, evaluations for both types of power continue to be, in terms of animal population, focused on decimation rather than on the ethics of using the habitats (air, water) of other species primarily for our own use and ignoring their presence.

As with the "empty lands" of indigenous people, we assume a right of presence and we simply take over. When we evaluate possible harm, we omit the option of not proceeding at all. Take, for example, the issue of whale and dolphin reserves. Whale and Dolphin Conservancy (WDC) states: "We urgently need to create effective marine protected areas and reserves—safe havens that help to preserve the habitat critical for whales and dolphins in all the oceans of the world. Why? To protect them from the dangers of pollution, fishing nets, hunting, live-capture."[24] New Zealand has just declared a new marine sanctuary,[25] which is excellent news.

But announcements like this beg the question—who do we think we are to simply move into their territory as if they weren't there and expect them to compress their lives into the area mandated by us? Does the idea of restrictive sanctuaries ring any bells in relation to how indigenous people have been treated?

Exercise: Recognizing Overlooked Harm

Over the next 24 hours see if you can identify:

1. One way in which women are routinely ignored or dismissed. What could you do about it?

2. One overlooked negative impact on wildlife in your community that could be addressed. What could you do about it?

3. One overlooked community practice that has a negative impact on the natural environment. What could you do about it?

Being Unperceived

A final type of depersonalization by invisibility is that of literally not "seeing" the other. One form is the case where we appear to make no distinction—so there is deniability—and yet a distinction is implicit. As mentioned earlier, we may use "man" to mean "everyone," but the underlying dichotomy of "man" and the invisible "woman" still exists. If questioned, the speaker would say, "Of course, 'man' includes women." Think back to the satire on the term "white" and the feeling tone of saying, "All Whites are created equal."

We often have a habit of not seeing people whose job it is to help us. We take their function for granted and excuse ourselves from having to consider their feelings or desires by ignoring them as individuals. When people talk disparagingly about "service jobs," it is not the actual service that is the problem. It is the invisibility that often goes with such an occupation. Ask yourself what you know about the service personnel upon whom you depend regularly—their name? their family composition? current concerns that they have for family members? their aspirations? For many of us, the answers to these questions would be, "I haven't a clue. I never bothered to ask."

A more nuanced form is what is known as "colorblindness"—a denial of any difference. "We're all just people," says the perpetrator. Sounds liberal and accepting, doesn't it? The problem is that it literally makes invisible the actual differences in experience that shape a person's behavior and future expectations. Let's take a Black woman: When her ethnicity or her gender is ignored, the consequences can include:

o An invalidation of her sense of identity ("it's not ok to be a Black woman").

o An invalidation of her experiences of prejudice and discrimination ("she's just overly sensitive").

o An equating of her identity with something negative or bad ("let's not talk about it").

o A narrowed world perspective that does not include the contributions of members of stigmatized groups.

Colorblind messages create problems for both the perpetrator and the target.[26] As a result of hearing such messages, the perpetrator is likely to express more negative feelings and act in a more discriminatory way towards members of a stigmatized group.[27] The target is left with lowered self-confidence and a sense of not being okay.

Another variation is that of a person's denying their own identity. Being closeted about a gay identity is the most common expression, but it can include hiding one's religious affiliation or political affiliation or ethnicity or level of education (e.g., as was important in China during the Cultural Revolution).

When one is closeted as a gay person, there is a separation between public self and private self.[28] Others view us as being part of the dominant in-group—heterosexual—which raises an internal sense of there being something wrong with who we are. An important part of our self-identity is literally invisible to those around us. If we are in an intimate relationship, that relationship is also invisible, and we are assumed to be unattached. And yet the dangers that arise from being fully visible, as we've mentioned before, are very real.

Finally, we have "intersectional" invisibility, or belonging to multiple subgroups, so that we are not fully visible in any of them.[29] Researchers have demonstrated that if someone is from a minority group, they are less likely to be noticed or heard. For example, if you are a Black woman, your face is less likely to be recognized and the statements you make are less likely to be heard or are attributed incorrectly.[30] Another less-studied group is that of third-culture kids, those who grow up outside their national culture and then emigrate "home" as adolescents or adults—for example, children of diplomats or military personnel or missionaries. In their national mainstream culture, the part of them shaped by other cultural experiences is invisible—indeed, often not even suspected—and they may feel a bit untethered, as though they belong everywhere and no place.[31]

Highlighting Backgrounding

Invisibility is the manner of harming ourselves and others that we most commonly ignore. While overt bigotry and negative stereotyping are painful and damaging, at least there is an activity that we can point to and say, "That's wrong." When we are simply dismissed or overlooked, it is truly as if we did not exist.

Failing to take ourselves or others seriously has long-range consequences, both in terms of our feelings of self-worth and in terms of lost contributions to our group and community. While it is unrealistic for us to be aware of everyone all of the time, at issue is the manner in which we are present in the world. Is it our intention to only "humanize" those in our inner circle? Or are we willing to extend that sense of being an important part of the world to all others that we meet, human and nonhuman?

EIGHT

"They're Ours to Use": Objectification

A young man flirts with one woman in order to make another woman jealous. An advertisement shows a feminine leg as the base of a lamp. A dolphin is trained to place mines on the hull of a ship. An elephant is chained in order to drag logs of wood. What do each of these examples have in common? They are all examples of objectifying another entity, of using them to meet a need that is not their own. In this chapter, we will be looking first at how objectification plays out with humans and then with nonhumans.

The Dynamic of Objectification

Depersonalization through objectification occurs when the target is treated like a commodity instead of with dignity and respect. This includes, at its extreme, all forms of forced labor and sexual exploitation. The dynamic of objectification is deeply entrenched in our social fabric and occurs almost without our awareness.

Oddly enough, though we objectify frequently, we are aware on some level collectively that it is immoral. In the UN Universal Declaration of Human Rights, we have enshrined three relevant principles:

Article 4: No one shall be held in slavery or servitude, and the slave trade shall be prohibited in all their forms.

Article 23: (1) Everyone has the right to work, to free choice of employment, to just and favourable conditions of work and to protection against unemployment.

(2) Everyone, without any discrimination, has the right to equal pay for equal work.

(3) Everyone who works has the right to just and favourable remuneration ensuring for himself and his family [sic] an existence worthy of human dignity, and supplemented, if necessary, by other means of social protection.

Article 24: Everyone has the right to rest and leisure, including reasonable limitation of working hours and periodic holidays with pay.

Objectification is a social process that occurs when a perpetrator in a position of power treats the target as an entity to be controlled and valued only as a means to an end. When we refer to objectification as a method of depersonalization, we are referring to a sustained practice of viewing the other as an object to be used. We are not referring to the episodic common exchanges of "could you..." or "would you..."

Let's take an example for illustration. Suppose I say to my partner, "Please bring me a glass of water." In that moment I am indeed using my partner to meet a need of mine. However, my use of "please" signals (or should signal) that this is a request, not an expectation. In a restaurant, the context would be different—I could ask the wait staff for a glass of water and it would be an expectation, not a request; however, I would simply be asking that wait staff perform a role that they have accepted and for which they are paid. It becomes objectification when I relate to my partner primarily as being available to do things for me (non-reciprocal) or I order my partner to comply (non-voluntary) or I fail to be thoughtful enough to thank the wait staff for doing their job.

We can summarize the differences between helpfulness and objectification in Table 5 below. Objectification occurs when the target is expected to perform in a particular manner that has not been mutually agreed and does not have the right or ability to refuse. It is a one-way dynamic, with the target viewed only in relation to their request fulfillment and not as a unique individual. Think of the table below as applying to interactions between two partners.

Table 5: Helpfulness and Objectification Compared

Dimension	Helpfulness	Objectification
Framing of request	no expectation	expectation
Voluntary response?	yes	no
Refusal is:	acceptable	not acceptable
Frequency of occurrence	episodic	sustained
Mutually-agreed role?	yes	no
Reciprocal action?	yes	no
Viewed as unique individual?	yes	no

Feminist Andrea Dworkin wrote of this form of depersonalization: "Objectification occurs when a human being, through social means, is made less than human, turned into a thing or commodity, bought and sold. When objectification occurs, a person is depersonalized, so that no individuality or integrity is available socially or in what is an extremely circumscribed privacy. Objectification is an injury right at the heart of discrimination: those who can be used as if they are not fully human are no longer fully human in social terms; their humanity is hurt by being diminished."[1]

We have already encountered examples of objectification, particularly of women, in other chapters. We have the compartmentalization of women as the cook, the parent, the chauffeur—expected "free work" that is not explicitly contracted for in relationships. We also have more extreme uses of women as debt payment, sold as virgins or child brides to provide family income, or indentured as compensation for murders committed by male relatives. We can add now the "bait and switch" work scenario—i.e., the woman is invited to a restaurant or bar to "talk business," though in fact the purpose is to have her perform sexually.

We can think of objectification as comprised of two threads: the use of the target as an object or instrument, and the denial of personhood. Filmmaker Jean Kilbourne was one of the first to focus attention on the role of advertising in portraying females as objects.[2] Her series, *Killing Us Softly* (begun in 1979, with the latest segment in 2010), argues that the superficial and unreal portrayal of females results in lowered self-esteem.

Women are more likely than men to be portrayed as bodies available for use (which could explain why the objectification dynamics show up more strongly in relation to women) and are then seen as less intelligent and competent.[3] Objectification does not imply, as one might think, that the target is seen only as a physical body with no mental capacities.[4] Rather the type of mental capacity is reduced to emotion and sensation ("experience"), with the ability to exercise control and take action ("agency") being diminished.

But the availability of fMRI technology has verified a disturbing trend. Males high on hostile sexism associate sexualized female images with being objects, not active agents—that is, their brain activity is the same as when they look at an object, not when they look at a person.[5] As well, the fMRI results show that these men do not associate sexualized female images with a person who is able to think through an issue and develop a plan of action.

Objectification results in people, particularly women, not being seen as individuals but instead being interchangeable (or "fungible"), like car tires of the same size. Research has shown that participants cannot correctly match the faces to the bodies of either women with ideal bodies or women with average bodies, though they did just fine in matching a face to the correct body when it was a male.[6]

Recent research has confirmed that as focusing on physical appearance increases, not only is the target less likely to be viewed as intelligent and purposeful but belief in their having moral standing is also withdrawn.[7] "Moral standing" refers back to the fifth component of what it means to be a person — that is, having "rights" or being "beyond use" as an object. So we see the direct link between objectification and depersonalization. The dynamic holds true for both genders though much of the research has focused on females.[8]

However, there is an added layer for females. Trying to be objective as per the Newtonian model, says philosopher Sally Haslanger, results in trying to discover a thing's nature.[9] In order to do that, we collect data on how the thing behaves under normal circumstances — that is, on observed regularities. What we observe in a sexist society is that women tend to behave in a submissive and deferential manner. (Note that this is their behavior, not necessarily their nature.)

Remember what we discussed in Chapter Two about our mind reviewing data and compressing it by removing inconsistencies? In that compression process, we can develop a schema of women that defines women's *nature* as being submissive and deferential, and thus their being available to be used as we wish. Then it is just a hop, skip and jump to interpret what we actually see through a "nature" lens. So women get caught in a self-fulfilling prophecy instead of being known as unique human beings in their own right.

Psychological Abuse as Objectification

One of the subtle forms of objectification that many of us adopt at some time is using another person psychologically to feel good about ourselves, to feel "better than" through a sense of superiority or domination or control. In other words, we allow our emotional self-control to slip, and we take our feelings of inferiority or frustration or rage out on the target. We allow ourselves to believe that it is just fine to use the target as a scapegoat. We forget that we are responsible for dissipating feelings like frustration or anger *without* taking them out on others.

The most common way that we do this is through verbal attacks—yelling, constant criticism, blaming, shaming, name calling, insults—all to make it clear that whatever has happened to trigger our unhappiness is their fault, not ours. An old *Saturday Evening Post* cover showed the resulting sequence clearly: the boss yells at the worker, the worker yells at the spouse, the spouse yells at the child, the child yells at the dog.

This form of objectification is bidirectional, or just as likely to be performed by females as by males.[10] It can range from verbally degrading to terrorizing the target. It is abusive when it becomes a pattern, even if unpredictable. In the U.S., researchers have shown that psychological abuse is pervasive in American families,[11] with fathers and mothers equally likely to be psychologically abusive towards their children.[12] But it is sons who, in turn, are most likely to be psychologically abusive toward elderly parents.[13]

Exercise: Managing Self-Talk

A common manifestation of psychological abuse is in our own self-talk. Try monitoring your thoughts (your self-talk) for three days and:

1. Make a record of times that you made an internal demeaning comment about yourself or your behavior. What did you say and what was the context?

2. Make a record of how you stopped the negative self-talk—did you just let time pass, or did you take a specific action?

At the end of the three days, look at what you have recorded. Are there patterns of when you are vulnerable to negative self-talk? Are there particular actions that are effective for you in stopping negative self-talk? What changes do you plan to make going forward in order to end psychological abuse to yourself?

Every year in the U.S. at least three million children are psychologically maltreated, usually by their parents.[14] The definition given of psychological maltreatment is "a repeated pattern of caregiver behavior or a serious incident that transmits to the child that s/he is worthless, flawed, unloved, unwanted, endangered or only of value in meeting another's needs."

This type of psychological abuse is particularly damaging because of the breach of the attachment bond between child and caregiver, resulting not only in the expected difficulty for the child with attention (due to constant monitoring for danger) but also aggression and noncompliance. Global studies indicate that it is the most widespread, most damaging, least reported, and least investigated form of child abuse.[15]

Sexual Objectification

Objectification theory[16] was originally developed to explain the common experiences of women and girls as a result of being viewed as sexual objects. Many assume that sexual objectification accounts for all gender inequalities, whereas we are seeing that there are a number of combined dynamics at work. Early studies demonstrated the negative impact of the "male gaze" — the objectifying visual inspection of the target's body by a male — often accompanied by lewd or disparaging remarks.[17] Current research verifies that, when subjected to the objectifying gaze, women performed less well at math and it increased the target's desire to interact with the perpetrator — in keeping with the dynamic of stereotype threat discussed previously.[18]

Sexual objectification refers to viewing and treating the target's body as a sex object, one that is evaluated for its sexual attractiveness (or lack thereof) and ability to arouse or gratify the perpetrator. The target's thoughts or feelings or abilities are ignored. As a result of sexual objectification, women and girls learn that their value lies in their physical appearance — as objects to be viewed, assessed, and consumed by others — and at the same time, they are presented with an ideal of feminine attractiveness that is unattainable for most women.

While in-person sexual objectification (whistles, catcalls) is not new, the explosion of more explicit sexual objectification in advertising, magazines, television shows and "reality" TV, movies, music videos, video games, and online sex sites has raised the stakes considerably. Those with high self-esteem can have a temporary sense of feeling very positively about themselves because of the type of adulation that typically accompanies in-person sexual objectification.[19] However, research shows that ongoing sexual objectification leads to feelings of inadequacy and shame, depression, habitual body monitoring and disgust with one's body, low self-worth, low life satisfaction, lowered cognitive and motor functioning, sexual dysfunction, and unhealthy eating and exercise routines.[20] So the stakes are high.

When research participants are "primed" to see females as sexual objects, women and girls are viewed as less competent and less worthy of empathy.[21] Over repeated exposures, males become more tolerant of sexual harassment. They begin to view rape as a myth ("because they always ask for it") and "putting her in her place," through physical violence, as acceptable. Two documentaries have been produced to alert us to the pervasiveness and dangers of this type of objectification: *Miss Representation*[22] and *Generation M: Misogyny in Media and Culture*.[23]

Several studies have shown that, while sexualized male images were perceived by both genders as persons ("configural processing"), sexualized female images were perceived as objects ("analytical processing").[24] But these dynamics are not only internal. When sexual objectification comes into play in real life, the target is judged to perform less well and is subjected to sexual harassment.[25] In addition, when known to be a victim of sexual assault, the target is perceived to be more responsible for the assault and less worthy of moral concern.[26]

One of the current controversies is what exactly is sexual objectification—i.e., how can we recognize it. Political scientist Caroline Heldman has developed a Sex Object Test to "measure the presence of sexual objectification in images," and she has provided graphic images from actual ad campaigns to support the seven variations we might see:[27]

1. *Does the image show only part(s) of a sexualized person's body?* (Example: headless woman)

2. *Does the image present a sexualized person as a stand-in for an object?* (Example: breasts as beer cans)

3. *Does the image show sexualized persons as interchangeable?* (Example: a series of breasts)

4. *Does the image affirm the idea of violating the bodily integrity of a sexualized person who can't consent?* (Example: an unconscious woman held on a leash)

5. *Does the image suggest that sexual availability is the defining characteristic of the person?* (Example: "now open" printed over a woman on her back with her legs spread apart)

6. *Does the image show a sexualized person as a commodity that can be bought and sold?* (Example: women shown in a vending machine with the sign "served chilled")

7. *Does the image treat a sexualized person's body as a canvas?* (Example: a nude woman's back covered in newsprint)

Another controversy is the causal relationship between sexual objectification of women and pornography. Lawyer Catharine MacKinnon defines pornography as "the graphic sexually explicit subordination of women through pictures or words that also includes women dehumanized as sexual objects, things, or commodities; enjoying pain or humiliation or rape; being tied up, cut up, mutilated, bruised, or physically hurt; in postures of sexual submission or servility or display; reduced to body parts, penetrated by objects or animals, or presented in scenarios of degradation, injury, torture;

shown as filthy or inferior; bleeding, bruised, or hurt in a context that makes these conditions sexual."[28]

We see here a dynamic that reinforces the view that women's role is to be available as (impossibly beautiful) sexual objects for men's consumption. Male sexuality becomes defined as the possession and consumption of the female, and female sexuality becomes defined as *being* consumed and possessed. According to MacKinnon, pornography contributes to both men's and women's view of women as objects available for men's consumption.

Those that deny that pornography is an objectification of women argue that the women portrayed consented to being used for men's sexual pleasure. MacKinnon and Andrea Dworkin[29] argue that the women's consent does not make it permissible to use a woman as a sexual object. This is particularly true if the women consented because of a lack of other options for self-support. MacKinnon writes: "The sex is not chosen for the sex. Money is the medium of force and provides the cover of consent."[30]

Even worse, notes MacKinnon, women in pornography are presented as enjoying being used, abused, and violated by men: "In pornography, women desire disposition and cruelty. Men…create scenes in which women desperately want to be bound, battered, tortured, humiliated, and killed. Or merely taken and used. Women are there to be violated and possessed, men to violate and possess us."[31] Dworkin warns, "The most enduring sexual truth in pornography is that sexual violence is desired by the normal female, needed by her, suggested or demanded by her."[32] So what we see, when pornography is analyzed, is a depersonalization intended to display females as objects to be used to satisfy aggressive and sexual desires.

MacKinnon's assertions about the impact of viewing pornography, especially hard-core pornography, have been verified by a range of researchers. Young people, especially boys, are intrigued by pornography, and they can find even hard-core pornography easily on the Internet. So what are the consequences of frequent viewing? As we know, our brains have the ability to adapt to our experiences (neuroplasticity).[33] When we experience something exciting, like pornography, our brain cells release a chemical known as dopamine, which makes us feel good. But the brain doesn't stop at making us feel good. It also starts to strengthen the connections between all the brain cells that fired.

If we continue to watch pornography regularly, our brain gets overwhelmed by the constant overload of chemicals that comes along with that watching. So it fights back by taking away some of the dopamine receptors that provided that good feeling.[34] As a result, we don't feel quite as excited, so we step up our porn intake.[35] And suddenly we are addicted—feeling depressed or uneasy if we go for very long without seeing porn. But that's not all. The addiction actually damages the part of the brain—shrinking the brain's frontal lobes—that helps us think things through and make good choices.[36] So the more porn we watch, the more we want to watch, the more our brain is damaged, and the more difficult it to stop. The good news is that by using the very neuroplasticity that caused the damage in the first place, the brain can heal itself if we stop looking at porn.

There are social consequences, as well, of viewing hard-core porn. Just as with playing violent video games, young males in particular start to become indifferent to the emotional or empathic aspect of relationships.[37] Their expectations become shaped by the endless stream of new, mind-blowing stimulation, and they find dating and relationship-oriented sex more work and more risky (because of potential rejection) and ultimately boring.[38] Research has found that, if men are exposed to media that objectify women, they report less satisfaction in intimate heterosexual relations.[39]

Increasingly young people's relationships are being played out online—flirting, wooing, communicating.[40] And sexting, or the sending of sexually-explicit self-images, has become increasingly common. In fact, popular magazines like *Cosmopolitan* and *Vogue* have published articles on how to make sexts spicy. While sexting with one's partner can be problematic, the dynamic has gone viral, so to speak. We now have not only middle school students on trial for the criminal act of disseminating child pornography (forwarding sexted images to school mates),[41] but also young rapists on trial who not only rape young girls, but film the target after the rape (as though she were a trophy) and text it around the target's school.[42]

The Internet Watch Foundation has estimated that 88 percent of sexted images are "stolen" from their original location and displayed not only to the social network of the target but also on porn sites that collect sexual images of the young.[43] We see in the news the disastrous consequences for the target, including blackmail and severe depression and even suicide. The other part of this trend, which is not discussed often, is that young people are becoming used to separating the physical body from the whole person and the context of a relationship.

Self-Objectification

The separation of self and body is known as self-objectification—so we become both the perpetrator and the target. Recently, the American Psychological Association has become concerned about the extent to which girls and women *self*-objectify and published a *Report of the APA Task Force on the Sexualization of Girls*.[44] Two of the dynamics that have become apparent in the self-objectification process are body surveillance (or the habitual monitoring of body appearance) and body shame (or the perceived failure to meet cultural body ideals).

Research has shown that, if women are exposed to objectifying images, over time they increase their body surveillance and begin to self-objectify.[45] As a result they feel more body shame and also begin to perform poorly as attentional resources are focused on managing their self-image. The same process has been confirmed in relation to music videos. When females are exposed to music videos high in sexual objectification—which many are—they are more likely to self-objectify.[46]

In the process of self-objectification, a woman focuses on her projection of how her body appears to others rather than on how she can perform actions using that body. Negative consequences include body shame, anxiety, eating disorders, depression, and sexual dysfunction. Social worker Sophia Rinaldis has identified nine ways in which women enact body shame, or a feeling that their body is not okay as is:[47]

o Focusing on dieting rather than on nutrition
o Refusing to indulge in pleasurable food choices
o Idolizing unrealistic body types seen in the media
o Shaming people who are "too skinny"
o Judging the variety of body types we see
o Judging others for conforming behaviors
o Judging expressions of sexuality
o Not knowing our bodies
o Defining beauty as a look instead of a state of mind

Neuroscientist Karen Rommelfanger gives an excellent illustration from her own professional experience when she quotes a highly successful male colleague's Facebook posting.[48] Her colleague wrote:

> My impression of the Conference of the Society for Neuroscience in New Orleans. There are thousands

of people at the conference and an unusually high concentration of unattractive women. The super model types are completely absent. What is going on? Are unattractive women particularly attracted to neuroscience? Are beautiful women particularly un-interested in the brain? No offense to anyone.

As she points out, it is disturbing that a senior academic — in a position to mentor students, review article submissions, make candidate selections, etc. — would believe that physical appearance is the most important attribute of a female scientist, and that he would share this perspective with the world. What is even more disturbing is the self-objectification response that occurred, with women rebutting that they were beautiful or that there are beautiful scientists, rather than questioning the objectification.

Exercise: Ending Self-Objectification

In the next 48 hours, notice any instance where you are treating yourself as an object and, if you are, try one of the following and note the results:

1. Visualize yourself as an out-of-focus picture that you bring back into focus.

2. Imagine an energetic line running from your navel to the top of your head.

Each of these are techniques for centering yourself back in your body, as the actor not the observer.

Earlier we mentioned the "male gaze" and its impact. In self-objectification, we see that male gaze internalized. When females self-objectify, they internalize a need to "correct" their bodies so that they live up to the ideals of feminine appearance, whatever those may be at the time. So they begin treating themselves as things to be decorated and gazed upon. Philosopher Sandra-Lee Bartky has grouped the practices that females (women and girls) use to produce a "feminine" body and ultimately to see themselves as follows:[49]

1. *Practices that produce a body of a particular size and shape*: If it is considered sexy to appear abnormally thin, then females become prone to eating disorders in order to manage their weight or thin their thighs. A glance at the statistics for anorexia and bulimia will show that the vast majority of sufferers are females. In addition, many women modify their bodies through plastic surgery such as breast enlargement, Botox, or liposuction.

2. *Practices to control the body's gestures, postures, and movements*: Females learn that they should take up very little space, while males tend to expand to fill the space available. In addition, women's fashion (tight or long skirts, high heels) is designed to restrict free and easy movement. Anyone who does not normally wear high heels, but then feels compelled to so at a particular social event, knows that practice is required if you don't want to trip and fall!

3. *Practices to display the body as an ornamented surface*: Retail establishments have large displays of cosmetics designed to make skin soft, smooth, hairless, and wrinkle-free—"like a baby's." There are admonitions against being seen without make-up, and females have greater pressure than males to adorn themselves (or be adorned) with jewelry.

These messages to self-objectify come from everywhere: parents, teachers, friends, online, the media, male partners. "Whatever else she [a woman] may become, she is importantly a body designed to please or to excite," says Bartky.[50] Political scientist Iris Marion Young adds, "Developing a sense of our bodies as beautiful objects to be gazed at and decorated requires suppressing a sense of our bodies as strong, active subjects."[51]

Human Trafficking

Human trafficking, even though illegal under several international conventions, is unfortunately alive and flourishing. In Chapter Four, we looked at the issue of the trafficking of at least 15.9 million women and girls as part of the pattern of sexual violence against women, but this is just the tip of the iceberg, so to speak. The Walk Free Foundation's *Global Slavery Index: 2014* estimates that 35.8 million adults and children are trafficked each year, with profits of $150 billion to those controlling the trade (primarily organized crime).[52] Trafficking includes sexual exploitation (53%), forced labor (40%), slavery or practices similar to slavery such as forced marriage or debt bondage, and exploitation through the removal of organs. Despite the efforts of Interpol and national law enforcement agencies, few perpetrators are convicted.

The UN Office on Drugs and Crime has issued a *Global Report on Trafficking in Persons: 2014*[53] indicating that while 49 percent of targets trafficked are women, another 33 percent are children of which two-thirds are girls (some as young as four years old). All children may be sold into hazardous physical labor (such as dangerous mine work), but girls are most frequently sold for sexual exploitation while forced military participation (child soldiers) is more common for boys.

Trafficking in general is a growth industry, with the fastest growing sector being the traffic in organs due to increasing demand for transplant organs, particularly kidneys. Most often the target is forced or deceived into giving up an organ, or does so out of economic necessity (much like selling blood). In some instances, though, the organ is removed while the target is being treated for another ailment. Implicated are not only the transporter, but also the staff of the hospital or clinic, the medical professionals, the agents and contractors, the buyers, and the banks where organs are stored.

Lest we think, "This couldn't happen in my country," we need to be clear that human trafficking is occurring in the thousands if not millions in *every* country. The target is often trafficked by someone they know and trust—including mothers selling daughters to brothels to pay off debts. While drug trafficking accounts for a large portion of the $850 billion in revenues for organized crime worldwide, revenues from human trafficking are rapidly increasing.

Objectifying Children

While there are now some conventions to protect children from abuse, historically children have been viewed and treated as property. Although an unfortunately high percent of children suffer from brutal violence of the type we discussed in Chapter Four, the motivation is usually not that the child is sinful or inhuman, but rather that they belong to the adult to treat as they will. This objectification is reinforced by laws and customs that give parents control of children and what happens to them.

We have already explored human trafficking in general. What are the issues specific to children? Child exploitation typically has three stages: recruitment, movement or engagement, and exploitation. The recruiter may be a stranger, the child's parents, or even the child themselves (if they are under pressure to contribute financially to their family). When the recruiter is a stranger, the child may be physically enticed or abducted, but increasingly recruitment is happening online. The Internet has been a boon to child recruiters as they are able to work with anonymity.

In order to gain the cooperation of the child, there is a recruitment phase known as "grooming" where the recruiter (stranger or family member) builds an emotional connection with the child in order to gain their trust. If a stranger, the recruiter can pretend to be the same age as the child with the same concerns, or can offer advice, gifts, or outings—always alert for leverage that can be used to force cooperation, especially if the child has low self-esteem or is otherwise vulnerable.

Next comes the transportation stage, if the child is to be physically moved (locally, regionally, or internationally), or the engagement stage if the activity is to take place online. Engagement activities include sending or posting sexually explicit images of themselves, taking part in sexual activities via webcam or smartphone, or having sexual conversations by text or online—all of which can then be used to blackmail the child into the exploitative activity.

Finally we have the actual exploitation. With the growth of the Internet, recruiters no longer need to run the risks associated with meeting the child in real life; instead, they can persuade or blackmail the child into taking part in online sexual activity. Sexual exploitation of children also includes child tourism (publicized provision of child prostitutes), the use of children in sex shows for voyeurs, and child pornography—the multibillion dollar industry wherein children are filmed being raped or performing sexual acts with other children, adults, and various objects.

One in seven children is forced into illegal non-sexual labor—primarily agriculture, but often with hazardous materials or in industries such as rug weaving where small hands are a plus (with children starting as young as four years old).[54] Girls' forced domestic work is the most invisible of all, and UNICEF indicates that there is evidence that girls may constitute the majority of child workers.[55] Other forms of forced labor include debt bondage, child begging, child soldiers, and accessories in the drug trade. In all instances, the recruiter views the child as a tool to obtain a particular end, overlooking the shattering of trust and innocence, as well as the loss of education and health.

While the trafficking and exploitation of children is horrifying, what is even worse is the knowledge that 90 percent of children are sexually exploited by someone they know and should be able to trust. The most common form of sexual exploitation, and perhaps the most traumatic, is incest by close family members. Here the very people entrusted with the child's well-being are the ones using that child for their own ends and using them in ways that will scar the child for life.

There is one other child objectification issue that we need to mention—the hypersexualization, or presentation as sexual objects, of girls. Referring back to the 2007 American Psychological Association report on the sexualization of girls as a result of media imagery,[56] there were four negative influences on girls' well-being noted, having to do with:

a. Difficulty concentrating and increased body shame.

b. Health issues, such as eating disorders, low self-esteem, and depression.

c. Diminished sexual health and unrealistic expectations regarding sexuality.

d. Believing that females are valued primarily for their physical appearance.

Since then, a 2011 study has found that almost 30 percent of clothing for young girls is sexualized (e.g., thongs for underwear) and, further, that there was a link between sexualized clothing and self-objectification.[57]

The Geena Davis Institute on Gender in Media has commissioned some ground-breaking international research that documents the gender inequality and rampant stereotyping in film and television today. For example, females are twice as likely as males to be shown in sexualized clothing, partially or fully nude; and the sexualized portrayal is as likely to occur at age 13 as at age 39.[58]

So far we have said little about bullying, which was covered extensively in *Positive Harmlessness in Practice,* or the repeated and habitual use of force or threats to intimidate the target into meeting the perpetrator's needs. Youth-on-youth bullying is receiving increased attention due to high profile cases focused particularly on cyber bullying. The dynamic of wanting to prove you are better than a peer is understandable, though not acceptable.

But what about the all-but-ignored arena of adult-on-youth bullying? Since a lot of the bullying goes on between parents and their children, it gets overlooked as part of "parents know best for their kids." But there are other adults — e.g., teachers, coaches, religious instructors — that also bully and get away with it as "disciplining." Research shows that teachers who bully retaliate, when confronted, by giving young students lower grades.[59] Bullying by sports coaches is still ubiquitous and reflects a common cultural belief that humiliation tactics (demeaning, shaming, name calling) are necessary for coaches to produce winning teams.[60] Unstated is the likelihood that the coach is using the team to glorify the coach's reputation — hence the need to avoid losing at all costs.

Objectifying Nonhumans

Because scientists have begun asserting that there are nonhuman beings who qualify for personhood and hence for moral standing, we are having to rethink our relationships with other species. Our operating premise has been anthropocentrism, or the belief that human are the most important species and higher moral standing. Recent research, however, demonstrated that young children do not view the world in an anthropocentric manner.[61] That perspective is learned by the time children are five years old from adults around them.

Our policies are primarily based on a "sustainability paradigm," which assumes that all of nature is a resource for humanity. We measure the success of our policies by the percentage of species that remain intact rather than become extinct, without regard to the moral rights of individuals harmed by humans. In fact, we exercise policies to "cull" (murder) populations of species that we view as predatory, such as bears or wolves, in order to control their numbers and hence the impact on our choices.

Anthropocentrism has led us to believe that it is just fine for us to destroy habitat as long as we do not remove something of immediate value to humans. As a result, we have escalated potential interspecies conflict by damaging or destroying habitat, polluting waterways, and blocking migratory pathways.

Here are some examples of the objectification strategies that we are using with plants and animals:

a. *Murdering animals for sport and trophies*: Of the species we know to be very intelligent and self-aware, dolphins are butchered by the hundreds each year in dolphin drives, at least one thousand minke and sperm whales are murdered (by Japan, Iceland, and Norway whale hunters), elephants are murdered on advertised "elephant hunt" safaris, and tigers are murdered despite being endangered.

b. *Murdering animals for parts*: Both elephant tusks and tiger organs are in high demand in Southeast Asia.

Elephants are often hunted for the illegal ivory and then left to die after hacking off the tusks.

c. *Murdering animals to counterbalance habitat destruction*: Having destroyed enough habitat that there are few places where wild species can live without conflict with humans, governments organize "culls" to restrict population growth of bears and wolves.

d. *Murdering animals for food*: At least two of the species that we eat regularly turn out to be intelligent and self-aware: pigs and chickens (see Appendix B).

e. *Holding animals captive for entertainment*: Some very intelligent and highly social animals are held in solitary confinement in aquariums, zoos, and circuses — namely, dolphins, whales, and elephants.

f. *Training animals to provide rides or perform tricks for humans*: This is a specialized form of entertainment captivity, usually involving the use of fear and pain to force the animal to perform as desired. Thus we have elephants trained to give rides on their backs (with the Thomas Cook Group being the largest enterprise to enforce this cruelty), and dolphins trained to allow humans to grab their dorsal fins.

g. *Holding animals captive for research*: Chimpanzees and other great apes have routinely been caged for (often fatal) scientific experimentation.

h. *Exploiting animals in forced labor without pay*: Because we tend to think of animals as objects for our use, we force them to perform for us without pay without their having consented to terms of employment. Examples include having dolphins patrol harbors, having elephants drag logs or assist with other heavy lifting, or using dogs to detect drugs or assist the blind. While personal relationships between the nonhumans and their handlers are often quite friendly and close, the reality is that the nonhumans have no say in when they work and what happens when their working life is over (as there are no wages accumulating to support them in retirement).

i. *Murdering "redundant" exhibit animals*: All too frequently animals that have earned revenues for zoos or marine exhibits are killed because they are "not needed" (e.g., for breeding programs), with no attempt to allocate part of the revenues earned toward a supportive retirement scenario.

j. *Destroying forests and other plant life*: Research has shown that trees and plants are also intelligent and highly social (see Appendix B). Habitat destruction not only affects the species that live within the habitat but also represents the destruction of intelligent vegetation.

k. *Uprooting/relocating plant life*: While research tells us that plant life organizes itself in communities and can tell relatives from non-relatives, we simply move plants wherever we please.

This brings us to our objectification of the Earth itself. Ecocide is the extensive damage to, destruction of, or loss of ecosystem(s) of a given territory, whether by human agency or by other causes, to such an extent that peaceful enjoyment by the inhabitants of that territory has been, or will be, severely diminished.[62]

In March 2010 international barrister and award-winning author Polly Higgins proposed to the United Nations that ecocide be made the fifth crime against peace, which would mean that cases of ecocide could be tried in the International Criminal Court.[63] It would also alert us to being more mindful in the manner in which we interact with the Earth.

Wildlife activists Nicholas Entrup and Margi Prideaux have pointed out: "Instead of human society being accountable to the biosphere, the biosphere has become accountable to us. A tree becomes timber; a mountain or gorilla family become ecotourism destinations; a school of bluefish tuna becomes a fishery; a dolphin is an entertainment exhibit; a whale is meat and blubber."[64] Sounds a bit backwards, doesn't it? We have a ways to go before we relate to other species and our biosphere as equals.

Recognizing Objectification

If we pause for a moment to consider motivation, it is actually quite easy to pinpoint when we are objectifying another. And there are so many examples! The challenge is choosing to act, to change the dynamic.

Our discussion of objectification brings us to the close of Part Two and our survey of the different ways in which we depersonalize others and even ourselves. Looking back to Chapter One and the dynamic of dichotomies, we can see that there is a wide range of ways in which we enact a person/non-person dichotomy—and these habits keep us wedded to a dualistic perspective. We are the ones, though, that have the ability to broaden our circle of care, to expand who and what we include morally, to live our lives in a more nuanced manner. If we do, we may be surprised by the wonders we experience.

Part Three

Moving Beyond the Dualistic Model

NINE

Remembering Who We Are

What would our lives be like if we refused to be trapped in our current illusion of duality? If we felt no need to depersonalize those who are different from us? If we lived the reality that we are all interconnected? What would we need to change in order to offset the dualistic patterns of centuries?

We saw in Part One that there are reasons why we start believing in duality. We explored the dynamics that make it seem real and lead to depersonalizing others. In Part Two, we examined the various ways in which we carry out that depersonalization—some of which are painful to bring to mind, involving as they do atrocities to our collective soul. So why bother to enumerate the apparently limitless ways in which we are willing to harm each other and ourselves?

Until we are willing to face how deeply damaging a dualistic philosophy of life is, it will be impossible for us to make the changes that are needed. It will always be easiest to repeat the familiar, to behave mindlessly, to slip into that tainted sense of satisfaction that we *are* better than others that comes from putting others down—psychologically or physically.

Dealing with the Illusion of Duality

You, the reader, have surely noticed that we have spent no time at all on analyzing the wide range of dualistic philosophies or the theories of non-duality or nondualism. When I began the research for this book, I reviewed hundreds of articles and books on duality and non-duality. But I eventually realized that, as Einstein has said, "We cannot solve our problems with the same thinking we used when we created them."

The concept of "non-duality" is itself part of a dichotomy—the complement to "duality" as the indication (if we refer back to our discussion of dichotomies in Chapter One). As in any dichotomy, the complement is defined by *not* being the indication—so in this case, "not duality." The Merriam-Webster dictionary does not define "non-duality" so we can turn to the parallel concepts of dualism/nondualism. The Merriam-Webster dictionary defines "nondualism" as "a doctrine of classic Brahmanism holding that the essential unity of all is real whereas duality and plurality are phenomenal illusion and that matter is materialized energy which in turn is the temporal manifestation of an incorporeal spiritual eternal essence constituting the innermost self of all things." Since that same dictionary defines "dualism" as "the quality or state of having two different or opposite parts," we can immediately see that "nondualism" is not the true complement of dualism because it does not include all options that are not dualism (e.g., pluralism) and it introduces a new element—that of a "spiritual eternal essence."

So the whole duality/non-duality debate is based on a false dichotomy. By assuming a dualistic worldview to start with, duality becomes the perspective (the indication, the assumption) from which we evaluate all other visions of reality. But duality is *not* our energetic, interconnected reality so the debate falls apart.

We need to approach the issue from a different perspective. What is at issue is *not* the number of divisions of reality— one (monism), two (dualism), three (triadism), or hundreds. What *is* at issue is the false and restrictive worldview represented by the term "duality"—the acceptance of patriarchy and the outdated Newtonian model as being reality, the description of a world in which it is not only okay but expected to have one group superior to other groups.

We have detailed in Part Two the harmful consequences of that false worldview — the cognitive bias and stereotyping and moral exclusion and violence. We don't need a new model or a different paradigm. We already have our *actual* reality — the surging sea of energy of which we are all equally important parts. If we want to give our reality a name, let's call it the One Life, as in the Ageless Wisdom tradition. That One Life is an interconnection of many unique and different entities — unity and diversity simultaneously.

Framing the Changes Needed

Positive Harmlessness in Practice (Volume Two in this series) provided us with a broad framework for how we harm ourselves and others — through commission and omission, through thoughts and words and actions — and introduced a model of harm and harmlessness. In this volume we have filled in the details of how we generate harm, the various depersonalization methods we adopt — hostile bigotry, benevolent bigotry, stereotyping, invisibility, and objectification.

The question before us is "where to from here"? How do we begin to peel back the false assumptions, to sort through what is real and what is false? How do we leverage a recognition of our actual reality in order to make the changes needed, particularly when key dynamics holding our assumption of duality in place operate outside of our awareness? *Positive Harmlessness in Practice* introduced a three-stage model for becoming consciously harmless: noticing, feeling, and acting. Referring back to this model can help us identify priority areas for change:

- o Noticing: mindfulness, focusing, embracing options, reducing cognitive bias

- o Feeling: emotional muscle, gratitude, empathy, compassion

- o Acting: motivation, filters, norms, role models, micro-affirmations

Many change strategies have focused on *intention* as the key to success—affirming what we want, visualizing our desires. But intention is only part of the answer because *what* we intend will still inevitably be shaped by our assumptions about reality. So we need ways to consciously experience and embrace our energetic reality. We need to choose activities that will create more than situation-specific change and will help us shed harmful habits permanently.

Intention is important because it intensifies our innate ability to change. We are most open to "rewiring" ourselves when we are young, but the ability to do so never leaves us. Neuroplasticity is our ally. It grounds us in a hope for a new way of being—one based on our actual reality, not mechanistic determinism. If we intentionally lay down new "tracks" through repetition, the way we behave and view the world will shift.

To move beyond dualistic thinking we have to be willing to reach past the simplicity of dichotomies while remembering the value of repetition or practice. The more frequently we purposely practice a new behavior, the faster it will become a permanent part of our repertoire. Remember that our memories are held within cells throughout our body. Since our body has a process of continuous cell renewal—for some cells as frequently as days or weeks[1]—we have multiple opportunities for a fresh start as memories of old approaches are replaced by our new behaviors. This ability to put in place cells with new memories is the basis for programs that ask you to practice a new behavior for a month.

What gets us into trouble is an attachment to simplicity instead of valuing complexity and detail in how we receive and process information. It's like the difference between a sandwich and a multicourse meal. The sandwich is fine if we want to be quick or expedient, but if we want a fine culinary experience, we will want more variety of textures and flavors. We can have a lot of fun experimenting with different recipes, trying out different restaurants, watching cooking shows and so forth. But, bottom line, we will only seek out those activities if we choose to have a more complex relationship with food than just grabbing a sandwich.

In the same way, we could stay with the simplistic way in which we categorize data and operate "us"/"them" dichotomies, or we can develop habits that will lead us to explore new concepts, behave mindfully, and add detail to commonly-used schemas.

President Barack Obama has said, "We are the ones we've been waiting for. We are the change that we seek." Absolutely true! But change is not easy. We have years of patterning to overcome. So we need to take it step by step, not rushing but being persistent. In a way it doesn't matter where we start, as long as we start!

Exercise: Identifying Your Change Strategy

Reflect back on the most successful changes you have made:

1. What triggered your decision to change?

2. What strategy did you use for repetition of the new behavior?

3. How did you stay motivated through the period of repetition necessary to embed the change?

Table 6: Evaluating Change Strategies

Strategy	Rating*	Priority?
Noticing		
Increase mindfulness		
Extend working memory capacity		
Maintain focus		
Increase tolerance for ambiguity		
Pose multiple options		
Identify examples of depersonalization		
Reduce cognitive bias		
Feeling		
Increase positive emotions		
Focus on gratitude		
Strengthen empathy		
Strengthen compassion		
Acting		
Motivation		
Accept social dynamics		
Provide new norms		
Provide positive role models		
Micro-affirmations		
Total		

Rating:
> 1 = already strong; no need for additional work
> 2 = somewhat strong; could use some work
> 3 = not strong; needs work

Table 6 provides a structure to help you get started. As you read through each of the sections below (on noticing, feeling, or acting), you can rate yourself in terms of how competent you feel in various strategies for ending depersonalization habits. These are not the only possible strategies—they are just suggestions. An extra line is provided in each section so that you can add your own strategies. First try rating how confident you feel in each of the strategies and then try identifying your priority areas for change. Generally speaking we find change easiest if we start with something where we can see the shift relatively quickly so that we gain confidence that change is possible.

The sections below describe options for how to stimulate change and begin to shift old patterns. Again, the ideas presented are not "the answer." They are only catalysts to help you find your own answers. You know what works best for you. There are many paths in the change process that can lead to the same outcome. What one or two or three habits could you focus on shifting now that would make a significant difference for you?

Strengthening Noticing

We have seen that our brain provides us with a number of tools for efficient data processing. Used mindlessly, they can result in inaccurate schemas or stereotypes, ignoring data that appears contradictory (cognitive bias), reworking memories to delete apparent redundancies, and a strong preference for simplicity due to limited working memory capacity.

Many approaches to social change start with behavior, with acting differently, in the belief that the gap (dissonance) between what we are doing and our implicit biases will lead to change—"fake it till you make it." While change is possible using this approach, we are just as likely to ignore or rationalize the dissonance. When we don't "make it," it is often because we underestimate the influence of unconscious processes—not the "unconscious" of Freud but rather the perceptual and data processing activities that operate routinely outside of our awareness, which we reviewed in Chapter One. Strategies for change need to help bring these reflexive approaches into our awareness if they are creating problems. Here are some examples of strategies we could adopt:

Mindfulness. Part of what helps us function cognitively is assigning a range of tasks to those parts of our brain that operate mindlessly, on automatic. It is neither realistic nor helpful to be mindful of everything every minute of the day — routine tasks would consume all of our time and energy! Just think of the mental resources that would be required if we had to consciously remember to breathe every five to ten seconds.

But being able to be mindful, or aware of our experience without judgment, can be extremely helpful. While we operate mindlessly, we will not be able to challenge old thinking and old assumptions. Learning to be mindful, on the other hand, can not only enhance our general well-being[2] but also help us be less emotionally reactive,[3] more cognitively flexible,[4] and better able to interact with others.[5]

Mindfulness meditation has received a lot of social and research attention. If meditation is an approach that appeals to you, there are a number of mindfulness meditation outlines available online. If you would prefer a different approach, here are other ways to improve mindfulness:

- o Active listening
  All too often we are thinking ahead to what we want to say instead of listening to the person we are with. Practice engaging actively by asking questions, summarizing to make sure you have understood the other person, and linking what you do say to what the other person has been saying.

- o Focus on breathing
  A good way to refocus into the present is to manage our breathing for a short period. If we breathe shallowly and very fast, we will soon become agitated and distracted. If, however, we breathe deeply and calmly, we will be able to relax into the present.

o Body awareness

We can supplement conscious breathing with becoming aware of other parts of our body that are usually outside of our awareness—the feel of the fork in our hand as we eat, the water on our body as we shower, the muscle sensations as we walk. Any practice in conscious awareness will generalize to help us process data more consciously.

o Thought management

A common way that we distract ourselves is by allowing our thoughts to ramble along "unsupervised." The result is "chatter" that either reinforces our current beliefs and stereotypes or replays interactions that we found very positive or very negative. Part of mindfulness is reining in this rambling self-talk and focusing on what is relevant and important. Remember that plasticity will help. Refocus enough times and that new focus will become your new mental habit pattern.

Working memory capacity. If we want to make changes, we need to be able to hold data in our conscious awareness so that we have choices about how to proceed. The research in the area of working memory capacity is primarily focused on improving fluid intelligence, or the ability to solve problems in novel situations. For our purposes, we are not so concerned with intelligence as we are in the basic ability to be aware of more than five things at once so that we have a richer decision-making environment.

We have already seen that various depersonalization scenarios have the effect of reducing the working memory available to process new data because we are preoccupied with scanning for threats and processing nonverbal cues. That scanning is adaptive as it can protect us from imminent physical or psychological danger. But reduced working memory capacity results in a companion reduction in the ability to hold new material in conscious memory long enough to process it and learn from it. If we can expand working memory capacity, we will be less handicapped in situations of threat and high stress.

A number of websites now promote "brain training," promising to utilize neuroplasticity to improve the capacity of the working memory, but the research results are mixed.[6] Perhaps users of the websites simply get better at the specific games. Perhaps the increasing complexity of the tasks helps users learn to "chunk" data more effectively rather than simply expanding working memory capacity. The one verifiable result is an increase in "useful field of view," or the space over which we can attend to information, which does suggest that at least the ability to screen out distractions can be improved.[7]

It is not only a matter of expanding working memory capacity but also a matter of not constricting our focus through fear or anxiety. Research has shown that, even in stressful situations that could otherwise compromise our working memory, mindfulness meditation can help us maintain and improve working memory capacity.[8] Alternately, we can query the fear or anxiety when it occurs, keeping in mind that it is a lingering habit pattern that began when such a reaction was useful. We can ask ourselves questions such as: What am I really afraid of? What is the worst that could happen? How have I managed successfully in the past? The idea is to help ourselves experience that the reaction is reflexive and outdated.

Focus. A downside of the growth in social media is the constant stimulation from a wide range of sources on a variety of topics, many of which are irrelevant to our current task. We discussed the tendency to reinforce exploration, the seeking out of new stimuli, rather than learning to focus intently on one topic. Again, mindfulness meditation can help improve all aspects of attention.[9] We all know the typical aids for focus: clear away clutter (mental or physical), create realistic To Do lists and time lines, build in mental breaks and physical activity. These can be supplemented with practices that support focus, like setting aside time for a particular project during which you turn off your phone and email.

Tolerance for ambiguity. One strategy for increasing the complexity of what we hold in working memory is being able to tolerate ambiguity. The simple, dualistic solution has little or no ambiguity—what you see is what you get with no options. Ambiguity, on the other hand, means allowing for uncertainty, for multiple meanings, for considering more than one option. Tolerance for ambiguity is similar to the "perceiving" type in the Myers-Briggs typology,[10] while intolerance for ambiguity is similar to the "judging" type, which signals that uncertainty is threatening and rapid closure is desired. To sustain a tolerance for ambiguity, we need to be willing to be uncomfortable, in a state of tension, resisting premature closure.

What is the relevance of tolerance of ambiguity for our discussion? First, there is research evidence that prejudice is directly linked to a discomfort with ambiguity.[11] People who are prejudiced make quick decisions about others, using their available schemas to categorize them and ignore any contradictory information. But this dynamic can be used to reduce prejudice if perpetrators are introduced to members of the out-group whom they like, thus modifying the schema applied to that group as a whole.

Second, without a tolerance for ambiguity, we will be closed to new information. Radio host Jeff Sanders writes in *Forbes* that tolerance for ambiguity is the critical trait for entrepreneurial success in order to hold a bold vision while also investigating other possibilities. He suggests that the best way to develop or increase our tolerance for ambiguity is "to make mistakes early, cheaply, and often. To learn that failure is a blessing if it helps you grow. To learn that failure in pursuit of a worthy goal is noble and that questions are more important than answers."[12]

Multiple options. There are always more than two options. The most straightforward way we can experience this is to *ask ourselves for a third option* when we hear ourselves say "either … or." For example, if we are about to say, "Shall we invite Sarah over for coffee or see if we can drop in on her," we could add, "…or see if she wants to meet us at the coffee shop or …" The other options may be less appealing, but getting in the habit of always mentioning at least three options is the quickest way to "rewire" our brain away from a dichotomous approach.

Identifying examples. Some depersonalizing behaviors are so common that we take them for granted and simply don't notice them. We know that identifying depersonalizing behaviors is the first step in confronting the perpetrator and ending the abuse. However, identification means that we must be able to differentiate between what we ourselves have caused and what is the abusive behavior of others.

Research shows that this differentiation between our own responsibility and the actions of others is difficult for anyone struggling with self-esteem issues.[13] So we can get caught in a double bind. Being the target of prejudice and abuse lowers self-esteem whether or not we are aware of those actions. But doing something about it requires us to have the self-confidence to say, "It's not me. It's the perpetrator."

Looking back at the research of Julia Becker and Janet Swim, we see the power of journaling or making daily notes about our experience.[14] Try picking a form of depersonalization (sexism, racism, ageism, etc.) and write down each day for a week:

o How often you noticed the bias directed at you.

o How often you noticed the bias directed at others.

o How often you yourself acted in a biased fashion.

Not only will you learn about the pattern of depersonalization and its frequency, but more importantly you will sensitize yourself to depersonalizing behaviors that had been outside your awareness so that you can move to change them.

Cognitive bias. Reducing cognitive bias can be very challenging, again because the bias occurs outside of our awareness. So we need conscious strategies to disrupt our automatic mental routines. Mindfulness meditation is one such strategy in that it helps us identify and delink automatic responses that we developed in prior learning and supports us in integrating data in new ways.[15] While there are many forms of bias, there are six that we could usefully focus on disrupting. Here are possible ways to do so:

o Attentional bias, or limits to what we focus on.
   Expand your attentional field by picking an unusual focus each day such as talking to a stranger, or reading on a new topic, or seeking out a new experience.

o Attribution error, or crediting in-group members with skills and talent while attributing out-group member success to luck.
   Retrain yourself by noticing the skills and talent of individual out-group members.

o Confirmation bias, or looking for data to confirm a desired outcome.
   Build in the habit of considering all data by picking a conclusion you've reached and consciously searching for disconfirming data.

o In-group bias, or assigning positive attributes to your in-group.

Learn to view in-group members accurately by noticing ways in which in-group members differ from each other and from you. Have a constructive and respectful conversation on a topic where you disagree.

o Negativity bias, or the tendency to focus more on the negative than on the positive.
Ask yourself what the positive aspects of the situation are when you find yourself focusing on the negative. Recall events that you experienced as negative and identify at least one positive outcome that emerged from the situation.

o Stereotyping, or out-group bias.
Pick an unfamiliar group and learn more about its members in order to add detail to overly simplistic schemas. Use a screen saver that rotates through the faces of persons from all ethnic backgrounds and scenes set in a range of cultures. Attend newcomer events to meet new immigrants.

One form of cognitive bias that we need to develop more direct access to is our assumptions regarding nonhumans. In Chapter Three we explored what it means to be a "person," and the research in Appendix B supports the assignment of personhood to a range of entities other than humans.

Here is a way to get started: Pick an animal or a plant type that matters to you and hold a mental image of the entity. Now read the research in Appendix B regarding that entity. Embellish your mental image with all of the attributes scientists have discovered until they become a "person" to you. You can do the same with the Earth — notice weather, sunsets, night skies, topography and imagine these as expressions of a sentient being.

Most of us have deeply-engrained human/nonhuman biases that will take time to untangle. To help gain some perspective on how humans might be viewed by other species, recall the interaction between the prince and the flower in Antoine de Saint-Exupéry's *The Little Prince*:[16] "Where are the people?" the little prince asked. The flower replied, "One never knows where to find them. The wind blows them away. They have no roots, and that makes their life very difficult."

Strengthening Feeling

How we filter data coming in depends in large part on our emotional predispositions. To the extent that we are geared to social acceptance and strongly influenced by peers, we will screen information to fit with those attitudes. If we are threatened by differences and distance ourselves from all but our close in-group, we will continue to depersonalize a wide range of persons. Strategies to strengthen our "emotional muscle" include:

Positive emotions. In *Positive Harmlessness in Practice*, we noted our tendency to pay more attention to negative emotions of fear and anger than to positive emotions like joy. Part of what supports depersonalization is the tendency to feel negative emotions when confronted by out-group members and to see out-group members as all the same (out-group homogeneity) rather than as individuals. Research has shown that, when we are feeling joyous this assumed out-group homogeneity disappears and we become aware of individual differences.[17] That feeling of joy promotes more inclusive social categorization and reduces distortion. Positive emotions broaden our scope of attention and our ability to take in more nuanced data.[18]

So feeling positive as much of the time as possible is the answer—or is it? Positive emotions have a positive effect only when they are appropriate to the situation.[19] The downside of positive emotions like happiness is that they also signal that we have fulfilled our goals and can coast a bit; as well, they can result in feeling less inhibited and more likely to take risks. So negative emotions also have their place in alerting us to difficulties and energizing us to take action.

The challenge is to achieve emotional balance so that we are able to experience and leverage both positive and negative emotions. This is particularly true when we are not feeling confident about ourselves. Research has found that making positive self-statements has a negative effect for those who are unsure of themselves instead of boosting self-esteem.[20] When we include both negative and positive self-statements, the experience feels more realistic and so feels better.

Gratitude. Gratitude is thought to be the most influential of the positive emotions since it focuses on noticing and appreciating the positive.[21] Researchers talk, though, about a gratitude gap—significantly more people say that they feel grateful than act on that feeling. While the feeling of gratitude has positive consequences for us individually, those benefits are magnified when we interact with others and gain a sense of social support and connection with others.[22] For our purposes, the importance of gratitude is that it leads to people being more open and receptive to new ideas.

Exercise: Feeling Gratitude

For one week, each evening name three things that you are grateful for and then reflect:

1. Did any involve something that someone else did for you? If so, did you thank them?

2. If not, select something the next day that you *can* thank someone else for—and thank them.

Empathy. Cultivating the ability to understand another's feelings and "walk in their shoes" helps us to expand our circle of care, our boundary of moral inclusion. Encouraging empathy also decreases the likelihood of violence because the two share the same neural circuitry and so each can suppress the other.[23] So practicing empathy crowds out our ability to be violent.

One of the consequences of our online connectedness is, ironically, a noticeable drop in empathy among younger people.[24] While we can share our experiences quickly and extensively, we can also ignore others' painful experiences. Social media like Facebook encourage us to focus on ourselves and to become accustomed to easy "friend"-ing with no corollary relational responsibilities. The Me generation is being described as self-centered, narcissistic, and individualistic. Some researchers believe this is reinforced by massive exposure to violence in TV, movies, and video games that help numb us to the pain of others.

The good news is that research has shown that the ability to empathize with others is part of our natural repertoire[25]-- our default response—as long as it is not suppressed by out-group bias.[26] Our degree of empathy is directly related to our feeling of a common bond and increases toward members of our in-group.[27] While our ability to empathize drops with strangers, it will rebound if we have some kind of positive interaction with that stranger or discover that we have things in common.[28]

Compassion. While empathy focuses on feeling along with the target, compassion includes a desire to help the target feel better. We tend to feel compassion toward individuals who are experiencing serious difficulties not of their own making and whose difficulties are ones that we can picture affecting us as well. Research with children three to five years old indicates that our basic impulse is to help the target of abuse, rather than punish the perpetrator.[29]

Researchers have also found that it is possible with training to build up people's "compassionate muscle," moving from friends to troublesome others, and have documented both an increase in neural activity related to emotion regulation and increased altruism.[30] So again the practice of this helping (prosocial) emotion makes it more likely that we will respond compassionately in the future. Because of the importance of compassion in motivating us to reach beyond stereotypes and bias in order to help others in need, TED speaker Karen Armstrong chose as her initiative the global adoption of a Charter for Compassion.[31]

While we may not be able to empathize with other species, we can certainly sympathize with mistreatment and want to make amends. The challenge that arises for us is to remain focused on actions in the target's own best interest rather than on what makes us feel better. Paternalistic "for their own good" treatment lies perilously close to benevolent bigotry.

Strengthening Acting

Our actions are shaped both by what we believe is true and by what we feel is possible. Historically, the Intergroup Contact Theory — that contact between in-group and out-group members is the best way to precipitate change — has shaped social action.[32] Of course the context for contact has to be positive, based on common goals and a need for intergroup cooperation.

Research is showing, though, that contact is not necessarily enough. Some of the research on what matters in taking action is presented below, along with a few examples to stimulate your own thinking of how others are making a difference. However, there are many other excellent examples. Publications like the newsletter of the Good News Agency[33] track governmental and community initiatives. Embracing who we are as energetic beings can be displayed in many ways. The key, though, is to act because that is what will ultimately "rewire" us. As anthropologist Margaret Mead said, "Never doubt that a small group of thoughtful, committed citizens can change the world; indeed, it's the only thing that ever has."

Motivation. What we believe about why people act the way that they do influences how we act and respond. Research has shown, for example, that if we believe that someone acted out of free will, we are more grateful to them.[34] The American Psychological Association has reported some encouraging research showing that if we believe that our behavior occurs as a result of effort or choice instead of being innate, we are more likely to perform well and be open to change.[35] Extending this dynamic to the realm of prejudice, if we believe that stereotypes are not fixed traits, we are more likely to question them and become less prejudiced.

Based on this research, it seems clear that a first practical step in social change is to educate people about neuroplasticity and the potential for change. Researchers have added another piece: If we believe that someone is unlikely to change, we in turn are unlikely to confront them on prejudiced behavior.[36] But if we believe that change is possible and that the other party might be motivated to change, then we are more likely to engage in educational exchanges that could lead the other party to make different, less prejudiced choices.

Social dynamics. One of the bases for negative judgments of others is a belief in meritocracy or that people are rewarded based exclusively on their performance; therefore, people who are not succeeding must be lazy or incompetent. Unfortunately, as we have seen repeatedly, that ideology is not realistic given the biases operating in our society. While people within a privileged in-group may be evaluated fairly based only on merit, those in the out-group will be evaluated in a biased fashion. Regardless of how skilled they are or how much they try, their opportunities will be limited by prejudice.

To address social inequities rooted in cognitive bias and stereotyping, we need to accept that prejudice is alive and well and operating largely unconsciously. In fact, research has demonstrated that less than ten percent of us are truly free of prejudice[37] and millennials are no less prejudiced than their parents.[38]

New social norms. To support any shift in worldview, we need formal agreements on what is and is not acceptable. One area where progress is being made is in enacting anti-bullying legislation. In the United States, all 50 states now have such laws in place, and there is a watchdog organization called Bully Police USA. In Canada bullying falls generally under the federal Criminal Code, and specific anti-bullying legislation is handled at the provincial level, although not all forms of bullying may be covered. The nonprofit, Stop a Bully, allows students who are victims or witnesses of bullying to safely report the details to school officials.

Gradually local communities such as Regina (Saskatchewan), Port Moody (British Columbia), and Blackfalds and Hanna (Alberta) are enacting local bylaws that impose fines and jail time and require attendance at anti-bullying courses. Hanna has gone a further step in its legislation and included bystanders who encourage a bully. Progress is being made in Europe, and the Philippines enacted an anti-bullying law in September 2013. This increasing momentum demonstrates that, if we decide it is important, we can build community consensus regarding unacceptable depersonalizing behavior and enshrine that consensus in legal instruments.

Another type of initiative that can set a new social norm is the development of educational resources for use in schools and communities. One such set of resources is the *Roots of*

Empathy course, developed in Canada for use with grades 1 to 8, which is now being used internationally.[39] It has a companion course, *Seeds of Empathy*, that is available for 3-5 year olds.

There are also websites to help shift our awareness and behavior, such as:

- o GreaterGood.berkeley.edu
- o RandomActsofKindness.org
- o ReducingStereotypeThreat.org
- o Understanding Prejudice.org

Social movements can also set new norms of behavior. One of the most engaging is the "Pay It Forward" movement that began when a novel of that name (later made into a movie) described a young boy who, as a social studies assignment to make a difference, launched the concept of helping someone for the reward of having them, in turn, help someone else in need. There is now a Pay It Forward Foundation, as well as a world Pay It Forward Day (April 28) that, in 2015, engaged people in 75 countries in small acts of kindness. Ongoing examples keep appearing in the news, like the six high school football players who, after having their meals paid for anonymously at a café, left enough money that eventually paid for meals for 30 more people.[40]

A challenging new norm just around the corner is the legal status of nonhumans. The Nonhuman Rights Project has as its mandate "through education and litigation, to change the common law status of at least some nonhuman animals from mere 'things,' which lack the capacity to possess any legal right, to 'persons,' who possess such fundamental rights as bodily integrity and bodily liberty, and those other legal rights to which evolving standards of morality, scientific discovery, and human experience entitle them."[41] Lawsuits have been filed in New York State on behalf of four chimpanzees held in captivity, with an elephant to be the next plaintiff.

The question for us is what will it mean to acknowledge the rights listed in Chapter Three in regard to at least some highly intelligent, self-aware nonhumans? The ramifications are far-reaching, and include not only treating nonhuman persons with dignity and respect but also a new approach to environmental issues such as noise pollution in the oceans.[42]

Positive role models. Hopefully the material in Part Two generated a strong and determined sense of "Never again." But just saying, "I'm not going to behave that way anymore" is not enough. Lasting change does not come from "should nots." We need a compelling vision of what we *can* do in order to ignite action.

One such realized vision has been the development of the YouTube campaign of "It Gets Better" statements from a range of well-known figures in response to the unfortunate number of gay teenager suicides. Research on the campaign has revealed that while heterosexuals saw no real difference between the types of messages posted, LGBTQ youth found that the messages focused on social change — that the situation can, should and will change — were the most comforting.[43] We each have the ability to initiate such campaigns in our communities, keeping in mind that support for the targets needs to be paired with proposals of concrete action for change.

There is also the possibility of an individual public stand on issues of unacceptable behavior. One such public statement occurred in September 2013. After learning about a pro-rape chant ("U is for underage, N is for no consent") being used to induct first-year students at St. Mary's University in Halifax, Nova Scotia, Daren Miller (a graduate of St. Mary's, living in Calgary) flew to Halifax and publicly returned his diplomas, saying, "For me this will go away. For someone who has been abused, that will live with them their entire lives....Men need to understand, particularly on a campus scene, that no means no."[44]

Micro-affirmations. Economist Mary Rowe began focusing attention on micro-messaging in 1973, beginning with micro-inequities or "apparently small events which are often ephemeral and hard-to-prove, events which are covert, often unintentional, frequently unrecognized by the perpetrator, which occur wherever people are perceived to be 'different.'"[45] Here we see an early definition of the dynamic of benevolent bigotry in action.

She then went on to focus attention on micro-affirmations, or the ingredients that precipitate the butterfly shift discussed in detail in *Positive Harmlessness in Practice*. We have the opportunity to shift our own awareness as well as to empower others through these "tiny acts of opening doors to opportunity, gestures of inclusion and caring, and graceful acts of listening,…consistently giving credit to others…providing comfort and support when others are in distress…Micro-affirmations include the myriad details of fair, specific, timely, consistent and clear feedback that help a person build on strength and correct weakness."

In the end, the benefits of these small acts will spread to others and will also help us "rewire" ourselves by blocking unconscious habits of depersonalization. Try taking a week and finding an opportunity each day for a micro-affirmation.

Moving Toward Abundance

Choosing to liberate ourselves from our archaic, dualistic worldview and its outmoded beliefs and damaging stereotypes involves deliberate effort. It requires putting down new grooves, new patterns, new connections in our brain so that we embrace complexity and live compassionately.

And so we come full circle. We saw the details of our actual energetic reality in *Principles of Abundance for the Cosmic Citizen*, described in seven principles that science has shown govern our lives: interconnectivity, participation, nonlinearity, nonduality, interdependence, adaptability, and cooperation. We explored what it would mean to experience harmlessness as a society and how we could begin to behave harmlessly in *Positive Harmlessness in Practice*. Now we have had an opportunity to apply the lens of harmlessness and moral inclusion to bring into focus the sweeping and, in fact, lethal ramifications of clinging to a dualistic "us"/"them" model. What is exciting is that we are on the cusp of being able to identify and eliminate the various ways in which we depersonalize ourselves and others, and embrace the relationships of dignity and mutual respect promised in the United Nations Universal Declaration of Human Rights.

The premise for this *Enough for Us All* trilogy is that there is indeed enough for us all, that we live in a context of cosmic abundance. We have the possibility to realize that abundant vision when we:

- o Curtail our sense of entitlement.

- o Switch to an inclusive "us" *and* "them" perspective.

- o Live mindfully and cooperatively.

- o Greet each day with gratitude for the diversity that surrounds us.

If we pay attention, if we notice the possibilities, if we open ourselves to feeling connected, we will experience the joyous flood of goodwill and well-being that is available to us all.

Now it is up to you, the reader. Will you choose to question assumptions of separativeness and open yourself to interconnections? Will you reach beyond the complacency of known habits to embrace the uncertainty that is our actual reality? Will you ask yourself the questions posed in the exercises and help a path forward to emerge? Will you challenge yourself to step out of centuries-old familiar patterns and toward the extraordinary future that may await us?

Let us take this step together as energetic parts of a multi-faceted, interconnected universe. To paraphrase Mahatma Gandhi, let us "be the change we want to see in the world." Yes, it will take effort to peel away the layers of learned attitudes and behaviors that have developed from our false, dualistic worldview. Yes, it will require time and patience. But, as Lao Tzu reminds us, "The journey of a thousand miles begins with a single step." *Remembering who we really are* will underscore for us how important each person's contributions are for the well-being of the whole (the One Life) of which we are all a part.

The Effects of Gendered Language

One of the strongest reinforcers of depersonalization is language.[1] English is a gendered language, and introducing gender-neutral terminology has not been easy. There are some notable successes in introducing more inclusive job titles: "fire fighter" instead of fireman, "police officer" instead of policeman, and so on. But despite research going back forty years or more that shows that language influences thought and that the impact is not trivial,[2] gendered language continues to be used, and those who object are met with "what's the fuss?"

The early work of Benjamin Lee Whorf and Edward Sapir on linguistic relativity, later known collectively as the Sapir-Whorf hypothesis, was instrumental in focusing attention on the role played by language in shaping how we view the world.[3] More recent research on the impact of language on behavior began with the now-famous observations by psychologist Sandra Bem in the early 1970s noting that adults handled and spoke to an infant differently based on whether they were told it was a boy or a girl. Both the American Psychological Association and the American Philosophical Association have determined that there is enough evidence of the negative impact of non-inclusive language that they have published professional guidelines on bias-free language.

While speakers of gendered languages, like English, may assume that gender designations are "natural" and required, there are in fact a number of languages and language families (e.g., Austronesian, Turkic, Uralic) that have no grammatical gender. All languages evolve over time, and one of the ways in which English has evolved is in the role that gender plays in determining how personal and relative pronouns are assigned. Old English was similar to modern French and German in that every noun was assigned to a grammatical gender class (masculine, feminine, neuter), and adjectives and pronouns related to the noun had to agree in gender. The gender specific third-person singular personal pronouns ("he," "she") are our current remnant of this older linguistic system.

Whereas up until recently it was still commonly-accepted practice to use gender-specific language in writing, both *The Publication Manual of the American Psychological Association* and *The Chicago Manual of Style* now have specific editing directives on the use of bias-free language. Writing in a bias-free manner with regard to gender has received particular attention both because gender-specific language is so pervasive and because scholarly research over the past 35 years has demonstrated repeatedly the negative psychological impact of gender-specific language and the insidious effects of gender bias on the attitudes and actions of people even when they are alert to that bias.

Research on Gendered Language

Starting in the 1970s, psychologists began demonstrating the negative effects of sexist language and how it helped to maintain sexist attitudes and behaviors.[4] Research on the use of the generic "he" has found that the pronoun is not neutral. A disproportionally high proportion of people picture a male when they hear "he."[5] To a lesser but still significant extent, they picture a male if the substitute "he/she" is used. The only pronoun producing a neutral, or gender balanced, image was the plural "they."

The same can be said of the word "man" and terms like "mankind." The generic "he" and similar words "not only reflect a history of male domination" but also "actively encourage its perpetuation."[6] Research has shown that a reduction in the use of "man" and "he" can lead to a long-term reduction in sexist thinking.[7]

The challenge is that the use of generic male terminology, particularly the use of "he" ("him", "himself", "his"), becomes embedded in our linguistic patterns at a very early age and its use is reinforced through frequent repetition. Juxtaposed against our daily experience, research has found that *every* use of the generic male is problematic, regardless of the author's intention.[8] There are instances where if women are not specifically included (e.g., female examples, the use of "she"), even gender-neutral language is interpreted as referring only to males.[9]

Psychologist Janice Moulton illustrates the non-neutrality of generic male terminology by changing "Some human beings are female" (gender neutral subject) to "Some men are female" (generic male subject) which has quite a different meaning![10] Research has found that if chapter titles are gender neutral (e.g., Society, Political Behavior), the illustrations selected will likely be evenly divided by gender; but if the chapter titles are gendered (e.g., Social Man, Political Man), the illustrations will be all male.[11]

A problematic area that is often overlooked concerns the examples that are used to illustrate points in spoken or written material. In addition to the obvious use of sex role stereotypes, there are also instances where the generic "he" results naturally in a male example and instances where no examples explicitly referencing women are included (and so they become invisible).

It is clear from the research that generic male language reinforces sexist thought through a linguistic bias in favor of male interpretation. But what about its influence on actions? Indeed, research has found that the bias from gendered language permeates both work and personal areas of our lives.[12]

But the bias goes deeper with potentially more serious consequences. Research has found that, with the use of gendered language, females almost disappear from those considered "persons" in males' minds.[13] And, perhaps even more disturbing, the effects of sexist language accumulate over time.

Research has found that, as girls become women, "the natural process of imagining oneself to be the subject of neutral human reference has somehow been short-circuited. Ninety percent of the women…reported no imagery in response to a sentence about a general human being, and the ten percent who did reported seeing pictures of males."[14]

Specific Problem Areas

In addition to the general use of the masculine as a generic reference, there are specific instances in which gendered language is problematic:

Forms of address. How we address someone in a public setting conveys a message about their status. If we use "Dr. Jones [male] and Mrs. Edwards [female]" to refer to two colleagues both of whom have doctorates, we infer that the female is less qualified. Even more denigrating would be "Dr. Jones and Marie Edwards," which assigns the female an inappropriate degree of informality. "Dr. Jones and Dr. Edwards" could be the proper form of address.

Occupational titles. We noted earlier some of the job titles that have changed. Others include "flight attendant" for steward/stewardess, "sales agent" for salesman, "supervisor" for foreman.

Gender-qualified occupational titles. When we qualify an occupational title by gender, we signal that there is something different (typically something "lesser") occurring. Examples include "woman doctor," "female lawyer," "male nurse."

Lack of parallel language. To ensure equal status, we need to use equivalent terminology. Examples include "guys and gals" or "ladies and gentlemen" rather than "guys and ladies," "men and women" rather than "men and girls" (when both groups are adults).

Sexist jokes. Sexist jokes function to normalize sexist behavior and, research has shown, result in a relaxing of male constraints on rape and other forms of violence against women and girls, a releaser of prejudice.[15] So objecting to them becomes critical. There are many reasons why women don't respond—for example, social pressure to be polite, normative pressure to be supportive, and concern about retaliation.[16]

Some people ask what would constitute a sexist joke. Here are some examples: (a) implied or explicit traits that demean a woman—e.g., not intelligent, easily fooled, inept, inferior, not attractive; (b) unflattering stereotypes—e.g., sexual teases, really just after a man's money, instantly available to be used for sex, barefoot and pregnant, belong in the kitchen; and (c) condones or refers indirectly to violence and physical abuse.

Addressing Generic Male Language

Early attempts to create gender-neutral, or bias-free, language were awkward, involving the use of constructions such as s/he or he/she. Gradually we have realized that English is a very flexible language and we actually have lots of inclusive alternatives from which to choose.

The easier issue is substituting for "man" or "men" or "mankind." In most cases, we can use "people" or "individuals" or "humanity" depending on the context. The more challenging issue has to do with the use of the masculine third-person pronoun to refer to someone of unspecified gender. Here are the four most common ways to make gendered sentences gender-neutral, using *"A student may need to consult his course schedule"* as the example:

1. Use a plural, rather than a singular, noun.
   Students may need to consult their course schedules.

2. Substitute a first- or second-person pronoun for a gender-specific third-person pronoun.
   Students may need to consult your course schedules.

3. Substitute articles ("a," "an," "the") for "he."
   A student may need to consult the course schedule.

4. Revise the sentence structure so that a pronoun is no longer needed.
   Consult your course schedules.

The language we use reflects how we think about ourselves and our world. It can be used to reinforce the status quo or to change it. If we use inclusive language, it opens the possibility to behave inclusively instead of dualistically.

APPENDIX B

Scientific Findings on Nonhuman Persons

Scientists are helping us understand that humans are not the only intelligent and self-aware species on the Earth. In legal terms, the entity that has legal rights and legal standing in regard to those rights is referred to as a "person." We already use "person" to denote both a human individual and a nonhuman corporate entity, but we do not yet extend these rights to nonhuman animals, plants, or even minerals.

Why does the status of "personhood" (which we discussed in Chapter Three) matter? Matthew Hiasl Pan is a case in point. This chimpanzee was abducted from Sierra Leone in 1982 and transported to Austria where he was placed in a shelter. In 2007, when the shelter threatened to go into bankruptcy and close friends of Matthew tried to intervene and establish a fund for his care, the Austrian courts found that Matthew existed only as an *asset* of the shelter and had *no moral/legal standing* to either receive funds or even to have a legal guardian appointed who could receive funds in his name. The case was appealed unsuccessfully to the European Court of Human Rights.

> If, however, Matthew were recognized as a person, the damage done to his life would count and he himself could start legal procedures against those responsible for it. He could sue the animal dealers, who abducted him and killed his mother. He could sue the company, who paid for his abduction in order to do experiments on him. And he could sue the governments of those countries, who gave permits for his abduction or for those experiments. All those are responsible for his situation, and all those

should…be held liable to undo the damage as best they can.[1]

Based on all of the scientific evidence available regarding the complex cognitive functioning and emotional intelligence of chimpanzees, Matthew qualifies for moral standing and hence for personhood; however, he faces an uncertain future because that status has not been acknowledged. So the matter of moral standing and personhood is not simply philosophical; there are life-altering consequences.

If an entity is a "person," then it is entitled to moral standing and moral inclusion. In other words, our relationship with such beings would need to change from paternalism or exploitation to one of dignity and mutual respect. Our present economic policies are primarily based on a "sustainability paradigm," which assumes that all of nature is a resource for humanity. We measure the success of those policies by the percent of species that do not become extinct, without regard to the moral rights of those species. In fact, we exercise policies to "cull" (murder) populations of species that we view as predatory, such as bears or wolves, in order to control their numbers and hence the impact on our own choices.

In considering how we might choose to change our laws and economic policies, the following are examples of research and legal rulings that support extending the definition of "personhood" to the Earth itself as a living biosphere, to animals, to plants, and perhaps even to minerals.

The Earth

Scientists have demonstrated that the planet Earth "behaves as a single, self-regulating system"[2] with the negative consequences of human actions that lead to environmental degradation of the biosphere and loss of biodiversity becoming more obvious. In recognition that what we call "nature" is in fact an interrelated series of living ecosytems, Ecuador asserted in Articles 10 and 71-74 of its 2008 Constitution of Ecuador the inalienable rights of ecosystems to exist and flourish. In addition, these Articles give people the right to petition on behalf of ecosystems and require the government to remedy violations of these rights.[3]

In 2010, Bolivia passed the Law of the Rights of Mother Earth, which includes the right of the Earth to not be polluted, to continue vital cycles unaltered, to be free of genetic alteration, and to be free of imbalance from mega-infrastructure and development projects. The law is administered by a Ministry of Mother Earth.[4] The United Nations is formally considering adopting a Universal Declaration of Rights for Mother Earth,[5] modeled on the Bolivian law.

British barrister, Polly Higgins, has led a group of researchers who have uncovered documents indicating that ecocide was to have been included in the Rome Statute as the fifth international Crime Against Peace but was withdrawn at the last minute.[6] Ecocide is defined as any large-scale destruction of the natural environment or overconsumption of critical non-renewable resources. Ecocide is already a crime in ten countries — Armenia, Belarus, Georgia, Kazakhstan, Kyrgyzstan, Moldova, Russian Federation, Tajikistan, Ukraine, Vietnam — and Higgins is lobbying the United Nations for its adoption as an international crime against peace.[7]

In September 2012, New Zealand declared the Whangangui River an "integrated, living entity" (Te Awa Tupua) with legal personhood status. Two guardians were appointed to act on its behalf, one representing the Maori (from a Whanganui River *iwi*) and one representing the Crown.[8] Thus we can see the beginning of a shift away from protection of the biosphere in order to ensure abundance for ourselves and towards respect for the environment and its components as living entities in their own right.

The Animal Kingdom: Vertebrates

We are learning more about the "personhood" of a wide range of animals as scientists shift away from imposing human assumptions on animals and instead learn how they interact in their own environment. As a consequence, we are realizing that we have grossly underestimated both the scope and the scale of animal intelligence.[9] Evolution would be inexplicably discontinuous if only humans, or only mammals, or only vertebrates were self-aware.[10] One of the measures of intelligence used is the mirror test for self-recognition, and elephants, chimpanzees, dolphins,[11] and magpies all passed with flying colors.

More important, though, than simple self-recognition is what is referred to as being the subject-of-a-life.[12] Does the entity have a sense of continuity over time, of engagement in a life process? If the answer is "yes," then harm would limit or cut short those future possibilities. A corollary of that sense of having one's own perspective is metacognition (thinking about thinking), which research has demonstrated occurs in at least cetaceans[13] and chimpanzees.[14]

Much of the focus of research has been in the arena of intelligence, decision-making, and problem solving, and the 2013 compilation of research articles, edited by Corbey and Lanjouw,[15] provides ample evidence that elephants and cetaceans (whales and dolphins) are very intelligent, second only to humans.

Cetaceans: Whales and Dolphins

Dolphins and whales live in highly complex matrilineal cultures,[16] including language, that vary from pod to pod, with cultural transmission of learned behavior.[17] They are also excellent examples of multiculturalism in that bottlenose dolphins, humpback whales, orcas, and sperm whales play together, cross species.[18] Humpback whales have been observed helping a baby grey whale in danger from a pod of orcas.[19]

Research has demonstrated repeatedly that dolphins are self-aware, have large complex brains,[20] and prodigious cognitive abilities.[21] Neuroscientist Lori Marino says that "dolphins are sophisticated, self-aware,[22] highly intelligent beings with individual personalities, autonomy and an inner life. They are vulnerable to tremendous suffering and psychological trauma."[23]

Dolphins are known for their problem solving skills, complex play patterns, ability to plan, and helpfulness to each other. They use sponges as tools to coax fish out from the sea floor, and the skill is taught by mothers to their offspring.[24] Advances are being made to communicate with dolphins primarily by teaching them sign language (a second language) or the use of iPad symbols rather than through decoding the dolphins' own communication.[25]

Sperm whales have the largest brain mass of any living animal; and whales generally have the greatest volume of cerebral cortex available for cognitive processing of any animal, along with a large and highly convoluted hippocampus (the portion of the limbic system that processes emotion and memory).[26] Sperm whales are organized into clans, each with its own dialect and culture.[27] Orca populations of the eastern North Pacific are structured into several social tiers that possess distinctive cultural attributes in vocal, social, feeding, and play behavior.

Cetaceans depend on sound to navigate and survive as well as communicate with others. One of the negative impacts of human activity is the rapidly increasing noise pollution in the world's oceans from tanker and ship traffic, sonic blasts, and the placement of wind and wave farm devices anchored offshore in the ocean floor. There is also the issue of ocean pollution, which not only injures cetaceans but also affects their food chain.

Despite all evidence regarding metacognitive abilities and social intelligence, we continue to treat cetaceans as non-sentient objects, commodities or resources. We capture and confine dolphins and whales to perform in marine parks or swim with tourists. Taiji, Japan is known for its annual dolphin slaughters (depicted in the 2009 documentary *The Cove*), and Japanese whalers continue to hunt minke whales in the Antarctic in defiance of the International Whaling Commission. In the Solomon Islands, "drive-hunting" of dolphins is common, with dolphins being killed for their teeth.[28] There needs to be a way to end these inhumane practices.[29]

Based on scientific evidence that cetaceans are extremely intelligent, insightful and self-aware, capable of a wide range of emotions, compassionate and altruistic, creative with problem solving ability, and cooperative both within and between species, scientists issued a Declaration of Rights for Cetaceans in 2010.[30]

Elephants

Research shows that elephants are very social and intelligent, insightful, self-aware,[31] capable of a range of emotions, compassionate, and able to use tools and create art. In the wild, they live in extended matriarchal groups with complex networks of individual relationships.[32] When members of their herd die, they grieve and engage in mourning rituals. In fact, dozens of elephants arrived at the home of Lawrence Anthony, the late "elephant whisperer," to mourn his death and stood in respectful silence for 48 hours before returning home.[33]

Elephants have complex social systems that value the ability to create harmony and problem-solving skills in their leaders over the more traditional traits of aggression and physical dominance.[34] Next to humans, elephants undergo the longest period of learning when young—around 10 years—with mothers teaching young elephants how to feed themselves, create and use tools, and behave appropriately in the complex, intensely matrilineal elephant society.

While elephants might appear handicapped from a human perspective, they deploy their trunk like an arm in order to use tools and produce abstract art; and they can radically change their behavior to cope with a new challenge. Highly altruistic, they actively aid each other and other species in distress and are predisposed to cooperate if treated with respect.

The intelligence and social culture of elephants is not open to dispute, but still zoos and other "owners" keep single elephants chained to stakes in concrete yards separated forever from their family herd, a practice that would be loudly condemned if perpetuated on humans. In addition, elephants at tourist venues are often subject to cruel training from a young age, controlled with fear and pain so that they'll perform and take people on their backs.

Great Apes and Other Primates

The primates known as the great apes include chimpanzees, gorillas, orangutans, and bonobos. Chimpanzees (along with other great apes) have demonstrated that they are intelligent, good problem solvers, and often better than humans at math. Great apes are known to have excellent long-term memory skills[35] and can anticipate events in a movie they have seen before.[36] They are highly social and have been shown to starve themselves rather than inflict pain on another chimp. When given the choice, they prefer outcomes that reward both themselves and their apparent opponent.[37]

Orangutan mothers stay with their young for eight to ten years, nurturing them.[38] The intelligence of orangutans is reflected in the way in which they learn complicated new skills, such as sawing wood or using a hammer and nail to put things together. Orangutans have the ability to understand their surroundings in a more abstract way than other animals so they know how to acclimate to some very harsh environments.

Other primates that have been researched include baboons — old world monkeys who live in complex social structures and have cognitive abilities very similar to chimpanzees and orangutans. Studies have shown that baboons are able to identify stress and cope with it, and can think critically when confronted with difficult situations. Rhesus Monkeys are extremely smart and resourceful, able to coordinate well-planned group attacks.

Introducing great apes to technology has had some surprising results. By providing chimpanzees with a customized video camera, the chimps created a movie as part of a project for researchers to understand how chimpanzees perceive the world and themselves.[39] Orangutans at an increasing number of zoos (e.g., Atlanta, Milwaukee, Phoenix, Smithsonian, Toronto) are using iPads to play games, watch videos, listen to music, and even Skype or FaceTime with each other.[40] At the Lake Superior Zoo, monkeys are also using iPads to create artwork.[41] Kanzi, a bonobo at the Ape Cognition and Conservation Initiative, has a 3,000 word English vocabulary, cooks, plays music, uses a computer, makes sarcastic jokes, and Skypes.[42]

A recent event regarding technology has raised the personhood issue from an intriguing angle. While photographer David Slater was in Indonesia taking pictures of endangered crested macaques, one of them used his camera to take a selfie, which has now gone viral as "Monkey Selfie."[43] Slater believes that he owns the copyright on the picture, which is part of his book *Wildlife Personalities*, as it was taken with his camera. However, PETA has filed suit in California saying that copyright should rest with the monkey, who should benefit from its proceeds.

The Great Ape Project, begun in 1994, was the first to address the issue more broadly of legal rights and legal standing or personhood. Its focus was on our closest genetic relatives, the Great Apes (chimpanzees, bonobos, gorillas, and orangutans). Based on their being intelligent, self-aware, and highly social, it launched the World Declaration on Great Primates that espouses the right to life, the right to individual freedom including protection from commercial exploitation or trading, and a prohibition of torture (including testing in research labs).[44]

In 1999, New Zealand granted basic rights to great apes, making their use in research, testing or teaching illegal. In 2007, the Balearic Islands granted legal personhood rights to all great apes. Meanwhile Switzerland amended its constitution in 1992 to recognize animals as *beings* rather than as *things* and added a law on respectful treatment of animals.[45] Germany followed in 2002 with a constitutional amendment guaranteeing rights to animals.

Bears

Bears are the most intelligent native nonhuman animals in North America, and many modern bear biologists credit them with intelligence that is the equivalent of the great apes or of a three-year-old human. Black bears in particular can count as well as primates.[46]

Bears have been shown to have excellent long-term memory, navigation skills superior to humans, the ability to use tools and perform complex tasks, and the capacity for subjective emotion including grief. They are also cunning in terms of their ability to locate food and evade predators including humans.

As highly evolved social animals, bears have well-structured relationships with each other in the wild, even sharing resources. The polar bear, for example, never loses track of other members of its community.[47] Cubs spend several years with their mother learning survival skills, including the location of various food sources. Despite the importance of community to their well-being, humans isolate bears from their family units, cage them, and force them to perform for entertainment purposes.

Birds

Avian intelligence is only recently getting extensive research attention.[48] The term "bird brain" is still often used as a derogatory term, but it turns out that a number of avian species are very intelligent. Magpies, for example, are not only smart but exhibit self-awareness as well.[49]

Crows are among the most intelligent birds in the world,[50] and have the problem-solving abilities of a seven-year-old human.[51] They have been shown to reason analytically, to fashion tools to gather otherwise inaccessible food,[52] and to adapt to difficult situations.[53] Ravens in particular have been shown to test out consequences mentally before acting and to enlist other animals to help them.[54] In the U.S., crows are protected as migratory birds and several species have been listed as endangered. But this has not prevented individuals and communities from launching campaigns to confine, kill, poison, immobilize, or harass crows.[55]

Parrots, particularly the African grey parrot and the Goffin's cockatoo, show the long-term decision-making skills of a human four-year-old.[56] Parrots have excellent memories, can count up to six,[57] categorize objects, and are capable of solving relatively complex problems.

Research has shown that pigeons have the intelligence of a human three-year-old and can differentiate a present self-image from one previously recorded.[58] They can name and categorize objects into multiple categories.[59] Pigeons are extremely good at geolocation and have been used as messengers repeatedly throughout history. In addition, they have excellent memories for both people and places. Their eyesight is better than that of humans, and the U.S. Coast Guard has trained pigeons to spot the orange life jackets of people lost at sea. In addition, they have excellent memories for both people and places.

While we treat chickens primarily as a food source, recent research shows that they are self-aware and more intelligent than human toddlers.[60] Chickens have demonstrated skills in numeracy, as well as the ability to plan ahead and exercise self-control. They engage in complex communication patterns, learn from others in their group, coordinate group activities, solve problems, and build long-term relationships.[61] Despite their intelligence and self-awareness, 95 percent of chickens in the U.S. in 2013 were still confined in "battery cages" (which have been outlawed in the

European Union), valued only for the eggs that are laid, with no room to move and no mental stimulation.[62]

Fish

Fish are sentient vertebrates; however, whether or not they feel pain is still open to debate.[63] What has been documented is reciprocal cooperation among rabbitfish pairs, with one standing on guard for the other while they forage for food.[64] This complex cognitive and social behavior is in sharp contrast to stereotypes of fish as cold, unsocial, and unintelligent.

Other Animal Species

While we may need no convincing of the intelligence of animals we adopt as pets — e.g., cats, dogs, horses--we are being confronted with a growing body of scientific literature on the unsuspected capabilities of a wide range of vertebrates.[65] Squirrels, for example, are fast learners, particularly when it comes to learning tasks that involve the same skills needed to remember where they have stored food.[66] A few others are described below.

Research shows that pigs are as smart as a three-year-old human being and more empathic and intelligent than species that humans routinely keep as pets (such as dogs and cats).[67] Pigs learn new skills easily and adapt to complex environmental situations. They have excellent long-term memories, live in complex social communities where they learn from one another, and are cooperative and empathic. Despite their intelligence and sociability, sows are often kept in "gestation crates" without room to turn around or any mental stimulation, expected to bear litter after litter until they are finally slaughtered.

Prairie dogs are social animals, living in small cooperative groups, with well-developed complex linguistic skills.[68] They can describe the physical features and location of predators to each other, as well as describe abstract shapes. Biologist Con Slobodchikoff, who decoded the language of prairie dogs, hopes to have developed a translation device for communication between humans and prairie dogs (and other animals) by 2020. In contrast to animals who move in order to avoid competition for resources, prairie dogs move when their kin disappear—in other words, they want to be in community.[69]

The Animal Kingdom: Invertebrates

Cephalopods are considered the most intelligent invertebrates, providing important examples of advanced cognitive evolution. The unsuspected leader in invertebrate intelligence is the octopus, which has been proven to have excellent problem-solving ability as well as a range of strategies for evading predators, including changing shape and color.[70] They are highly skilled problem solvers and hunters who use well developed strategies when finding food. They also feel pain.[71]

Squid, another cephalopod group, have a brain structure that is different from other invertebrates in the ocean and instead share complex features similar to the human brain.[72] They can be formidable predators, are very curious about their environment and have the ability to learn new skills and develop the capacity to use tools in order to both protect them from harm and relieve boredom.

Among other invertebrates shown to be sentient[73] are crustaceans. Scientists are divided on whether lobsters feel pain when plunged into boiling water, but agree that they do cringe.[74] The research raises ethical issues as we would certainly condemn plunging a human into water of killing temperatures.

Ants are able to work cooperatively in large groups to forage for food and build nests, which helps them withstand calamities that would wipe another species. Ants accommodate to their environment very well. Research shows that bees can rapidly solve complex mathematical problems.[75] Spiders are among the smallest creatures to possess a proportionately high level of intelligence, particularly the white-mustached portia spiders who have demonstrated special learning skills. Research shows that they hunt with intention.

All in all, we can see that a wide range of animals, vertebrates and invertebrates, are intelligent, self-aware, and engaged in complex relationships within their own communities. Hopefully we will begin to rethink our relationship with the animal kingdom and respect them in their own habitats.

The Vegetable Kingdom

While we may have experience in thinking about mammals like whales or elephants as intelligent and highly social, we are less likely to view the vegetable kingdom in that manner. Science is demonstrating through studies of plant neurobiology that many plants are autonomous, able to differentiate between self and non-self, capable of complex and adaptive behaviors, able to communicate and warn other plants of danger, and are able to enlist allies to aid them. Many forms of plant life, including trees and forests, are entitled to be treated with dignity because they are sensing, highly social organisms that communicate extensively, interact with their surroundings, learn from experience, are able to integrate diverse sources of information and act accordingly, and can distinguish between self and not-self and between kin and non-kin.[76]

Research shows that plants appear to be able to make complex decisions, being able to distinguish between inner and outer conditions and anticipate future risks.[77] They are able to adapt to temperature and environmental change without requiring a lengthy evolutionary change.[78] Relying on odors emitted by threatening species, plants can prime defenses ahead of time[79] and cry for help.[80]

We are only recently appreciating the complex social development of plants and have not yet had public discussions about the implications of practices we impose on this kingdom (e.g., forest clearcutting, genetic modification) in the context of viewing plants as "nonhuman persons." Indeed, we have strategies to exploit the intelligence of plants—for example, harnessing their ability to seek out their fair share of sunlight in order to ensure high-yield crops.[81]

Switzerland has again been a leader in creating a Bill of Rights for Plants, which states that "living organisms should be considered morally for their own sake because they are alive."[82]

The Mineral Kingdom

It is probably with the mineral kingdom that we, as humans, feel the least affinity although we are increasingly appreciative of the energetic communication of crystals and other gem stones. Bolivia is the first nation to legally protect the inherent worth of minerals, calling them "blessings."

To date, we have little experience in appreciating the mineral kingdom for its own contribution rather than as resources for human use and exploitation. Ordinances on the rights of nature are now in place in over thirty U.S. municipalities, including Pittsburgh.[83] However, the discussions about the negative impact of processes like fracking or tar sands oil extraction are being framed primarily in terms of impact on humans rather than on the mineral kingdom itself.

Implications for the Rights of Nonhuman Persons

If debates within the scientific community are examined, humans' vested interests are clearly at play. Once we concede personhood and moral/legal standing, certain rights follow that impinge on our ability to exploit nonhuman persons in whatever way we like. To offset this vested interest, the work of the Nonhuman Rights Project to obtain legal standing for nonhuman persons, beginning with chimpanzees, is vitally important.[84]

APPENDIX C

American Anthropological Association
Excerpts from "Statement on 'Race'"

[adopted May 17, 1998]

It has become clear that human populations are not unambiguous, clearly demarcated, biologically distinct groups. Evidence from the analysis of genetics (e.g., DNA) indicates that most physical variation, about 94%, lies *within* so-called racial groups. Conventional geographic "racial" groupings differ from one another only in about 6% of their genes. This means that there is greater variation within "racial" groups than between them....

"Race"... evolved as a worldview, a body of prejudgments that distorts our ideas about human differences and group behavior....we conclude that present-day inequalities between so-called "racial" groups are not consequences of their biological inheritance but products of historical and contemporary social, economic, educational, and political circumstances.

[For the full text, go to http://www.americananthro.org/ConnectWithAAA/ Content.aspx?ItemNumber=2583/]

Notes

Preface

1. D.I. Riddle, "Evolving Notions of Nonhuman Personhood: Is Moral Standing Sufficient?" *Journal of Evolution & Technology* 24, no. 3 (2014): 4-19.

2. U.N., "Ending Violence Against Women and Girls," http://www.un.org/en/globalissues/briefingpapers/endviol/.

3. M. Nussbaum, "Objectification," *Philosophy and Public Affairs* 24, no. 4 (1995): 249-291.

4. V. Plumwood, *Feminism and the Mastery of Nature* (London: Routledge, 1993).

Chapter 1: Creating the Illusion of Duality

1. A. H. C. Van der Heijden, "Perception for Selection, Selection for Action, and Action for Perception," *Visual Cognition* 3, no. 4 (1996): 357-361; M. Atienza, J.L. Cantero, & C. Escera, "Auditory Information Processing During Human Sleep as Revealed by Event-Related Brain Potentials," *Clinical Neurophysiology* 112, no. 11 (2001): 2031-2045.

2. R.C. Atkinson & R.M. Shiffrin, "Human Memory: A Proposed System and Its Control Processes," in *The Psychology of Learning and Motivation, Vol. 8*, ed. K.W. Spence & J.T. Spence (London: Academic Press, 1968).

3. G.A. Miller, "The Magical Number Seven, Plus or Minus Two: Some Limits on Our Capacity for Processing Information," *Psychological Review* 63 (1956): 81-97.

4. D.J. Simons, "Attentional Capture and Inattentional Blindness," *Trends in Cognitive Sciences* 4, no. 4 (April 2000): 147-155.

5. Wellcome Trust, "How Memory Load Leaves Us 'Blind' to New Visual Information," *ScienceDaily* (1 October 2012), http://www.science daily.com/releases/2012/10/21001095900.htm/.

6. J.G. Marsh, "Exploration and Exploitation in Organizational Learning," *Organizational Science* 2, no. 1 (1991): 71-87.

7. E. Ophir, C. Nass, & A.B. Wagner, "Cognitive Control in Media Multitaskers," *PNAS* 106, no. 37 (2009): 15583-15587.

8. J. Thomas, "Chronic Media Multi-Tasking Makes It Harder to Focus," *HealthDay* (24 August 2009), http://health.usnews. com/health-news/family-health/brain-and-behavior/articles/2009/08/24/chro nic-media-multi-tasking-makes-it-harder-to/; Science Beta, "The Truth About Chronic Media Multi-tasking and How to Monotask," *Science Beta* (10 February 2015), http://sciencebeta.com/truth-chronic-media-multitasking -monotask/.

9. C. Wallis, "The Multitasking Generation," *Time* (19 March 2006).

10. J. O'Dell, "For Students, What Is the 'Facebook Effect' on Grades?" *Mashable* (27 April 2011), http://mashable.com/2011/04/27/face book-effect-students/; Ohio State University, "Multitasking Hurts Performance But Makes You Feel Better," *ScienceDaily* (30 April 2012), http://www.sciencedaily.com/releases/2012/04/120430124618.htm/; University of Utah, "Frequent Multitaskers Are Bad At It: Can't Talk and Drive Well," *ScienceDaily* (23 January 2013), http://www.science daily.com/releases/ 2013/01/130123195101.htm/.

11. R. Mantell, "Multitasking: More Is Less," *The Wall Street Journal* (10 July 2011).

12. I. Lapowsky, "Don't Multitask: Your Brain Will Thank You," *Time* (17 April 2013).

13. C. Nass, "The Myth of Multitasking," *National Public Radio* interview (10 May 2013).

14. "Students Hooked on Social Media, Study Reveals," *CTV.ca* (28 April 2010).

15. University of New Hampshire, "Multitasking Can Be efficient at Certain Optimal Times," *ScienceDaily* (4 September 2008), http:// www. sciencedaily.com/releases/2008/09/080902104856.htm/.

16. University of Basel, "How Multitasking Can Improve Judgments," *ScienceDaily* (13 May 2013), http://www.science daily.com/releases/ 2013/05/13051 308047.htm/.

17. G. Allport, *The Nature of Prejudice* (Reading, MA: Addison-Wesley, 1954), 20.

18. P.C. Quinn, "Development of Subordinate-Level Categorization in 3-to-7-Month-Old Infants," *Child Development* 75, no. 3 (2004).

19. The original concept of schemata is linked with that of reconstructive memory as proposed and demonstrated in a series of experiments by F.C. Bartlett, *Remembering: A Study in Experimental and Social Psychology* (Cambridge: Cambridge University Press, 1932).

20. J. Kang, *Implicit Bias: a Primer for the Courts, National Center for State Courts* (August 2009), http://wp.jerrykang.net.s110363.gridserver. com/wp-content/uploads/2010/10/kang-Implicit-Bias-Primer-for-courts-09.pdf.

21. Michigan State University, "People Learn While They Sleep, Study Suggests," *ScienceDaily* (27 September 2011), http://www.science daily.com/releases/2011/09/110927124653.htm/.

22. R. Fisher & W.L. Ury, *Getting to Yes: Negotiating Agreement Without Giving In* (London: Penguin, 1981).

23. Historically intersex persons as infants (and thus unable to consent) have been surgically assigned to one gender or the other. However, there are now advocacy groups such as Accord Alliance (formerly the Intersex Association of North America) and Organisation Intersex International, an Intersex Awareness Day (October 26) and an Intersex Day of Remembrance (November 8), and conferences such as the International Intersex Forum all focused on gaining recognition for intersex as a normal variant of human sexuality.

24. See Public Statement by the Third International Intersex Forum, issued 1 December 2013, http://aiclegal.org/public-statement-by-the-third-international-intersex-forum/.

25. J.A. Bargh, M. Chen, & L. Burrows, "Automaticity of Social Behavior: Direct Effects of Trait Construct and Stereotype Activation on Action," *Journal of Personality and Social Psychology* 71, no. 2 (1996): 230-244.

26. D. Ropeik, "The Consequences of Fear," *EMBO Reports* 5 (2004): S57.

Chapter 2: Perpetuating the Illusion of Duality

1. Drawn in part from J.M. Grohol, "15 Common Cognitive Distortions," *Psych Central* (2009), http://psychcentral com/ lib/2009/15-common-cognitive-distortions/.

2. A. Fausto-Sterling, *Sexing the Body: Gender Politics and the Construction of Sexuality* (New York: Basic Books, 2000).

3. A.A. Bailey, *From Bethlehem to Calvary* (New York: Lucis Publishing, 1937), 203.

4. B. Lipton, *The Biology of Belief: Unleashing the Power of Consciousness, Matter, & Miracles* (Santa Rosa, CA: Mountain of Love, 2005).

5. Ibid., 87.

6. R.B. Zajonc, "Feelings and Thinking: Preferences Need No Inferences," *American Psychologist* 35, no. 2 (1980): 151-175.

7. J. Lehrer, *How We Decide* (New York: Houghton Mifflin, 2009), xvi.

8. Institute of HeartMath, "The Power of Emotions," http://store. heartmath.org/store/solutions-for-stress/the-power-of-emotion, 4.

9. E.A. Phelps, K.M. Lempert, & P. Solo-Hessner, "Emotion and Decision Making: Multiple Modulatory Neural Circuits," *Annual Review of Neuroscience* 37 (2014): 263-287.

10. See http://www.psych.nyu.edu/phelpslab/publications. html for Elizabeth Phelps' extensive bibliography of publications on the neuroscience of affect, learning and decisions.

11. C. Pert, *Molecules of Emotion: The Science Behind Mind-Body Medicine* (New York: Scribner, 1997), 312.

12. See the concept of thin-slicing, or generalizing based on a tiny segment of information, in M. Gladwell, *Blink: The Power of Thinking Without Thinking* (New York: Little, Brown, 2005).

13. S. Fiske, "Are We Born Racist? in *Are We Born Racists? New Insights from Neuroscience and Positive Psychology*, ed. J. March, R. Mendoza-Denton, & J.A. Smith, 7-16 (Boston: Beacon Press, 2010).

14. N. Chater, "The Search for Simplicity: A Fundamental Cognitive Principle?" *Quarterly Journal of Experimental Psychology* 52A, no. 2 (1999): 273-302.

15. B. Rasch & J. Born, "About Sleep's Role in Memory," *Physiological Reviews*, 93, no. 2 (2013): 681–766.

16. N. Chater & P. Vitányi, "Simplicity: A Unifying Principle in Cognitive Science?" *TRENDS in Cognitive Sciences* 7, no. 1 (2003): 19-22.

17. J. Winters, "Why We Fear the Unknown," *Psychology Today* (1 May 2002).

18. University of British Columbia, "Infants Raised in Bilingual Environments Can Distinguish Unfamiliar Languages," *ScienceDaily* (20 February 2011), http://www.sciencedaily.com/releases/2011/ 02/10218092539.htm/.

19. E. Sapir, *Language* (New York: Harcourt, Brace, & World, 1921); B.L. Whorf, *Language, Thought, and Reality: Selected Writings of Benjamin Lee Whorf*, ed. John B. Carroll (Cambridge, MA: MIT Press, 1956).

20. L. Margulis & D. Sagan, *Microcosmos* (Berkeley: University of California Press, 1997), 29.

21. Ibid., 124.

22. A. Novotney, "Awakening the Child Inside, " *American Psychological Association* 42, no. 1 (2011): 34.

23. J.K. Hamlin, K. Wynn, & P. Bloom, "Social Evaluation by Preverbal Infants," *Nature* 450, no. 22 (November 2007): 557-560.

24. J.T. Kubota, J. Li, E. Bar-David, M.R. Banaji, & E.A. Phelps, "The Price of Racial Bias: Intergroup Negotiations in the Ultimatum Game," *Psychological Science* 4, no. 12 (2013): 2498-2504.

25. L.M. Maatz, "The Awful Truth Behind the Gender Pay Gap," *Forbes* (07 April 2014), http://www.forbes.com/sites/forbeswomanfiles/2014/04/07/the-awful-truth-of-the-gender-pay-gap-it-gets-worse-as-women-age/; Association of American University Women, *The Simple Truth About the Gender Pay Gap* (Fall 2015).

26. See R. Eisler, *The Chalice and the Blade: Our History, Our Future* (New York: Harper & Row, 1989); M.J. Yin, *The Chalice and the Blade in Chinese Culture* (Beijing: China Social Sciences Publishing House, 1995).

27. R. Miles, *Who Cooked the Last Supper? The Women's History of the World* (New York: Crown/Archetype, 2007).

28. U. LeGuin, "Women/Wildness," in *Healing the Wounds,* ed. J. Plant (New Society: Philadelphia, 1989), 45.

Chapter 3: Avoiding Disconfirmation of Duality

1. B.D. Perry, "The Neurodevelopmental Impact of Violence in Childhood," in *Textbook of Child and Adolescent Forensic Psychiatry* (Chapter 18), ed. D. Schetky & E.P. Benedek, 221-238. (Washington, DC: American Psychiatric Press, 2001).

2. Using functional magnetic resonance imaging (fMRI) and positron emission tomography (PET) techniques.

3. L. Sanders, "The Brain Sorts Words During Sleep," *Science News* 186, no. 8 (18 October 2014).

4. P. Barrouillet, S. Bernardin, & V. Camos, "Time Constraints and Resource Sharing in Adults' Working Memory Spans," *Journal of Experimental Psychology: General* 133, no. 1 (2004): 83–100; M.A. Just & P.A. Carpenter, "A Capacity Theory of Comprehension: Individual Differences in Working Memory," *Psychological Review* 99, no. 1 (1992): 122–49; J.N. Towse, G.J. Hitch, & U. Hutton, "On the Interpretation of Working Memory Span in Adults," *Memory & Cognition* 28, no. 3 (2000): 341–348.

5. R. Hooper, "Four Ways You Can See the Multiverse," *New Scientist* (25 September 2014), https://www.new scientist.com/article/dn26267-four-ways-you-can-see-the-multiverse/; University College London. "Is Our Universe Inside a Bubble? First Observational Test of the 'Multiverse'," *ScienceDaily* (3 August 2011), http://www.sciencedaily. com/releases/2011/08/110803 102844.htm.

6. See the science summarized in D. I. Riddle, *Principles of Abundance for the Cosmic Citizen* (AuthorHouse, 2010).

7. Ibid., see Chapter 4, "Principles of Interconnectivity" for a summary of this quantum physics research.

8. B. Swimme, *The Hidden Heart of the Cosmos: Humanity and the New Story* (Maryknoll,NY: Orbis, 1996), 100.

9. D.I. Riddle, *Service-Led Growth: The Role of the Service Sector in World Development* (New York: Praeger, 1986); see also articles listed at http://www.servicegrowth.com.

10. M. Waring, *If Women Counted: A New Feminist Economics* (New York: Harper & Row, 1988).

11. J.F. Helliwell, R. Layard, & J.D. Sachs, eds., *World Happiness Report*, http://worldhappiness.report/.

12. D. Peña, "Monsanto and DuPont Lose Initial Appeals Over Mexico GM Maize Ban," *Sustainable Pulse* (20 March 2015), http://sustainable pulse.com/2015/03/20/monsanto-and-du pont-lose-initial-appeals-over-mexico-gm-maize-ban/#.Vh0C irmFMdU.

13. L. Thomas in Margulis & Sagan, op.cit., 10.

14. Cardiff University. "Astronomers Unravel the History of Galaxies for the First Time," *ScienceDaily* (27 August 2015), http://www.sciencedaily.com/releases/2015/08/150827083534.htm; University of Vermont, "Chameleon Star Baffles Astro-nomers," *ScienceDaily* (24 January 2013), http://www.science daily.com/releases/2013/01/130124183444.htm.

15. M. Brooks, "How to Be in Two Places at Once," *New Scientist* (19 July 2011), https://www.newscientist.com/article/dn20712-how-to-be-in-two-places-at-the-same-time/.

16. University of Innsbruck, "Quantum physics: Flavors of Entanglement," *ScienceDaily* (14 October 2010), http://www.sciencedaily.com/releases/2010/09/100927083907.htm.

17. Association for Psychological Science, "Surprising Connection Between Two Types of Perception," *Science Daily* (22 June 2011), http://www.sciencedaily.com/releases/2011/06/11061411563 8.htm.

18. University of Bristol, "Particle and Wave-Like Behavior of Light Measured Simultaneously," *ScienceDaily* (1 November 2012), http://www.science.daily.com/releases/2012/11/1211011411 07.htm.

19. University of Vienna, "Can Future Actions Influence Past Events? Experiment mimics Quantum Physics' 'Spooky Action into the Past'," *ScienceDaily* (23 April 2012), http://www.sciencedaily.com/releases/2012/04/120423131902.htm.

20. Margulis & Sagan, 1997, op.cit., 30-31.

21. Weizmann Institute of Science, "Quantum Theory Demonstrated: Observation Affects Reality," *ScienceDaily* (27 February 1998), http://www.sciencedaily.com/releases/1998/ 02/980227055013.htm.

22. Griffith University. "Quantum Experiment Verifies Einstein's 'Spooky Action at a Distance'," *ScienceDaily* (24 March 2015), http://www.sciencedaily.com/releases/2015/03/15032408480 8.htm.

23. B.P. Stein, "Two Physicists Share Nobel Prize for Detecting Changes in Neutrino Identities," *Inside Science* 6 October 2015), https://www.insidescience.org/content/two-phyicists-share-nobel-prize-detecting-changes-neutrino-identities/3281.

24. S. Loughnan, N. Haslam, T. Murnane, J. Vaes, C. Reynolds, & C. Suitner, "Objectification Leads to Depersonalization: The Denial of Mind and Moral Concern to Objectified Others," *European Journal of Social Psychology* 40 (2010): 709-717.

25. B. Bastian, S.M. Laham, S. Wilson, N. Haslam, & P. Koval, "Blaming, Praising, and Protecting Our Humanity: The Implications of Everyday Dehumanization for Judgments of Moral Status," *British Journal of Social Psychology* 50 (2011): 469-483; S.T. Fiske, A.J.C. Cuddy, & P. Glick, "Universal Dimensions of Social Cognition: Warmth and Com petence, *TRENDS in Cognitive Sciences* 11, no. 2 (2007): 77-83; N. Haslam, "Dehumanization: An Integrative Review," *Personality and*

Social Psychology Review 10, no. 3 (2006): 252-264; S. Loughnan, N. Haslam, T. Murnane, J. Vaes, C. Reynolds, & C. Suitner, "Objectifi cation Leads to Depersonalization: The Denial of Mind and Moral Concern to Objectified Others," *European Journal of Social Psychology* 40 (2010): 709-717; D.I. Riddle, "Evolving Notions of Nonhuman Personhood: Is Moral Standing Sufficient?" *Journal of Evolution & Technology* 24, no. 3 (2014): 4-19.

26. S. Opotow, "Moral Exclusion and Injustice: An Introduction," *Journal of Social Issues* 46, no. 1 (1990): 1-20.

27. S.M. Wise, *Drawing the Line: Science and the Case for Animal Rights* (New York: Basic Books, 2003).

28. See http://earthjuris.org/about/.

29. See http://www.nonhumanrightsproject.org/.

30. See http://www.wildlawuk.org/index.html.

31. See http://therightsofnature.org/.

32. "India Bans Captive Dolphin Shows as 'Morally Unacceptable'," *International Daily Newswire* (20 May 2013).

33. See *Proposed Universal Declaration of the Rights of Mother Earth,* adopted 22 April 2010 by the People's Conference on Climate Change and the Rights of Mother Earth, Cochabamba, Bolivia, http://therightsof nature.org/universal-declaration/.

34. See *Declaration of Rights for Cetaceans: Whales and Dolphins*, adopted 22 May 2010 at the Helsinki Collegium for Advanced Studies, University of Helsinki, Finland, Cetacean Rights: Conference on Fostering Moral and Legal Change, http://www.cetaceanrights.org/.

35 A. Reiss & J. Roth, eds., *Understanding and Preventing Violence* (Washington, DC: National Academy Press,1993), 116.

36. See http://www.who.int/mediacentre/factsheets/fs239/en/.

37. N. Stuch & S. Schwartz, "Intergroup Aggression: Its Predictors and Distinctness from In-Group Bias," *Journal of Personality and Social Psychology* 56, no. 3 (1989): 364-373.

38. These categories have been developed based primarily on the work of P. Glick & S. Fiske, "The Ambivalent Sexism Inventory: Differentiating Hostile and Benevolent Sexism," *Journal of Personality and Social Psychology* 70, no. 3 (1996): 491–512; M. Nussbaum, "Objectification,"

Philosophy and Public Affairs 24, no. 4 (1995): 249-291; V. Plumwood, *Feminism and the Mastery of Nature* (London: Routledge, 1993).

39. S. Lehman, "The Implicit Prejudice" *Scientific American* (6 May 2006), http://www.scientificamerican.com/article/the-implicit-prejudice/.

40. C.S. Taber & M. Lodge, "Motivated Skepticism in the Evaluation of Political Beliefs," *American Journal of Political Science* 50, no. 3 (2006): 755–769.

41. C.S. O'Sullivan & F.T. Durso, "Effect of Schema-Incongruent Information on Memory for Stereotypical Attributes, *Journal of Personality and Social Psychology* 47, no. 1 (1984): 55-70.

42. N. Chater & P. Vitányi, "Simplicity: A Unifying Principle in Cognitive Science?" *TRENDS in Cognitive Sciences* 7, no. 1 (2003): 19-22.

43. H.M. Kleider, K. Pezdek, S.D. Goldinger, & A. Kirk, "Schema-Driven Source Misattribution Errors: Remembering the Expected from a Witnessed Event," *Applied Cognitive Psychology* 22, no. 1 (2008): 1-20; M. Tuckey & N. Brewer, "The Influence of Schemas, Stimulus Ambiguity, and Interview Schedule on Eyewitness Memory Over Time," *Journal of Experimental Psychology: Applied* 9, no. 2 (2003): 101-118.

44. S. Lehman, "The Implicit Prejudice," *Scientific American* (6 May 2006), http://www.scientificamerican.com/article/the-implicit-prejudice/.

45. E.F. Loftus, "Creating False Memories," *Scientific American* 277 (1997): 70–75; D.A. Pizarro, C. Laney, E.K. Morris, & E.F. Loftus, "Ripple Effects in Memory: Judgments of Moral Blame Can Distort Memory for Events," *Memory & Cognition* 34 (2006): 550–555; D.L. Schacter, *The Seven Sins of Memory: How the Mind Forgets and Remembers* (New York, NY: Houghton Mifflin, 2001).

46. P.H. Ditto, D.A. Pizarro, & D. Tannenbaum, "Motivated Moral Reasoning," in *Psychology of Learning and Motivation, Vol. 50: Moral Judgment and Decision Making*, ed. D. M. Bartels, C. W. Bauman, L. J. Skitka, & D. L. Medin, 307–338 (San Diego, CA: Academic Press, 2009).

47. D.L. Ames & S.T. Fiske, "Outcome Dependency Alters the Neural Substrates of Impression Formation," *NeuroImage* 83 (2013): 599-608.

48. P. Barrouillet, S. Bernardin, & V. Camos, "Time Constraints and Resource Sharing in Adults' Working Memory Spans," *Journal of Experimental Psychology: General* 133, no. 1 (2004): 83–100.

49. P. Barrouillet, S. Bernardin, S. Portrat, E. Vergauwe, & V. Camos, "Time and Cognitive Load in Working Memory," *Journal of*

Experimental Psychology: Learning, Memory, and Cognition 33, no. 3 (2007): 570-585; G.S. Halford, R. Baker, J.E. McCredden, & J.D. Bain, "How Many Variables Can Humans Process?" *Psycho logical Science* 16, no. 1 (2005): 70–76; K. Oberauer, & R. Kliegl, "A Formal Model of Capacity Limits in Working Memory," *Journal of Memory and Language* 55, no. 4 (2006): 601–626.

50. D.L. Ames & S.T. Fiske, "Intentional Harms Are Worse, Even When They're Not," *Psychological Science* 20, no. 10 (2013): 1-8.

51. J. Knobe, "Intentional Action and Side Effects in Ordinary Language," *Analysis* 63 (2003): 190–193.

52. T. Pyszczynski & J. Greenberg, "Toward an Integration of Cognitive and Motivational Perspectives on Social Inference: A Biased Hypothesis-Testing Model," in *Advances in Experimental Social Psychology, Vol. 20*, ed. L. Berkowitz, 297–340 (New York: Academic Press, 1987).

53. J.C. Becker & J.K. Swim, "Seeing the Unseen: Attention to Daily Encounters with Sexism as Way to Reduce Sexist Beliefs," *Psychology of Women Quarterly* 35 (2011): 227-242.

Chapter 4: Hostile Bigotry

1. See various definitions in E.B. Royzman, C. McCauley, & P. Rozin, "From Pluto to Putnam: Four Ways to Think about Hate," in *The Psychology of Hate*, ed. R.J. Sternberg, 3-35 (Washington, DC: American Psychological Association, 2005).

2. T.W. Adorno, E. Frenkel-Brunswick, D.J. Levinson, & R.N. Sanford, *The Authoritarian Personality* (New York: Harper, 1950).

3. F. Pratto, J. Sidanius, L.M. Stallworth, & B.F. Malle, "Social Dominance Orientation: A Personality Variable Predicting Social and Political Attitudes," *Journal of Personality and Social Psychology* 67, no. 4 (1994): 741-763; J. Sidanius, S. Levin, J. Liu & F. Pratto, "Social Dominance Orientation, Anti-Egalitarianism and the Political Psychology of Gender: An Extension and Cross-Cultural Replication," *European Journal of Social Psychology* 30, no. 1 (2000): 41-67.

4. W.A. Cunningham, J.B. Nezlek, & M.R. Banaji, "Implicit and Explicit Ethnocentrism: Revisiting the Ideologies of Prejudice," *Personality and Social Psychology Bulletin* 30, no. 10 (2004): 1332-1346.

5. V. Plumwood, *Environmental Culture: The Ecological Crisis of Reason* (London: Routledge, 2002), 32.

6. T.E. Nelson, M. Biernat, & M. Manis, "Everyday Base Rates (Sex Stereotypes): Potent and Resilient," *Journal of Personality and Social Psychology* 59 (1990): 664-675.

7. B.D. Perry, "The Neurodevelopmental Impact of Violence in Child hood," in *Textbook of Child and Adolescent Forensic Psychiatry* (Chapter 18), ed. D. Schetky & E.P. Benedek, 221-238 (Washington, DC: American Psychiatric Press, 2001).

8. W.J. Cromie, "Music Videos Promote Adolescent Aggression," *Harvard University Gazette* (9 April 1998), http://news.harvard.edu/gazette/1998/04.09/MusicVideosProm.html.

9. A. Parks, "Little by Little, Violent Video Games Make Us More Aggressive," *Time* (24 March 2014), http://time.com/34075/ how-violent-video-games-change-kids-attitudes-about-aggression/.

10. L. Bowen, "Certain Video Games May Lead Teens to Drive Recklessly," *APA Monitor on Psychology* 43, no. 10 (2012): 15.

11. T. Greitemeyer, "Effects of Playing Video Games on Perceptions of One's Own Humanity," *Journal of Social Psychology* 153, no. 4 (2013): 499-514.

12. American Psychological Association, *APA Task Force on Violent Media* (Washington, DC: American Psychological Association, 2015).

13. Western Carolina University, "Sexist Humor No Laughing Matter, Psychologist Says," *ScienceDaily* (7 November 2007), http://www.sciencedaily.com/releases/2007/11/071106083038.htm; T.E. Ford & M.A. Ferguson, "Social Consequences of Disparagement Humor: A Prejudiced Norm Theory," *Personality and Social Psychology Review* 8, no. 1 (2004): 79-94.

14. M. Thomae & G.T. Viki, "Why Did the Woman Cross the Road? The Effect of Sexist Humor on Men's Rape Proclivity," *Journal of Social, Evolutionary, and Cultural Psychology* 7, no. 3 (2013): 250-269.

15. See http://www.splcenter.org/.

16. Crimes against humanity are committed through murder, extermi nation, enslavement, deportation, imprisonment, torture, rape, persecutions on political, racial & religious grounds, and other acts.

17. G.H. Stanton, "The 8 Stages of Genocide," *Genocide Watch*, http://www.genocidewatch.org/genocide/8stagesofgenocide.htm/1.

18. See reports of the U.S. Federal Bureau of Investigation at https://www.fbi.gov/stats-services/crimestats.

19. See http://www.aaanet.org/stmts/for a listing of the various official American Anthropological Association statements, & http://www. understandingrace.org/for its *RACE: Are We So Different?* project.

20. Anti-Defamation League, *ADL Global 100: An Index of Anti-Semitism* (2015).

21. See http://global100.adl.org/.

22. See http://www.trc.ca/websites/trcinstitution/index.php? p=3

23. See D.E. Stannard, *American Holocaust: The Conquest of the New World* (New York: Oxford University Press, 1994).

24. C. Silva, "Undocumented Immigrants Taking Jobs From Citizens? Most Americans Believe Immigration Is Bad for Economy," *International Business Times* 14 (August 2015), http://www.ibtimes. com/undocumented-immigrants-taking-jobs-us-citizens-most-ameri cans-believe-immigration-2054509/.

25. A. Wordsworth, "Swedes Surprised When Immigrant Rage Explodes on Their Doorstep," *National Post*, (24 May 2013), http://news. nationalpost.com/full-comment/swedes-surprised -when-immigrant-rage-explodes-on-their-doorstep; also news items from the UK: http://www.bnp.org.uk/news/national/more-racial-unrest-sheffield; http://www.telegraph.co.uk/news/uknews/immigration/10555158/ Id-rather-be-poorer-with-fewer-migrants-Farage-says.html; http:// www.telegraph.co.uk/news/uknews/immigration/11210687/Immigr ation-the-real-cost-to-Britain.html/.

26. "Behind the Murderous Anti-Immigrant Rage in South Africa," *Daily Beast* (15 April 2015), http://www.thedailybeast. com/articles/2015/ 04/20/behind-the-murderous-anti-immigrant-rage-in-south-africa.ht ml#/.

27. "Quick Facts: What You Need to Know About the Syria Crisis" (2 Sep tember 2015), http://www.mercycorps.org/articles/turkey-iraq-jor dan-lebanon-syria/quick-facts-what-you-need-know-about-syria-crisis

28. "Global Discrimination Against LGBT Persons: 2015 United Nations Report," *Journalist's Resource* (8 June 2015), http://journalists resource.org/studies/international/human-rights/global-discrimina tion-against-lgbt-persons-2015-united-nations-report/.

29. N. Hensley, "'Gay Cure' Treatments Violate Fraud Laws by Labeling Homosexuality an Illness: New Jersey Judge," *Daily News* (18 February 2015), http://www.nydaily news.com/news/national/

gay-cure-treatments-violate-new-jersey-fraud-laws-judge-article-1.2120122/.

30. L. Hazelton, "Raped for Being Gay: Scourge of South African Rape Attacks Which Men Claim Will 'Cure' Women of Being Lesbian," *Mail Online* (31 October 2011), http://www.daily mail.co.uk/news/article-2055289/Corrective-rape-South-Africa-women-attacked-cure-lesbians.html; N. Mabuse, "Horror of South Africa's 'Corrective Rape'," *CNN* (28 October 2011), http://www.cnn.com/2011/10/27/world/wus-sa-rapes/index.html; P. Strudwick, "Crisis in South Africa: The Shocking Practice of 'Corrective Rape' — Aimed at 'Curing' Lesbians," *The Independent* (4 January 2014), http://www.independent.co.uk/news/world/africa/crisis-in-south-africa-the-shocking-practice-of-corrective-rape-aimed-at-curing-lesbians-9033224.html/.

31. R. Jain, "Parents Use 'Corrective Rape' to 'Straight'en Gays," *The Times of India* (1 June 2015), http://timesofindia.indiatimes.com/life-style/relationships/parenting/Parents-use-corrective-rape-to-straightenays/articleshow/47489949.cms?utm_source=twitter.com&utm_medium=referral&utm_campaign=timesofindia/.

32. S.S. Kilborne, "Hate on Trial: What the Case Against Scott Lively Really Means," *Slate* (16 December 2014), http://www.slate.com/blogs/outward/2014/12/16/scott_lively_alien_tort_statute_means_lgbt_ugandans_can_sue_him_in_america.html/.

33. See https://ccrjustice.org/home/what-we-do/our-cases/sexual-minorities-uganda-v-scott-lively/.

34. See U.S. statistics released by the National Coalition of Anti-Violence Programs, http://www.avp.org/resources/avp-resources/405.

35. Southern Poverty Law Center, *Misogyny: The Sites* (1 March 2012), https://www.splcenter.org/fighting-hate/intelligence-report/2012/misogyny-sites.

36. See http://www.unwomen.org/en/what-we-do/ending-violence-against-women/facts-and-figures/.

37. Ibid.

38. N.D. Kristof, "A Rite of Torture for Girls," *New York Times* (12 May 2011): A24.

39. S. Nolen, "Women Without a Choice," *The Globe and Mail* (19 September 2015), A16.

40. "UN Calls Contraception Access a 'Universal Human Right'," CBS News (14 November 2012), http://www.cbsnews.com/news/un-calls-contraception-access-a-universal-human-right/.

41. "Indian Man Convicted of Gang Rape Blames Victim," *CBS News* (3 March 2015), http://www.cbsnews.com/news/india-bus-gang-rape-convict-blames-victim/.

42. L. Smith, "Corrective Rape: The Homophobic Fallout of Post-Apartheid South Africa," *The Telegraph* (21 May 2015), http://www.telegraph.co.uk/women/womens-life/11608361/Corrective-rape-The-homophobic-fallout-of-post-apartheid-South-Africa.html/.

43. D. Bolger, "Where Rape Gets a Pass," *NY Daily News* (5 July 2014), http://www.nydailynews.com/opinion/rape-pass-arti cle-1.185 4420

44. T. Callahan, "Students From Dalhousie Dentistry Scandal Working as Dentists, Says Lawyer," *CTV News* (10 July 2015), http://www.ctv news.ca/canada/students-from-dalhousie-dentistry-scandal-working-as-dentists-says-lawyer-1.2462784; S. Choise, "Dalhousie Made String of Errors in Dentistry Probe, Report Finds," *Globe and Mail* (29 June 2015), http://www.theglobeandmail.com/news/national/report-says-dalhousie-did-not-treat-female-students-fairly-transparently-in-dentistry-scandal/article 25174977/.

45. P. Glick & S.T. Fiske, "Hostile and Benevolent Sexism," *Psychology of Women Quarterly* 21 (1997): 119–135.

46. M. Potok, "The 'Philosophy' of Rape," *Intelligence Report* (20 March 2015), https://www.splcenter.org/fighting-hate/intelligence-report/2015/%E2%80%98philosophy%E2%80%99-rape/.

47. J. Younis, "What Happened When I Started a Feminist Society at School," *The Guardian* (20 June 2013).

48. C. Dell'Amore, "Bikinis Make Men See Women as Objects, Scans Confirm," *National Geographic News* (16 February 2009).

49. See http://www.hiik.de/en/konfliktbarometer/

50. "There Can Be No Hiding Place for Perpetrators of Sexual Violence in Conflict: UN Official," *United Nations Radio* (11 April 2013), http://www.unmultimedia.org/radio/english/2013/04/there-can-be-no-hiding-place-for-perpetrators-of-sexual-violence-in-conflict-un-official/.

51. See http://www.who.int/mediacentre/factsheets/fs357/en/.

52. See http://www.who.int/disabilities/violence/en/.

53. World Health Organization, *Violence Against Adults and Children with Disabilities*, http://www.who.int/disabilities/violence/en/.

54. "Metal Studs Treat the Homeless 'Like Animals'," *Sky News* (8 June 2014), http://news.sky.com/story/1277765/metal-studs-treat-the-homeless-like-animals/.

55. Y. Alcindor, "Cities' Homeless Crackdown: Could It Be Compassion Fatigue?" *USA Today* (10 June 2012), http://usatoday30.usatoday.com/news/nation/story/2012-06-10/cities-crack-down-on-homeless/55479912/1?siteID=je6 NUbpO bpQ-E6HWdFQVHWMsbt4nKEFbUg

56. National Law Center on Homelessness & Poverty, "Homelessness in America: Overview of Data," http://www.nlchp.org/documents/Homeless_Stats_Fact_Sheet/.

57. E. Badger, "It's Unconstitutional to Ban the Homeless from Sleeping Outside, the Federal Government Says," *Washington Post* (13 August 2015), http://www.washingtonpost.com/news/wonkblog/wp/2015/08/13/its-unconstitutional-to-ban-the-homeless-from-sleeping-outside-the-federal-government-says/ .

58. The four Crimes Against Peace are genocide, war crimes, crimes of aggression (such as unprovoked war), and crimes against humanity.

59. J. Jowit, "British Campaigner Urges UN to Accept 'Ecocide' as International Crime," *The Guardian* (9 April 2010).

60. See http://www.ecojustice.ca/tar-sands-ceos-guilty-of-ecocide -after-mock-trial/.

61. "Interventions," *TeachSafeSchools.org*, http://www.teachsafeschools.org/bully_menu5-2.html/.

Chapter 5: Benevolent Bigotry

1. A.R. Pearson, J.F. Dovidio, & S.L. Gaertner, "The Nature of Contemporary Prejudice: Insights from Aversive Racism," *Social and Personality Psychology Compass* 3 (2009): 1-25.

2. A.G. Greenwald, & M.R. Banaji, "Implicit Social Cognition: Attitudes, Self-Esteem, and Stereotypes," *Psychological Review* 102 (1995): 4–27.

3. M.R. Banaji, C. Hardin & A.J. Rothman, "Implicit Stereotyping in Person Judgment," *Journal of Personality and Social Psychology* 65, no. 2 (1993): 272-281; R.H. Fazio, J.R. Jackson, B.C. Dunton, & C.J. Williams, "Variability in Automatic Activation as an Unobtrusive Measure of Racial Attitudes: A Bona Fide Pipeline?" *Journal of Personality and Social*

Psychology 69, no. 6 (1995): 1013-1027; S.L. Gaertner & J.P McLaughlin, "Racial Stereotypes: Association and Ascriptions of Positive and Nega tive Characteristics" *Social Psychology Quarterly* 46, no. 1 (1983): 23-30.

4. C. Cozzarelli, A.V. Wilkinson & M.J. Tagler, "Attitudes Toward the Poor and Attributions for Poverty," *Journal of Social Issues* 57, no. 2 (2001): 207-227.

5. L. Bradshaw, "Why Luck Has Nothing to Do With It," *Forbes* (8 November 2011), http://www.forbes.com/sites/lesliebradshaw/ 2011/11/08/why-luck-has-nothing-to-do-with-it/; N.F. Russo, R.M. Kelly, & M. Deacon, "Gender and Success-Related Attributions: Beyond Individualistic Conceptions of Achievement," *Sex Roles* 25, no. 5/6 (1991): 331-350.

6. E. Winkler, "Children Are Not Colorblind: How Young Children Learn Race," *PACE*, no. 3 (2009), http://www.academia.edu/3094721 /Children_Are_Not_Colorblind_How_Young_Children_Learn_Race.

7. See https://implicit.harvard.edu/implicit/education. html/.

8. See https://implicit.harvard.edu/implicit/takeatest.html/.

9. See http://www.lookdifferent.org/what-can-i-do/bias-cleanse/.

10. J.F. Dovidio, K. Kawakami, & S.L Gaertner, "Implicit and Explicit Prejudice and Interracial Interaction," *Journal of Personality and Social Psychology* 82, no.1 (2002): 62-68.

11. J.F. Dovidio, "Racial Bias, Unspoken but Heard," *Science* 326 (2009): 1641-1642.

12. Ohio State University, "Racial Biases Fade Away Toward Members of Your Own Group," *ScienceDaily* (23 March 2009), http://www.science daily.com/releases/2009/03/ 09032311045 60456.htm; Association for Psychological Science. "Why Few People Are Devoid Of Racial Bias," *ScienceDaily* (26 September 2007), http://www.sciencedaily.com/ releases/2007/ 09/0709 24122814.htm/.

13. For example, M.J. Monteith, N.E. Deneen & G.D. Tooman, "The Effect of Social Norm Activation on the Expression of Opinions Concerning Gay Men and Blacks," *Basic and Applied Social Psychology* 18, no. 3 (1996): 267-288.

14. J. Kang, *Implicit Bias: A Primer* (National Center for State Courts, August 2009), http://wp.jerrykang.net.s110363.gridserver. com/wp-content/uploads/2010/10/kang-Implicit-Bias-Primer-for-courts-09. pdf/.

15. Ibid., 6.

16. Kirwan Institute, *Implicit Bias in School Discipline,* http://kirwaninstitute.osu.edu/initiatives/school-discipline/.

17, J.A. Sabin & A.G. Greenwald, "The Influence of Implicit Bias on Treatment Recommendations for 4 Common Pediatric Conditions: Pain, Urinary Tract Infection, Attention Deficit Hyperactivity Dis order, and Asthma," *American Journal of Public Health* 102, no. 5 (2012): 988-995.

18. M. Woo, "How Science Is Helping America Tackle Police Racism," *Wired* (21 January 2015), http://www.wired.com/ 2015/01/implicit-bias-police-racism-science/.

19. For example, J.K. Swim, M.J. Ferguson, & L.L. Hyers, "Avoiding Stig ma by Association: Subtle Prejudice Against Lesbians in the Form of Social Distancing," *Basic and Applied Social Psychology* 21, no. 1 (1999): 61-68.

20. M. Shepherd, M. Erchull, A. Rosner, L. Taubenberger, E. Forsyth Queen, & J. McKee, "'I'll Get That for You': The Relationship Between Benevolent Sexism and Body Self-Perceptions," *Sex Roles* 64, no. 1/2 (2011): 1-8.

21. See http://www.breakfreenow.com/Theory.html/.

22. D.M. Frost & I.H. Meyer, "Internalized Homophobia and Relationship Quality Among Lesbians, Gay Men, and Bisexuals," *Journal of Consulting Psychology* 56, no 1 (2009): 97-109.

23. I.H. Meyer, "Prejudice, Social Stress, and Mental Health in Lesbian, Gay, and Bisexual Populations: Conceptual Issues and Research Evidence," *Psychological Bulletin* 129, no. 5 (2003): 674-697.

24. P. Glick & S.T. Fiske, "An Ambivalent Alliance: Hostile and Benevolent Sexism as Complementary Justifications for Gender Inequality," *American Psychologist* 56, no. 2 (2001), 109.

25. S. Shiffrin, "Paternalism, Unconscionability Doctrine, and Accom modation," *Philosophy and Public Affairs* 29, no. 3 (2000): 205-250.

26. S. Plous, & T. Williams, "Racial Stereotypes from the Days of American Slavery: A Continuing Legacy," *Journal of Applied Social Psychology* 25 (1995): 795-817.

27. J.F. Dovidio & S.L. Gaertner, "Aversive Racism and Selection Deci sions: 1989 and 1999," *Psychological Science* 11 (2000): 319–323; J.F. Dovidio & S.L. Gaertner, "Aversive Racism," in *Advances in Experi*

mental Social Psychology, Vol. 36, ed. M.P. Zaanna, 1–51 (San Diego, CA: Academic Press, 2004); G. Hodson, J.F. Dovidio, & S.L. Gaertner, "Processes in Racial Discrimination: Differential Weighting of Conflict ing Information," *Personality and Social Psychology Bulletin* 28 (2002): 460–471.

28. A.P. Brief, J. Dietz, R.R. Cohen, S.D. Pugh, & J.B. Vaslow, "Just Doing Business: Modern Racism and Obedience to Authority as Explanations for Employment Discrimination," *Organizational Behavior and Human Decision Processes* 81 (2000): 72–97.

29. R.W. Meertens & T.F. Pettigrew, "Is Subtle Prejudice Really Prejudice?" *Public Opinion Quarterly* 61 (1997): 54-71.

30. B. Dardenne, M. Dumont, & T. Bollier, "Insidious Dangers of Benevolent Sexism: Consequences for Women's Performance," *Journal of Personality and Social Psychology* 93, no. 5 (2007): 764-779.

31. J.C. Becker & J.K. Swim, "Seeing the Unseen: Attention to Daily Encounters with Sexism as Way to Reduce Sexist Beliefs," *Psychology of Women Quarterly* 35 (2011): 227-242.

32. B.M. Masser & D. Abrams, "Reinforcing the Glass Ceiling: The Consequences of Hostile Sexism for Female Managerial Candidates," *Sex Roles* 51, no. 9–10 (2004): 609–616.

33. J.B. Nezlek, A. Schutz, & I. Sellin, "Self-Presentational Success in Daily Social Interaction," *Self and Identity* 6 (2007): 361–379.; S.T. Fiske, A.J. Cuddy, & P. Glick, "Universal Dimensions of Social Cognition: Warmth and Competence," *Trends in Cognitive Sciences* 11 (2007): 77–83.

34. A.E. Abele & B. Wojciszke, "Agency and Communion from the Perspective of Self Versus Others," *Journal of Personality and Social Psychology* 93 (2007): 751–763; J. Willis & A. Todorov, "First Impressions: Making Up Your Mind After a 100-ms Exposure to a Face," *Psychological Science* 17, no. 7 (2006): 592-598.

35. M.R. Leary, 2010, "Affiliation, Acceptance, and Belonging: The Pursuit of Interpersonal Connection," in *Handbook of Social Psychology*, Vol. 2, ed. S. T. Fiske, D. T. Gilbert, & G. Lindzey, 864–897 (Hoboken, NJ: John Wiley & Sons); D.S. Holoien & S.T. Fiske, "Downplaying Positive Impressions: Compensation Between Warmth and Competence," *Journal of Experimental Social Psychology* 49, no. 1 (2013): 33-41.

36. R.W. Meertens, & T.F. Pettigrew, "Is Subtle Prejudice Really Prejudice?" *Public Opinion Quarterly* 61 (1997): 54-71.

37. M. Kite & B. Whitley, *The Psychology of Prejudice and Discrimination* (Wadsworth, Cengage Learning, 2010).

38. S. Fischer, "Elephant 'Speaks' Like a Human—Uses Trunk to Shape Sound," *National Geographic* (3 November 2011), http://news.national geographic.com/news/2012/11/121102-korean-speaking-elephant-talk-human-science-weird-animals/.

39. J. Honeyborne, "Elephants Really Do Grieve Like Us: They Shed Tears and Even Try to 'Bury' Their Dead—A Leading Wildlife Film-Maker Reveals How the Animals Are Like Us," *Daily Mail* (13 January 2013), http://www.dailymail.co.uk/news/article-2270977/Elephants-really-grieve-like-They-shed-tears-try-bury-dead--leading-wildlife-film-ma ker-reveals-animals-like-us.html/; "Wild Elephants Gather Inexpli cably to Mourn Death of 'Elephant Whisperer'," *Beliefnet,* http:// www.beliefnet. com/Inspiration/Home-Page-News-and-Views/Wild-Elephants-Mourn-Death-of-famed-Elephant-Whisperer.aspx?p=1/.

40. H. Scales, "'Talking Whale' Could Imitate Human Voice," *National Geographic News* (23 October 2012), http://news.nationalgeographic. com/news/2012/10/121022-whales-voices-science-animals-humans-marine-mammals/.

41. P. Glick & S.T. Fiske, "The Ambivalent Sexism Inventory: Differen-tiating Hostile and Benevolent Sexism," *Journal of Personality and Social Psychology* 70 (1996): 491-512.

42. P. Glick & S.T. Fiske, "Hostile and Benevolent Sexism," *Psychology of Women Quarterly* 21 (1997): 119–35.

43. A.H. Eagly & A. Mladinic, A. "Are People Prejudiced Against Women? Some Answers from Research on Attitudes, Gender Stereotypes, and Judgments of Competence," in *European Review of Social Psychology,* Vol. 5, ed. W. Stroebe & M. Hewstone, 1–35 (New York: Wiley, 1993).

44. A.H. Eagly & V.J. Steffen, "Gender Stereotypes Stem From the Distribution of Women and Men into Social Roles," *Journal of Personality and Social Psychology* 46 (1984): 735-754.

45. M.R. Jackman, "Gender, Violence, and Harassment," in *Handbook of the Sociology of Gender*, ed. J.S. Chafetz, 275-317 (New York: Springer, 1999).

46. M. Tannenbaum, "If It Looks Like a Compliment, and Sounds Like a Compliment…Is It Really a Compliment?" *Scientific American* (31 January 2012), http://blogs.scientificamerican. com/guest-blog/if-it-

looks-like-a-compliment-and-sounds-like-a-compliment-is-it-really-a-compliment/.

47. P. Glick, S.T. Fiske, A. Mladinic, J.L. Saiz, D. Abrams, B. Masser, B. Adetoun, J.E. Osagie, A. Akande, A. Alao, B. Brunner, T.M. Willemsen, K. Chipeta, B. Dardenne, A. Dijksterhuis, D. Wigboldus, T. Eckes, I. Six-Materna, F. Expósito, M. Moya, M. Foddy, H-J. Kim, M. Lameiras, M.J. Sotelo, A. Mucchi-Faina, M. Romani, N. Sakalli, B. Udegbe, M. Yamamoto, & M. Ui, "Beyond Prejudice as Simple Antipathy: Hostile and Benevolent Sexism Across Cultures," *Journal of Personality and Social Psychology* 79, no. 5 (2000): 763–775.

48. P. Glick, J. Diebold, B. Bailey-Werner, & L. Zhu, "The Two Faces of Adam: Ambivalent Sexism and Polarized Attitudes Toward Women," *Personality and Social Psychology Bulletin* 23, no. 12 (1997): 1323–1334.

49. J.C. Becker, P. Glick, M. Ilic, & G. Bohner, "Damned If She Does, Damned If She Doesn't: Consequences of Accepting Versus Confronting Patronizing Help for the Female Target and Male Actor," *European Journal of Social Psychology* 41, no. 6 (2011): 761-773.

50. R.L. Wiener, R. Reiter-Palmon, R.J. Winter, E. Richter, A. Humke, & E. Maeder, "Complainant Behavioral Tone, Ambivalent Sexism, and Perceptions of Sexual Harassment," *Psychology, Public Policy, and Law* 16, no. 1 (2010): 56-84.

51. S.P. Stermer & M. Burkley, "SeX-Box: Exposure to Sexist Video Games Predicts Benevolent Sexism," *Psychology of Popular Media Culture* 4, no. 1 (2015): 47-55.

52. M. Infanger, J. Bosak, & S. Sczesny, "Communality Sells: The Impact of Perceivers' Sexism on the Evaluation of Women's Portrayals in Advertisements," *European Journal of Social Psychology* 42, no. 2 (2012): 219-226.

53. J.J. Begany & M.A. Milburn, "Psychological Predictors of Sexual Harassment: Authoritarianism, Hostile Sexism, and Rape Myths," *Psychology of Men & Masculinity* 3, no. 2 (2002): 119-126.

54. M. Mikolajczak & J. Pietrzak, "Ambivalent Sexism and Religion: Connected through Values," *Sex Roles* 70, no. 9 (2014): 387-399.

55. Glick, Diebold, Bailey-Werner, & Zhu, 1997, op.cit.

56. C.G. Sibley & J.C. Becker, "On the Nature of Sexist Ambivalence: Profiling Ambivalent and Univalent Sexists," *European Journal of Social Psychology* 42, no. 5 (2012): 589-601.

57. P. Glick, M. Wilkerson, & M. Cuffe, "Masculine Identity, Ambivalent Sexism, and Attitudes Toward Gender Subtypes: Favoring Masculine Men and Feminine Women," *Social Psychology* 46 (2015): 210-217.

58. M. Barreto & N. Ellemers, "The Burden of Benevolent Sexism: How It Contributes to the Maintenance of Gender Inequalities," *European Journal of Social Psychology* 35 (2005): 633-642.

59. B. Dardenne, M. Dumont, & T. Bollier, "Insidious Dangers of Benevolent Sexism: Consequences for Women's Performance," *Interpersonal Relations and Group Processes* 93 (2007): 764-779.

60. P. Glick & S.T. Fiske, "The Ambivalent Sexism Inventory: Differentiating Hostile and Benevolent Sexism," *Journal of Personality and Social Psychology* 70, no. 3 (1996): 491-492.

61. A. Fischer, "Women's Benevolent Sexism as Reaction to Hostility," *Psychology of Women Quarterly* 30, no. 4 (2006): 410-416; K. Connelly & M. Heesacker, "Why Is Benevolent Sexism Appealing? Associations with System Justification and Life Satisfaction," *Psychology of Women Quarterly* 36, no. 4 (2012): 432-443.

62. J. Becker, & S. Wright, "Yet Another Dark Side of Chivalry: Benevolent Sexism Undermines and Hostile Sexism Motivates Collective Action for Social Change," *Journal of Personality and Social Psychology* 101, no. 1 (2011): 62-77.

63. P. Glick & S.T. Fiske "Ambivalent Sexism Revisited," *Psychology of Women Quarterly* 35, no. 3 (2011): 530-535.

64. The term was coined in July 1979 by Katherine Lawrence and Maryanne Schreiber of Hewlett-Packard.

65. M.K. Ryan & S.A. Haslam, "The Glass Cliff: Evidence That Women Are Over-Represented in Precarious Leadership Positions," *British Journal of Management* 16 (2005): 81–90; A. Cook & C. Glass, "Glass Cliffs and Organizational Saviors: Barriers to Minority Leadership in Work Organizations?" *Social Problems* 60, no. 2 (2013): 168–187.

66. N.C. Overall, C.G. Sibley, & R. Tan, "The Costs and Benefits of Sexism: Resistance to Influence During Relationship Conflict," *Journal of Personality and Social Psychology* 101, no. 2 (2011): 271-290.

Chapter 6: Stereotyping

1. J. Lehrer, *How We Decide* (New York: Houghton Mifflin, 2009), xvi; R.B. Zajonc, "Feelings and Thinking: Preferences Need No Inferences," *American Psychologist* 35, no. 2 (1980): 151-175.

2. D.T. Gilbert & J.G. Hixon, "The Trouble of Thinking: Activation and Application of Stereotypic Beliefs," *Journal of Personality and Social Psychology* 60, no. 4 (1991): 509-517.

3. Adapted from S.T. Fiske, A.J.C. Cuddy, P. Glick, & J. Xu, "A Model of (Often Mixed) Stereotype Content: Competence and Warmth Respectively Follow From Perceived Status and Competition," *Journal of Personality and Social Psychology* 82, no. 6 (2002): 878–902.

4. S.T. Fiske, "Managing Ambivalent Prejudices: The Smart-but-Cold, and the Warm-but-Dumb Stereotypes," *Annals of the American Academy of Political and Social Sciences* 639, no. 1 (2012): 33-48.

5. H. Tajfel, *Social Identity and Intergroup Relations* (Cambridge: Cambridge University Press, 1982).

6. J. Winters, "Why We Fear the Unknown," *Psychology Today* (1 May 2002), https://www.psychologytoday.com/articles/ 200305/why-we-fear-the-unknown/.

7. H. Tajfel & J.C. Turner, "The Social Identity Theory of Inter-Group Behavior," in *Psychology of Intergroup Relations*, ed. S. Worchel & L.W. Austin (Chicago: Nelson-Hall, 1986).

8. M.J. Gill, "When Information Does Not Deter Stereotyping: Prescriptive Stereotyping Can Foster Bias Under Conditions That Deter Descriptive Stereotyping," *Journal of Experimental Social Psychology* 40 (2004): 619-632.

9. Ibid.

10. M.E. Heilman, "Description and Prescription: How Gender Stereotypes Prevent Women's Ascent Up the Organizational Ladder," *Journal of Social Issues* 57, no. 4 (2001): 657–674.

11. J.L. Berdahl & J.-A. Min, "Prescriptive Stereotypes and Work place Consequences for East Asians in North America," *Cultural Diversity and Ethnic Minority Psychology* 18, no. 2 (2012): 141-152.

12. D.A. Stanley, P. Sokol-Hessner, M.R. Banaji, & E.A. Phelps, "Implicit Race Attitudes Predict Trustworthiness Judgments and Economic Trust Decisions," *PNAS* (2011): 1-6.

13. Association for Psychological Science, "Racism's Cognitive Toll: Subtle Discrimination is More Taxing on the Brain." *ScienceDaily* (24 September 2007), http://www.sciencedaily.com/releases/2007/09/070919093316.htm.

14. C. Good, A. Rattan, & C.S. Dweck, "Why Do Women Opt Out? Sense of Belonging and Women's Representation in Mathematics," *Journal of Personality and Social Psychology* 102, no. 4 (2012): 700-717.

15. S.T. Fiske & M.S. North, "Measures of Stereotyping and Prejudice: Barometers of Bias," in *Measures of Personality and Social Psychological Constructs*, ed. G.J. Boyle, D.H. Saklofske, & G. Matthews (New York: Elsevier/Academic, 2014).

16. J. Bosak & A. Diekman, "Malleability of Intergroup Stereotypes and Attitudes," *Social Psychology* 41, no. 3 (2010): 111-112; P.B. Carr, C.S. Dweck, & K. Pauker, "'Prejudiced' Behavior Without Prejudice? Beliefs About the Malleability of Prejudice Affect Interracial Interactions," *Journal of Personality and Social Psychology* 103, no. 3 (2012): 452–471.

17. W.T.L. Cox & P.G. Devine, "Stereotypes Possess Heterogeneous Directionality: A Theoretical and Empirical Exploration of Stereotype Structure and Content," *PLoS ONE* 10, no. 3 (2015).

18. L.A. Rudman & E. Borgida, "The Afterglow of Construct Accessibility: The Behavioral Consequences of Priming Men to View Women as Sexual Objects," *Journal of Experimental Social Psychology* 31 (1995): 493–517.

19. B.A. Nosek, F.L. Smyth, N.N. Sriram, N.M. Lindner, T. Devos, A. Ayala, & A.G. Greenwald, "National Differences in Gender–Science Stereotypes Predict National Sex Differences in Science and Math Achievement," *PNAS* 106, no. 26 (2009): 10593-10597.

20. L.A. Rudman, A.G. Greenwald, & D.E. McGhee, "Implicit Self-Concept and Evaluative Implicit Gender Stereotypes: Self and In-Group Share Desirable Traits," *Personality and Social Psychology Bulletin* 27, no. 9 (2001): 1164-1178.

21. B. Wittenbrink, C.M. Judd, & B. Park, "Evidence for Racial Prejudice at the Implicit Level and Its Relationship with Questionnaire Measures," *Journal of Personality and Social Psychology* 72, no. 2 (1997): 262-274.

22. M.J. White, & G.B. White, "Implicit and Explicit Occupational Gender Stereotypes," *Sex Roles*, 55, no. 3 (2006): 259-266.

23. J. Agerström, & D. Rooth, "The Role of Automatic Obesity Stereotypes in Real Hiring Discrimination," *Journal of Applied Psychology* 96, no. 4 (2011): 790-850.

24. K.C. Yam, R. Fehr, & C.M. Barnes, "Morning Employees Are Perceived as Better Employees: Employees' Start Times Influence Supervisor

Performance Ratings," *Journal of Applied Psychology* 99, no. 6 (2014): 1288-1299.

25. P.A. Goff, J.L. Eberhardt, M.J. Williams, & M.C. Jackson, "Not Yet Human: Implicit Knowledge, Historical Dehumanization, and Contemporary Consequences," *Journal of Personality and Social Psychology* 94, no. 2 (2008): 292-306.

26. J.F. Kihlstrom, "The Psychological Unconscious," in *Handbook of Personality: Theory and Research*, ed. L. Pervin, 445-464 (New York: Guilford, 1990).

27. J. Bargh, M. Chen, & L Burrows, "Automaticity of Social Behavior: Direct Effects of Trait Construct and Stereotype Activation on Action," *Journal of Personality and Social Psychology* 71, no. 2 (1996): 230–244.

28. Z. Kunda, P.G. Davies, B.D. Adams, & S.J. Spencer, "The Dynamic Time Course of Stereotype Activation: Activation, Dissipation, and Resurrection," *Journal of Personality and Social Psychology* 82, no. 3 (2002): 283-299.

29. L. Ashburn-Nardo, C.L. Voils, & M.J. Monteith, "Implicit Associations as the Seeds of Intergroup Bias: How Easily Do They Take Root?" *Journal of Personality and Social Psychology* 81, no. 5 (2001): 789-799.

30. S.C. Wheeler & R.E. Petty, "The Effects of Stereotype Activation on Behavior: A Review of Possible Mechanisms," *Psychological Bulletin* 127, no. 6 (2001): 797-826.

31. Z. Kunda, P.G. Davies, B.D. Adams, & S.J. Spencer, "The Dynamic Time Course of Stereotype Activation: Activation, Dissipation, Resurrection," *Journal of Personality and Social Psychology* 82, no. 3 (2002): 283-299.

32. C.M. Steele, "A Threat in the Air: How Stereotypes Shape Intellectual Identity and Performance," *American Psychologist* 52, no. 6 (1997): 613–629.

33. C.M. Steele & J. Joshua, "Stereotype Threat and the Intellectual Test Performance of African Americans," *Journal of Personality and Social Psychology* 69, no. 5 (1995): 797–811.

34. C.M. Steele, S.J. Spencer, & J. Aronson, "Contending with Group Image: The Psychology of Stereotype and Social Identity Threat," *Advances in Experimental Social Psychology* 34 (2002): 379-440.

35. University of Kent, "How Negative Stereotyping Affects Older People," *ScienceDaily* (29 January 2015), http://www.sciencedaily.com/releases/2015/01/150129104221.htm/.

36. Steele, 1997, op.cit.

37. M. Shih, T.L. Pittinsky, & N. Ambady, "Stereotype Susceptibility: Identity Salience and Shifts in Quantitative Performance," *Psychological Science* 10, no. 1 (1999): 80-83.

38. S.L. Beilock, R.J. Rydell, & A.R. McConnell, "Stereotype Threat and Working Memory: Mechanisms, Alleviation, and Spillover," *Journal of Experimental Psychology: General* 136, no.2 (2007): 256–276.

39. University of Toronto, "Stereotyping Has a Lasting Negative Impact, New Research Finds," *ScienceDaily* (11 August 2010), http://www.sciencedaily.com/releases/2010/08/10081012221 0.htm/.

40. M.C. Steffens, P. Jelenec, & P. Noack, "On the Leaky Math Pipeline: Comparing Implicit Math-Gender Stereotypes and Math Withdrawal in Female and Male Children and Adolescents," *Journal of Educational Psychology* 102, no. 4 (201): 947-963.

41. R. Baumeister & K. Vohs, ed. "Intergroup Anxiety," *Encyclopedia of Social Psychology* (Thousand Oaks, CA: Sage, 2007), 492–493.

42. D.M. Amodio & H.K. Hamilton, "Intergroup Anxiety Effects on Implicit Racial Evaluation and Stereotyping," *Emotion* 12, no. 6 (2012): 1273-1280; C.M. Judd & B. Park, "Out-Group Homogeneity: Judgments of Variability at the Individual and Group Levels," *Journal of Personality and Social Psychology* 54, no. 5 (1988): 778-788; P.W. Linville, "Polarized Appraisals of Out-Group Members," *Journal of Personality and Social Psychology* 38, no.5 (1980): 689-703.

43. P.W. Linville, "The Heterogeneity of Homogeneity," in *Attribution and Social Interaction: The Legacy of Edward E. Jones*, ed. J.M. Darley & J. Cooper, 423-487 (Washington, DC: American Psychological Association, 1998).

44. P.C. Lee & C.J. Moss, "Wild Female African Elephants (*Loxodonta africana*) Exhibit Personality Traits of Leadership and Social Integration," *Journal of Comparative Psychology* 126, no. 3 (2012): 224-232.

Chapter 7: Invisibility

1. B. Chai, "Richard Gere Plays Homeless Man in New Film," *The Wall Street Journal* (10 Oct 2014) http://www.wsj.com/articles/richard-gere-plays-homeless-man-in-new-film/.

2. N. Morton, *The Journey Is Home* (Boston: Beacon Press, 1985).

3. National Alliance to End Homelessness, *The State of Homelessness in America: 2015* (1 April 2015), http://www.endhomelessness.org/library/entry/the-state-of-homelessness-in-america-2015/. Note that while over 578,000 were sleeping rough or in shelters, an additional 7.7 million were living doubled up (overcrowded), 6.4 million were paying more than 50 percent of their income towards housing and at risk of losing it, and an additional 4.8 million were living below the poverty line, placing housing at risk.

4. Children's Defense Fund, *The State of American's Children: 2014*, http://www.childrensdefense.org/library/state-of-americas-children/#resources/.

5. See http://www.who.int/mediacentre/factsheets/fs357/en/.

6. Ibid.

7. M. Hewstone, "The 'Ultimate Attribution Error'? A Review of the Literature on Intergroup Causal Attribution," *European Journal of Social Psychology* 2, no. 4 (1990): 311-335.

8. B.G. Sims & J. Kienzle, *Farm Power and Mechanization for Small Farms in Sub-Saharan Africa* (Rome: Food and Agriculture Organization of the United Nations, 2006).

9. A. Yusufzai & D. Nelson, "Pupils Return to Pakistani School Where Taliban Killed 150," *The Telegraph* (12 January 2015), http://www.telegraph.co.uk/news/worldnews/asia/pakistan/11339184/Pupils-return-to-Pakistani-school-where-Taliban-killed-150.html/.

10. I. Hussain & F. Drury, "Pictured: Three Little Girls Strangled to Death by Their Father in Pakistan Because He Didn't Want to 'Waste Money' on Their Education," *Daily Mail* (9 June 2015), http://www.dailymail.co.uk/news/article-3117167/Pictured-Three-little-girls-strangled-death-father-Pakistan-didn-t-want-waste-money-education.html/.

11. P. Reaney, "Unequal Access to 'Hot Jobs' Obstructs Women's Careers: Reports," *Globe and Mail* (16 November 2012).

12. S. Lane, "Female Stars Relegated to the Underclass," *The Sydney Morning Herald* (20 July 2012).

13. J.R. Angelini, P.J. MacArthur, & A.C. Billings. "What's the Gendered Story? Vancouver's Prime Time Olympic Glory on NBC," *Journal of Broadcasting & Electronic Media* 56, no. 2 (2012): 261.

14. J.R. Angelini, A.C. Billings, & P.J. MacArthur, "The Nationalistic Revolution Will Be Televised: The 2010 Vancouver Olympic Games on NBC," *International Journal of Sport Communication* 5, no. 2 (2012): 193-209.

15. A. Bainbridge, "Gender Inequality of Olympic Proportions," *The Drum* (27 July 2012), http://www.abc.net.au/ news/2012-07-26/bainbridge-gender-inequality-of-olympic-proportions/ 4156158/.

16. Dartmouth College, "Oil-Dwelling Bacteria Are Social Creatures in Earth's Deep Biosphere," *ScienceDaily* (12 December 2014), http://www.sciencedaily.com/releases/2014/12/141212150315.htm/; University of Colorado at Boulder, "Microbes Discovered in Extreme Environment on South American Volcanoes," *ScienceDaily* (8 June 2012),http://www.sciencedaily.com/releases/2012/06/120608160119.htm/.

17. "Garbage in St. Lawrence River Drawing Complaints," *Cornwall News watch* (10 Sept 2015), http://www.cornwallnewswatch.com/2015/09/10/garbage-in-st-lawrence-river-drawing-complaints/.

18. See http://www.nrdc.org/oceans/plastic-ocean./

19. L. Parker, "Eight Million Tons of Plastic Dumped in Ocean Every Year," *National Geographic* (13 February 2015), http://news.nationalgeographic.com/news/2015/02/150212-ocean-debris-plastic-garbage-patches-science/.

20. See http://www.eurekalert.org/pub_releases/2015-09/epr-ocr0929 15.php/.

21. J. Giles & L. Kaufman, "After Oil Spills, Hidden Damage Can Last for Years," *New York Times* (17 July 2010), http://www.nytimes.com/2010/07/18/science/earth/18enviro.html?_r=0/; S. Almasy, "Consequences of Spills Can Last for Decades," *CNN* (3 May 2010).

22. Georgia Institute of Technology, "Gulf of Mexico Clean-Up Makes 2010 Spill 52-Times More Toxic," *Phys.org* (30 November 2012), http://phys.org/news/2012-11-gulf-mexico-clean-up-times-toxic.html/.

23. V. James, *Marine Renewable Energy: A Global Review of the Extent of Marine Renewable Energy Developments, the Developing Technologies and Possible Conservation Implications for Cetaceans* (WDC: November 2013).

24. See http://us.whales.org/issues/homes-for-whales-and-dolphins/.

25. See http://us.whales.org/news/2015/09/new-zealand-declares- new-marine-sanctuary/.

26. M.T. Williams, "Colorblind Ideology Is a Form of Racism," *Psychology Today* (27 December 2011), https://www.psychologytoday.com/blog/culturally-speaking/201112/colorblind-ideology-is-form-racism; K. Tarca, "Colorblind in Control: The Risks of Resisting Difference Amid Demographic Change," *Educational Studies* 38, no. 2 (2005): 99-120; E. Bonilla-Silva, "Color-Blind Racism: Toward an Analysis of White Racial Ideology," in *White Supremacy and Racism in the Post-Civil Rights Era*, ed. E. Bonilla-Silva, 137-146 (Lynne Rienner Publishers, Inc, 2001); S.A. Fryberg & N.M. Stephens, "When the World is Colorblind, American Indians Are Invisible: A Diversity Science Approach," *Psychological Inquiry* 21 (2010): 115-119.

27. D.S. Holoien & J.N. Shelton, "You Deplete Me: The Cognitive Costs of Colorblindness on Ethnic Minorities," *Journal of Experimental Social Psychology* 48 (2012): 562-565.

28. A. Sedlovskaya, V. Purdie-Vaughns, R.P. Eibach, M. LaFrance, R. Romero-Canyas, & N.P. Camp, "Internalizing the Closet: Conceal-ment Heightens the Cognitive Distinction Between Public and Private Selves," *Journal of Personality and Social Psychology* 104, no. 4 (2013): 695-715.

29. V. Purdic-Vaughns & R.P. Eibach, "Intersectional Invisibility: The Distinctive Advantages and Disadvantages of Multiple Subordinate-Group Identities," *Sex Roles* 59, no.5 (2008): 377-391; S.K. Kang & A.L. Chasteen, "Beyond the Double-Jeopardy Hypothesis: Assessing Emotion on the Faces of Multiple-Categorizable Targets of Prejudice," *Journal of Experimental Social Psychology* 45, no 6 (2009): 1281-1285.

30. A.K. Sesko & M. Biernat, "Prototypes of Race and Gender: The Invisibility of Black Women," *Journal of Experimental Social Psychology* 46, no 2 (2010): 356-360.

31. D.I. Riddle, "Multiculturalism: Moving Beyond Cultural Definition," *The Quadrangle* (Fall 1982): 9-11; 24.

Chapter 8: Objectification

1. A. Dworkin, "Against the Male Flood: Censorship, Pornography and Equality," in *Oxford Readings in Feminism: Feminism and Pornography*, ed. D. Cornell, 30-31 (Oxford: Oxford University Press, 2000).

2. J. Kilbourne, *Deadly Persuasion: Why Women and Girls Must Fight the Addictive Power of Advertising* (New York: Free Press, 1999).

3. D. Archer, B. Iritani, D.D. Kimes, & M. Barrios, "Face-ism: Five Studies of Sex Differences in Facial Prominence," *Journal of Personality and Social Psychology* 45 (1983): 725–735.

4. K. Gray, J. Knobe, M. Sheskin, P. Bloom, & L.F. Barrett, "More Than a Body: Mind Perception and the Nature of Objectification," *Journal of Personality and Social Psychology* 101, no. 6 (2011): 1207-1220.

5. M. Cikara & J.L. Eberhardt, "From Agents to Objects: Sexist Attitudes and Neural Responses to Sexualized Targets," *Journal of Cognitive Neuroscience* 23, no. 3 (2011): 540-551.

6. S.J. Gervais, T.K. Vescio, & J. Allen, "When Are People Interchangeable Sexual Objects? The Effect of Gender and Body Type on Sexual Fungibility," *British Journal of Social Psychology* 51, no. 4 (2011): 499-513.

7. S. Loughnan, N. Haslam, T. Murnane, J. Vaes, C. Reynolds, & C. Suitner, "Objectification Leads to Depersonalization: The Denial of Mind and Moral Concern to Objectified Others," *European Journal of Social Psychology* 40, no. 5 (2010): 709-717.

8. J. Aubrey, "Effects of Sexually Objectifying Media on Self-Objectification and Body Surveillance in Undergraduates: Results of Two-Year Panel Study," *Journal of Communication* 56 (2006): 1-21.

9. S. Haslanger, "On Being Objective and Being Objectified," in *A Mind of One's Own: Feminist Essays on Reason and Objectivity*, eds. L.M. Antony & C. Witt, 209–253 (Boulder: Westview Press, 1993).

10. S. Basile, "Comparison of Abuse by Same and Opposite-Gender Litigants as Cited in Requests for Abuse Prevention Orders," *Journal of Family Violence* 19 (2004): 59-68.

11. M.A. Straus, & C.J. Field, "Psychological Aggression by American Parents: National Data on Prevalence, Chronicity, and Severity," *Journal of Marriage and Family* 65 (2003): 795–808.

12. D.J. English, J.C. Graham, R.R. Newton, T.L. Lewis, R. Thompson, J.B. Kotch, & C. Weisbart, "At-Risk and Maltreated Children Exposed to Intimate Partner Aggression/Violence: What the Conflict Looks Like and Its Relationship to Child Outcomes," *Child Maltreatment* 14, no. 2 (2008): 157-171.

13. N.G. Choi & J. Mayer, "Elder Abuse, Neglect, and Exploitation: Risk Factors and Prevention Strategies," *Journal of Gerontological Social Work* 33, no. 2 (2000).

14. J. Spinazzola, H. Hodgdon, L.-J. Liang, J.D. Ford, C.M. Layne, R. Pynoos, E.C. Briggs, B. Stolbach, & C. Kisiel, "Unseen Wounds," *APA Monitor on Psychology* 46, no. 7 (2015): 68.

15. K. Covell & R.B. Howe, "Psychological Maltreatment and Children's Right to Health" (September 2012), http://www.ohchr.org/Docu ments/Issues/Children/Study/RightHealth/CapeBretonUniversityC anada.pdf/.

16. B.L. Fredickson & T.-A. Roberts, "Objectification Theory: Toward Understanding Women's Lived Experiences and Mental Health Risks," *Psychology of Women Quarterly* 21 (1997): 173-206.

17. R.M. Calogero, "A Test of Objectification Theory: The Effect of Male Gaze on Appearance Concerns in College Women," *Psychology of Women Quarterly* 28 (2004): 16-21.

18. S.J. Gervais, T.K. Vescio, & J. Allen, "When What You See Is What You Get: The Consequences of the Objectifying Gaze for Women and Men," *Psychology of Women Quarterly* 35, no. 1 (2011): 5-17.

19. J. Breines, "Do Women Want to Be Objectified?" *Psychology Today* 29 November 2012), https://www.psychology today.com/blog/in-love-and-war/201211/do-women-want-be-objectified/.

20. For a concise summary of research, see C. Heldman, "Sexual Objecti-fication, Part 2: The Harm" *Ms.* (6 July 2012), http://msmagazine. com/blog/2012/07/06/sexual -objectification-part-2-the-harm/.

21. M.A. Yao, C. Mahood, & D. Linz, "Sexual Priming, Gender Stereotyping, and Likelihood to Sexually Harass: Examining the Cognitive Effects of Playing a Sexually-Explicit Video Game," *Sex Roles* 62, no. 1 (2010): 77-88.

22. See http://therepresentationproject.org/films/miss-representation/.

23. See http://www.cinemapolitica.org/film/generation-m-misogyny-media-culture/.

24. P. Bernard, S.J. Gervais, J. Allen, S. Campomizzi, & O. Klein, "Integrating Sexual Objectification with Object Versus Person Recognition: The Sexualized-Body-Inversion Hypothesis," *Psycho-logical Science* 23, no. 5 (2012): 469-471; S.J. Gervais, T.K. Vescio, J. Forster, A. Maass, & C. Suitner, "Seeing Women As Objects: The Sexual Body Part Recognition Bias," *European Journal of Social Psychology* 42, no. 6 (2012): 743-753.

25. R. L. Wiener, S.J. Gervais, J. Allen, & A. Marquez, "Eye of the Beholder: Effects of Perspective and Sexual Objectification on Harassment," *Psychology, Public Policy and Law* 19, no. 2 (2013): 206-221.

26. S. Loughnan, A. Pina, E.A. Vasquez, & E. Puvia, "Sexual Objectification Increases Rape Victim Blame and Decreases Perceived Suffering," *Psychology of Women Quarterly* 37, no. 4 (2013): 455-461.

27. C. Heldman, "Sexual Objectification, Part 1: What Is It?" *Ms.* (3 July 2012), http://msmagazine.com/blog/2012/07/03/sexual-objectification-part-1-what-is-it/.

28. C. MacKinnon, *Feminism Unmodified* (Cambridge: Harvard University Press, 1987), 176.

29. A. Dworkin, *Pornography: Men Possessing Women* (New York: Dutton, 1989).

30. C. MacKinnon, *Only Words* (Cambridge: Harvard University Press, 1993), 28.

31. MacKinnon, 1987, op. cit., 148.

32. Dworkin, 1989, op. cit., 166.

33. N. Doidge, *The Brain That Changes Itself* (New York: Penguin Books, 2007).

34. D.L. Hilton, & C. Watts, "Pornography Addiction: A Neuroscience Perspective," *Surgical Neurology International* 2 (2011): 19; D.H. Angres & K. Bettinardi-Angres, "The Disease of Addiction: Origins, Treatment, and Recovery," *Disease-a-Month* 54 (2008): 696–721; T.M. Mick & E. Hollander, "Impulsive-Compulsive Sexual Behavior" *CNS Spectrums* 11, no. 12 (2006): 944-955; E.J. Nestler, "Is There a Common Molecular Pathway for Addiction?" *Nature Neuroscience* 9, no. 11 (2005): 1445–1449.

35. Angres & Bettinardi-Angres, 2008, op. cit.; D. Zillmann, "Influence of Unrestrained Access to Erotica on Adolescents' and Young Adults' Dispositions Toward Sexuality," *Journal of Adolescent Health* 27, no. 2 (2008): 41–44.

36. Hilton & Watts, 2011, op. cit.; A. Leshner, "Addiction Is a Brain Disease and It Matters," *Science* 278 (1997): 45–47.

37. C. Greenwood, "Porn's Effect on Youth 'Is Catastrophic': Top Met Officer Despairs of Boys and Girls Brutalised by Extreme Films Online," *Daily Mail* (16 September 2015), http://www.dailymail.

co.uk/news/article-3236083/Porn-s-effect-youth-catastrophic-Met-officer-despairs-boys-girls-brutalised-extreme-films-online.html/.

38. R. Weiss, "Sexual and Relationships Dysfunction Is the True Cost of Porn," *Huffington Post* (31 January 2013), http://www.huffington post.com/robert-weiss/sexual-dysfunction-pornography_b_2536216. html/.

39. E.L. Zurbriggen, L.R. Ramsey, & B.K. Jaworski, "Self- and Partner-Objectification in Romantic Relationships: Associations with Media Consumption and Relationship Satisfaction," *Sex Roles* 64, no 7 (2011): 449-462.

40. A. Lenhart, "Teens, Smartphones, & Texting," *Pew Research Center* (19 March 2012), http://www.pewinternet.org/ 2012/03/19/teens-smart phones-texting/; A. Lenhart, M. Anderson, & A. Smith, "Teens, Tech nology and Romantic Relationships," *Pew Research Center* (1 October 2015), http://www.pewinternet.org/2015/10/01/teens-technology-and-romantic-relationships/.

41. J. Hoffman, "A Girl's Nude Photo, and Altered Lives," *New York Times* (26 March 2011), http://www.nytimes.com/2011/03/27/us/ 27sexting.html?_r=0/.

42. E. Rezetti, "Rehtaeh Parsons Shows Connectedness Has Driven Us Apart," *Globe & Mail* (12 April 2013).

43. F. Martinez, "Study: 88 Percent of Sexual Pics Uploaded by Teens Are Stolen by Jailbait-Style Porn Sites," *The Daily Dot* (23 October 2012), http://www.dailydot.com/society/majority-teen-pics-jailbait-style-porn-sites-study/.

44. See https://www.apa.org/pi/women/programs/girls/report-full. pdf/.

45. T. McKay, "Female Self-Objectification: Causes, Consequences and Prevention," *McNair Scholars Research Journal* 6, no. 1 (2013).

46. J.S. Aubrey, & A. Gerding, "The Cognitive Tax of Self-Objectification: Examining Sexually Objectifying Music Videos and Female Emerging Adults' Cognitive Processing of Subsequent Advertising," *Journal of Media Psychology: Theories, Methods, and Applications* 27, no. 1 (2015): 22-32.

47. S. Rinaldis, "9 Body-Shaming Behaviors We All Need to Stop," (11 September 2014), http://www.mindbody green.com/0-15240/9-body-shaming-behaviors-we-all-need-to-stop.html/.

48. K.S. Rommelfanger, "Does This Lab Coat Make Me Look Fat?" *The Chronicle of Higher Education* (23 October 2012), http://chronicle.com/blogs/conversation/2012/10/23/does-this-lab-coat-make-me-look-fat/.

49. S.-L. Bartky, *Femininity and Domination: Studies in the Phenomenology of Oppression* (New York: Routledge, 1990).

50. Ibid., 80.

51. I.M. Young, "Is There a Woman's World? Some Reflections on the Struggle for Our Bodies," *Proceedings of The Second Sex – Thirty Years Later: A Commemorative Conference on Feminist Theory* (New York: The New York Institute for the Humanities, 2009).

52. See http://www.globalslaveryindex.org/; https://www.walkfree.org/modern-slavery-facts/

53. See http://www.unodc.org/documents/data-and-analysis/glotip/GLOTIP_2014_full_report.pdf/.

54. "Child Labor and the Rug Industry," http://www.goodweave.org/child_labor_campaign/child_labor_handmade_rugs_carpets/.

55. See http://www.unicef.org/education/index_focus_exploitation.html/.

56. American Psychological Association, *Report of the Task Force on the Sexualization of Girls*, https://www.apa.org/pi/women/programs/girls/report-full.pdf/.

57. S.M. Goodin, A. Van Denburg, S.K. Murnen, & L. Smolak, "'Putting on' Sexiness: A Content Analysis of the Presence of Sexualizing Characteristics in Girls' Clothing," *Sex Roles* 65 (2011): 1-12.

58. S.L. Smith, *Gender Bias Without Borders: An Investigation of Female Characters in Popular Films in 11 Countries.* http://see jane.org/wp-content/uploads/gender-bias-without-borders-executive-summary.pdf/.

59. J. Olsen, "Take Action When Adults Bully Young People," (21 May 2012), http://msue.anr.msu.edu/news/take_action_when_adults_bully_young_people/.

60. K. Roberts, "7 Actions Parents Can Take When Sports Coaches Act Like Bullies," *Huffington Post* (19 March 2014), http://www.huffingtonpost.com/dr-kate-roberts/7-actions-parents-can-take-when-sports-coaches-act-like-bullies_b_4954 874.html/.

61. P. Hermann, S.R. Waxman, & D.L. Medin, "Anthropocentrism Is Not the First Step in Children's Reasoning about the Natural World," *Proceedings of the National Academy of Sciences* (June 2010).

62. See http://eradicatingecocide.com/.

63. J. Jowit, "British Campaigner Urges UN to Accept 'Ecocide' as International Crime," *The Guardian* (9 April 2010).

64. N. Entrup & M. Prideaux, "Cetacean Rights: Confronting the Sustainability Paradigm and Deciding Who Is 'Beyond Use'." Paper presented at the Helsinki Conference on Cetacean Rights: Fostering Moral and Legal Change, May 2010.

Chapter 9: Remembering Who We Are

1. See a listing in *Cell Biology by the Numbers*, http://book. bionumbers.org/how-quickly-do-different-cells-in-the-body-replace-themselves/.

2. R. Walsh & S.L. Shapiro, "The Meeting of Meditative Disciplines and Western Psychology: A Mutually Enriching Dialogue," *American Psychologist* 61, no. 3 (2006): 227-239.

3. C.N.M. Ortner, S.J. Kiner, & P.D. Zelazo, "Mindfulness Meditation and Reduced Emotional Interference on a Cognitive Task," *Motivation and Emotion* 31 (2007): 271–283.

4. B.R. Cahn, & J. Polich, "Meditation States and Traits: EEG, ERP, and Neuroimaging Studies," *Psychological Bulletin* 132 (2006): 180-211.

5. M. Dekeyser, F. Raes, M. Leijssen, S. Leyson, & D. Dewulf, "Mindfulness Skills and Interpersonal Behavior," *Personality and Individual Differences* 44 (2008): 1235–1245.

6. S.F. Dingfelder, "A Workout for Working Memory," *APA Monitor on Psychology* 36, no. 8 (2005): 48; E. Day, "Online Brain-Training: Does It Really Work?" *The Guardian* (21 April 2013), http://www.the guardian.com/science/2013/apr/21/brain-training-online-neuro science-elizabeth-day/.

7. D.Z. Hambrick, "Brain Training Doesn't Make You Smarter," *Scientific American* (2 December 2014), http://www. scientificamerican.com/ article/brain-training-doesn-t-make-you-smarter/.

8. A.P. Jha, E.A. Stanley, A. Kiyonaga, L. Wong, & L. Gelfand, "Examining the Protective Effects of Mindfulness Training on Working Memory Capacity and Affective Experience," *Emotion* 10, no.

1 (2010): 54-64; Association for Psychological Science, "Brief Mindfulness Training May Boost Test Scores, Working Memory," *ScienceDaily* (26 March 2013), http://www.science daily.com/releases/2013/03/130326133335.htm/.

9. A. Moore & P. Malinowshi, "Meditation, Mindfulness and Cognitive Flexibility," *Conscious Cognition* 18 (2009): 176-186.

10. See http://www.myersbriggs.org/my-mbti-personality-type/mbti-basics/.

11. Association for Psychological Science, "Prejudice Comes From a Basic Human Need and Way of Thinking, New Research Suggests," *ScienceDaily* (21 December 2011), http://www.sciencedaily.com/releases/2011/12/111221140627.htm/.

12. J. Sanders, "The One Key Trait for Successful Entrepreneurs: A Tolerance for Ambiguity," *Forbes* (17 May 2012), http://www.forbes.com/sites/acton/2012/05/17/the-one-key-trait-for-successful-entrepreneurs-a-tolerance-for-ambiguity/.

13. M. D. Seery & W. J. Quinton, "Targeting Prejudice: Personal Self-Esteem as a Resource for Asians' Attributions to Racial Discrimination," *Social Psychological and Personality Science* 6, no. 6 (2015): 677-684.

14. J.C. Becker & J.K. Swim, "Seeing the Unseen: Attention to Daily Encounters with Sexism as a Way to Reduce Sexist Beliefs," *Psychology of Women Quarterly* 35, no. 2 (2011): 277-242.

15. D.J. Siegel, "Mindfulness Training and Neural Integration: Differentiation of Distinct Streams of Awareness and the Cultivation of Well-Being," *Social Cognitive & Affective Neuroscience* 2, no. 4 (2007): 259-263.

16. A. de Saint-Exupéry, *The Little Prince* (New York: Reynal & Hitchcock, 1943).

17. K.J. Johnson & B.L. Fredrickson, "'We All Look the Same to Me': Positive Emotions Eliminate the Own-Race Bias in Face Recognition," *Psychological Science* 16, no. 11 (2005): 875-881.

18. B.L. Fredrickson & C. Branigan, "Positive Emotions Broaden the Scope of Attention and Thought-Action Repertoires," *Cognition and Emotion* 19 (2005): 313–332.

19. J. Gruber, "Four Ways Happiness Can Hurt You," (3 May 2012), http://greatergood.berkeley.edu/article/item/four_ways_happiness_can_hurt_you/.

20. J.V. Wood, W.Q. E. Perunovic, & J.W. Lee, "Positive Self-Statements: Power for Some, Peril for Others," *Psychological Science* 20, no. 7 (2009): 860-866.

21. A.M. Wood, S. Joseph, & J. Maltby, "Gratitude Predicts Psychological Well-Being Above the Big Five Facets," *Personality and Individual Differences* 46 (2009): 443-447.

22. A.M Wood, J. Maltby, R. Gillett, P.A. Linley, & S. Joseph, "The Role of Gratitude in the Development of Social Support, Stress, and Depression: Two Longitudinal Studies," *Journal of Research in Personality* 42 (2008): 854-871.

23. FECYT (Spanish Foundation for Science and Technology), "Empathy and Violence Have Similar Circuits in the Brain, Research Suggests," *ScienceDaily* (11 April 2010), http://www.science daily.com/releases/2010/04/100409093405.htm/.

24. University of Michigan, "Empathy: College Students Don't Have as Much as They Used to, Study Finds," *ScienceDaily* (29 May 2010), http://www.sciencedaily.com/releases/2010/05/10052 8081434.htm/

25. F. de Waal, "The Evolution of Empathy," Greater Good (1 September 2005), http://greatergood.berkeley.edu/article/item/the_evolution_of_empathy/.

26. J. Interlandi, "The Brain's Empathy Gap," *New York Times* (19 March 2015), http://www.nytimes.com/2015/03/22/maga zine/the-brains-empathy-gap.html?_r=0/.

27. Society for Neuroscience, "Less Empathy Toward Outsiders: Brain Differences Reinforce Preferences For Those In Same Social Group," *ScienceDaily* (1 July 2009), http://www.sciencedaily.com/releases/2009/06/090630173815.htm/.

28. McGill University, "The Secret of Empathy: Stress from the Presence of Strangers Prevents Empathy, in Both Mice and Humans," *ScienceDaily* (15 January 2015), http://www.science daily.com/releases/2015/01/150115122005.htm; Northwestern University, "Race and Empathy Matter on Neural Level," *ScienceDaily* (27 April 2010), http://www.sciencedaily. com/releases/2010/04/100426182002.htm/.

29. J.D. Knudsen, "Are We Born Vengeful?" (27 July 2015), http://greatergood.berkeley.edu/article/item/are_we_born_vengeful/.

30. Association for Psychological Science, "Brain Can Be Trained in Compassion, Study Shows," *ScienceDaily* (22 May 2013), http://www.sciencedaily.com/releases/ 2013/05/130522160352.htm/.

31. See http://www.charterforcompassion.org/.

32. R. Brown, & M. Hewstone, "An Integrative Theory of Intergroup Contact," in *Advances in Experimental Social Psychology*, Vol. 37, ed. M.P. Zanna, 255–343 (San Diego, CA: Elsevier Academic Press, 2005); Cell Press, "Racial Bias Clouds Ability to Feel Others' Pain, Study Shows," *ScienceDaily* (27 May 2010), http://www.sciencedaily.com/releases/2010/05/10052 7122141.htm/.

33. See http://www.goodnewsagency.org/en/newsletter.php?gclid=CO ecw-XKusgCFUxufgodhXgC7g/.

34. M. MacKenzie, K. Vohs, & R. Baumeister, "You Didn't Have to Do That: Belief in Free Will Promotes Gratitude," *Personality and Social Psychology Bulletin* 40, no. 11 (2014): 1423-1434.

35. T. DeAngelis, "A New Way to Combat Prejudice," *APA Monitor on Psychology* 42, no. 9 (2011): 40.

36. Association for Psychological Science, "People Confront Prejudice Only When They Believe Others' Personalities Can Change, Study Finds," *ScienceDaily* (28 July 2010), http:// www.science daily.com/releases/2010/07/100728121335.htm/.

37. Association for Psychological Science, "Why Few People Are Devoid of Racial Bias," *ScienceDaily* (26 September 2007), http://www.sciencedaily.com/releases/2007/09/ 07092412281 4.htm/.

38. S. Clement, "Millennials Are Just About as Racist as Their Parents," *Washington Post* (7 April 2015), http://www.washingtonpost.com/news/wonkblog/wp/2015/04/07/white-millennials-are-just-about-as-racist-as-their-parents/.

39. See http://www.rootsofempathy.org/en.html/.

40. M. Spinelli, "High School Football Players 'Pay It For-ward,' Start Chain Reaction at Michigan Restaurant," *ABC News* (9 October 2015), http://abcnews.go.com/US/high-school-football-players-pay-forward- start-chain/story?id= 34344232/.

41. See http://www.nonhumanrightsproject.org/about-us-2/.

42. Elsevier, "Shhh…To Make Ocean Conservation Work We Should Keep the Noise Down: Quiet Marine Zones Would Support Ecological Research, Says New Study," *ScienceDaily* (8 October 2015), http://www.sciencedaily.com/releases/2015/ 10/151008101436.htm/.

43. A. Rattan & N. Ambad, "How 'It Gets Better': Effectively Communicating Support to Targets of Prejudice," *Personality and Social Psychology Bulletin* 40, no. 5 (2014): 1-12.

44. H. Ryan, "Former Saint Mary's Student Returns Degrees," *Metro News* (18 September 2013), 8.

45. M. Rowe, "Micro-Affirmations and Micro-Inequities," *Journal of the International Ombudsman Association* 1, no. 1, (2008), http://ombud. mit.edu/sites/default/files/documents/micro-affirm-ineq.pdf/.

Appendix A: Gendered Language

1. R. Lakoff, *Language and Women's Place* (New York: Harper & Row, 1975).

2. D.G. MacKay, "Language, Thought and Social Attitudes," in *Language: Social Psychological Perspectives*, ed. H. Giles, 89-96 (New York: Pergamon Press, 1980).

3. B. Whorf, *Language, Thought, and Reality* (Cambridge, MA: MIT Press, 1956).

4. J. Briere & C. Lanktree, "Sex-Role Related Effects of Language," *Sex Roles* 9, no. 5 (1983): 625-632.

5. Some of the research includes J. Gastil, "Generic Pronouns and Sexist Language: The Oxymoronic Character of Masculine Generics," *Sex Roles* 23, no. 11/12 (1990): 629-643; V.A. Kidd, "A Study of the Images Produced Through the Use of a Male Pronoun as the Generic," *Movements: Contemporary Rhetoric and Communication* 1 (1971): 25-30; D.G. MacKay & D.C. Fulkerson, "On the Comprehension and Production of Pronouns," *Journal of Verbal Learning and Verbal Behavior* 18 (1979): 661-673; W. Martyna, "What Does 'He' Mean?" *Journal of Communication* 238 (1978): 131-138; J. Schneider & S. Hacker, "Sex-Role Imagery and Use of the Generic 'Man' in Introductory Texts: A Case in the Sociology of Sociology," *The American Sociologist* 8 (1973): 12-18.

6. J. Sniezek & C. Jazwinski, "Gender Bias in English: In Search of Fair Language," *Journal of Applied Social Psychology* 16, no. 7 (1986): 642-662.

7. J. Silveira, "Generic Masculine Words and Thinking," *Women's Studies International Quarterly* 3, no. 2/3 (1980): 165-178.

8. D. Spender, *Man Made Language* (London: Routledge & Kegan, 1980); W. Martyna, "Beyond the 'He/Man' Approach: The Case for Non-sexist Language," *Signs* 5, no. 3 (1980): 482-493.

9. J.S. Hyde, "Children's Understanding of Sexist Language," *Develop mental Psychology* 20, no. 4 (1984): 697-706.

10. J. Moulton, "The Myth of the Neutral 'Man'," in *Sexist Language: A Modern Philosophical Analysis*, ed. M. Vetterling-Braggin, 100-116 (New York: Littlefield Adams, 1981).

11. C. Miller & K. Swift, *Words and Women* (Garden City, NY: Anchor Press/Doubleday, 1976).

12. Some of the research includes S. Bem & D. Bem, "Does Sex-Biased Job Advertising 'Aid and Abet' Sex Discrimination?" *Journal of Applied Social Psychology* 3 (1973): 6-18; J. Briere & C. Lanktree, "Sex-Role Related Effects of Sex Bias in Language," *Sex Roles* 9 (1983): 625-632; P.K. Chew & L.K. Kelley-Chew, "Subtly Sexist Language," *Pitt Law Legal Studies Research Paper Series, Working Paper No. 2008-30*, October 2008 (downloadable from http://ssrn.com/ abstract=1285570); L. Brooks, "Sexist Language in Occupational Information: Does It Make a Difference?" *Journal of Vocational Behavior* 23 (1983): 227-232; A. Stericker, "Does This 'He or She' Business Really Make a Difference? The Effect of Masculine Pronouns as Generics on Job Attitudes," *Sex Roles* 7 (1981): 637-641.

13. Sniezek & Jazwinski, 1986, op.cit.

14. W. Martyna, "Beyond the 'He/Man' Approach: The Case for Nonsexist Language," in *Language, Gender, and Society*, ed. B. Thorne, C. Kramarae, & N. Henley (Rowley, MA: Newbury House, 1983), 137.

15. M. Thomae & G.T. Viki, "Why Did the Woman Cross the Road? The Effect of Sexist Humor on Men's Rape Proclivity," *Journal of Social, Evolutionary, and Cultural Psychology* 7, no. 3 (2013): 250-269.

16. J.K. Swim & L.L. Hyers, "Excuse Me—What Did You Just Say?! Women's Public and Private Response to Sexist Remarks," *Journal of Experimental Social Psychology* 35, no. 1 (1999): 68-88.

Appendix B: Research

1. M. Balluch, "Personhood Trial for Chimpanzee Matthew Pan" (2008), http://www.vgt.at/publikationen/texte/artikel/20080118 Hiasl.htm

2. See the 2001 Amsterdam Declaration on Global Change, signed by 1,500 scientists from over 100 countries, http://www.essp.org/index.php?id=41/.

3. C.L. Madden, "Laws Gone Wild in Ecuador: Indigenous People and Ecosystems Gain Rights," *Policy Innovations*, 2 (October 2008), http://www.policyinnovations.org/ideas/briefings/data/000077/.

4. C. Jamasmie, "New Bolivian Law Poses Serious Challenges for Mining Companies," *Mining.com* (29 October 2012), http://www.mining.com/new-bolivian-law-poises-serious-challenges-for-mining-companies-34199/.

5. See the Universal Declaration of the Rights of Mother Earth introduced at the United Nations in April 2010, http://climateandcapitalism.com/2010/04/27/universal-declaration-of-the-rights-of-mother-earth/; T. Deen, "Global Campaign to Bestow Legal Rights on Mother Earth" (24 May 2011), https://www.commondreams.org/headline/2011/05/24-7/.

6. See http://eradicatingecocide.com/2012/08/14/un-ecocide-was-the-5th-crime-against-peace/.

7. J. Jowit, "British Campaigner Urges UN to Accept 'Ecocide' as International Crime," *The Guardian* (9 April 2010), http://www.guardian.co.uk/environment/2010/apr/09/ecocide-crime-genocide-un-environmental-damage/; P. Higgins, "Ecocide Was to Be the 5th Crime Against Peace," *Common Ground* (August 2011), http://commonground.ca/2012/08/ecocide-crime-against-peace/.

8. "New Zealand's Whanganui River Gets Personhood Status," *Environmental News Service* (13 September 2012), http://ens-newswire.com/2012/09/13/new-zealands-whanganui-river-gets-personhood-status/; K. Shuttle worth, "Agreement Entitles Whanganui River to Legal Identity," *The New Zealand Herald* (30 August 2012).

9. C. Siebert, "Animals Like Us," *Popular Science* (January 2015): 52-55.

10. J. Dunayer, "The Rights of Sentient Beings: Moving Beyond Old and New Speciesism," in *The Politics of Species: Reshaping Our Relationships with Other Animals*, ed. R. Corbey & A. Lanjouw, 27-39 (Cambridge: Cambridge University Press, 2013).

11. D. Reiss & L. Marino, "Mirror Self-Recognition in the Bottlenose Dolphin: A Case of Cognitive Convergence," *PNAS* 98 (2001): 5937-5942.

12. T. Regan, *The Case for Animal Rights* (Berkeley: University of California Press, 1983).

13. L. Marino, R.C. Connor, R.E. Fordyce, L.M. Herman, P.R. Hof, L. Lefebvre, D. Lusseau, B. McCowan, E.A. Nimchinsky, A.A. Pack, L. Rendell, J.S. Reidenberg, D. Reiss, M.D. Uhen, E. Van der Gucht, & H.

Whitehead, "Cetaceans Have Complex Brains for Complex Cognition," *PLoS: Biology* 5, no. 5 (2007), http://journals.plos.org/plosbiology/article?id=10.1371/jour nal.pbio.0050139/.

14. M.J. Beran, J.D. Smith, & B.M. Perdu, "Language-Trained Chimpanzees (Pan Troglodytes) Name What They Have Seen But Look First at What They Have Not Seen," *Psychological Science* 24, no. 5 (2013): 660-666.

15. R. Corbey & A. Lanjouw (eds.), *The Politics of Species: Reshaping Our Relationships with Other Animals* (Cambridge: Cambridge University Press, 2013).

16. Florida Atlantic University, "Just Like Humans, Dolphins Have Complex Social Networks," *ScienceDaily* (5 May 2015), http://www.sciencedaily.com/releases/2015/05/15050509 80 7.htm/.

17. L. Marino, "Humans, Dolphins, and Moral Inclusivity," in *The Politics of Species: Reshaping Our Relationships with Other Animals*, ed. R. Corbey & A. Lanjouw, 95-105 (Cambridge: Cambridge University Press, 2013).

18. M. Bekoff, "Whales and Dolphins at Play: A Great Lift That Will Make Your Day," *Psychology Today* (12 January 2012), http://www.psychologytoday.com/blog/animal-emotions/ 201201/whales-and-dolphins-play-great-lift-thatll-make-your-day/.

19. M. Bekoff, "Humpback Whales Protect a Gray Whale from Killer Whales," *Psychology Today* (8 May 2012), http://www.psychology today.com/blog/animal-emotions/201205/humpback-whales-pro tect-gray-whale-killer-whales/.

20. P.R. Hof, R. Chanis, & L. Marino, "Cortical Complexity in Cetacean Brains," *The Anatomical Record* 287 (2005): 1142–1152.

21. L. Marino, "Cetacean Brain Evolution: Multiplication Generates Complexity," *International Journal of Comparative Psychology* 17 (2004): 1-16.

22. D. Reiss & L. Marino, "Mirror Self-Recognition in the Bottlenose Dolphin: A Case of Cognitive Convergence," *PNAS* 98: (2001): 5937-5942.

23. Emory University, "Dolphin Cognitive Abilities Raise Ethical Questions, Says Emory Neuroscientist," *Science Daily*, (27 Feb. 2010), http://www.sciencedaily.com/releases/2010/02/1002 18173112.htm

24. J. Owen, "Dolphin Moms Teach Daughters to Use Tools," *National Geographic* (7 June 2005), http://news.nationalgeographic.com/news/2005/06/0607_050607_dolphin_tools.html/.

25. C. Dillow, "Early-Adopting Dolphin Uses iPad Touchscreen to Communicate with Humans," *Popular Science* (2 June 2010), http://www.popsci.com/science/article/2010-06/early-adopting-dolphin-uses-ipad-touchscreen-communicate-humans/; J. Foer, "It's Time for a Conversation: Breaking the Communication Barrier Between Dolphins and Humans," *National Geographic* (May 2015), http://ngm.nationalgeographic.com/2015/05/dolphin-intelligence/foer-text/.

26. A. Coghlan, "Whales Boast the Brain Cells That 'Make Us Human'," *New Scientist* (27 November 2006).

27. J.J. Lee, "Sperm Whales Language Reveals Hints of Culture," *National Geographic* (8 September 2015), http://news. nationalgeographic.com/2015/09/150908-sperm-whale-culture-vocalizations-animals-oceans-galapagos-science/.

28. Oregon State University, "Solomon Islands Dolphin Hunts Cast Spotlight on Small Cetacean Survival," *ScienceDaily* (6 May 2015), http://www.sciencedaily.com/releases/2015/05/150506164242.htm/.

29. "Whales Are People, Too: A Declaration of the Rights of Cetaceans," *Economist* (25 February 2012).

30. See the *Declaration of the Rights of Cetaceans: Whales and Dolphins*, agreed in Helsinki on 22 May 2010 (http:// www.cetaceanrights.org).

31. P. Aldhous, "Elephants See Themselves in the Mirror," *New Scientist* (30 Oct 2006), http://www.newscientist.com/article/dn10402-elephants-see-themselves-in-the-mirror.html/.

32. L. Gruen, "The Moral Status of Animals," in *The Stanford Encyclopedia of Philosophy*, ed. E. N. Zalta (2012), http://plato.stanford.edu/archives/win2012/entries/moral-animal/.

33. R. Kerby, "Wild Elephants Gather Inexplicably, Mourn Death of 'Elephant Whisperer'," *Beliefnet* (2012), http://www.beliefnet.com/Inspiration/Home-Page-News-and-Views/Wild-Elephants-Mourn-Death-of-famed-Elephant-Whisperer.aspx?p=1/.

34. "Elephant Personalities Revealed by Scientists," *The Telegraph* (19 November 2012), http://www.telegraph.co.uk/earth/wildlife/9638340/Elephant-personalities-revealed-by-scientists.html/; P.C. Lee & C.J. Moss, "Wild Female African Elephants (Loxodonta Africana) Exhibit Personality Traits of Leadership and Social Integration," *Journal of Comparative Psychology* 126, no. 3 (August 2012): 224-232.

35. Cell Press, "Chimpanzees and Orangutans Remember Distant Past Events," *ScienceDaily* (18 July 2013), http://www.sciencedaily.com/releases/2013/07/130718130613.htm/.

36. Cell Press, "Apes Know a Good Thriller When They See One," *ScienceDaily* (17 September 2015), http://www.sciencedaily.com/releases/2015/09/150917134634.htm/.

37. F. de Waal, "The Brains of the Animal Kingdom," *The Wall Street Journal* (22 March 2013), http://online.wsj.com/news/articles/SB10001424127887323869604578370574285382756/.

38. Gruen, 2012, op.cit.

39. M. Walker, "Movie Made by Chimpanzees to Be Broadcast," *BBC Earth News* (25 January 2010), http://news.bbc.co.uk/earth/hi/earth_news/newsid_8472000/8472831.stm/.

40. S. Anthony, "Orangutans to Skype Between Zoos with iPads," *ExtremeTech* (30 December 2011), http://www.extreme tech.com/extreme/111143-orangutans-to-skype-between-zoos-with-ipads/; R. Boyle, "FaceTime for Apes: Orangutans Use iPads to Video Chat With Friends In Other Zoos," *Popular Science* (3 January 2012), http://www.popsci.com/gadgets/article/2012-01/facetime-apes-zoo-orangutans-will-video-chat-using-ipads/; K. Fernandez-Blance, "Toronto Zoo Orangutans Go Ape for iPad," *The Star* (23 August 2012), http://www.thestar.com/news/gta/2012/08/23/toronto_zoo_orangutans_go_ape_for_ipad.html/.

41. B. Henry, "Monkeys Connect to the Digital Age at Lake Superior Zoo," *nncnow.com* (13 February 2015), http://www.northlandsnewscenter.com/news/local/Monkeys-at-Lake-Superior-Zoo-use-iPad-Face-time-291921061.html/.

42. T. Leonard, "He Can Cook, Play Music, Use a Computer - and Make Sarcastic Jokes Chatting with His 3,000-Word Vocabulary: My Lunch with the World's Cleverest Chimp (Who Skyped Me Later for Another Chat)," *Daily Mail* (6 June 2014), http://www.dailymail.co.uk/news/article-2651004/He-cook-play-music-use-computer-make-sarcastic-jokes-chatting-3-000-word-vocabulary-My-lunch-worlds-cleverest-chimp.html/.

43. H. Yan, "PETA Suit Claims Money Holds Copyright to Famous Selfie," *CNN* (23 September 2015), http://www.cnn.com/2015/09/23/world/monkey-selfie-peta-lawsuit/.

44. See the World Declaration on Great Primates at http://www.great apeproject.org/en-US/oprojetogap/Declaracao/declaracao-mundial-dos-grandes-primatas/.

45. Swiss Federal Ethics Committee for Non-Human Biotechnology, *The Dignity of Animals* (February 2001) http://www.ekah.admin.ch/fileadmin/ekah-dateien/dokumentation/publikationen/EKAH_Wu erde_des_Tieres_10.08_e_EV3.pdf); L. Hickman, "The Lawyer Who Defends Animals," *The Guardian*, (05 March 2010), http://www.guardian.co.uk/world/2010/mar/05/lawyer who defends animals/; "Life Looks Up for Swiss Animals," *Swiss info.ch* (23 April 2008), http://www.swiss info.ch/eng/Home/Archive/Life_looks_up_for_Swiss_animals.html? cid=6608378/.

46. C. Dell'Amore, "Black Bears Can 'Count' as Well as Primates," *National Geographic Daily News* (29 August 2012), http://news.national geographic.com/news/2012/08/120829-black-bears-cognition-ani mals-science/.

47. "Artic Bears: Bear Intelligence," *Nature* (10 June 2008), http://www.pbs.org/wnet/nature/arctic-bears-bear-intelligence/ 779/.

48. See the summary of research in A. Lamey, "Primitive Self-Consciousness and Avian Cognition," *The Monist* 95, no. 3 (2012): 486-510.

49. A. Motluk, "Mirror Test Shows Magpies Aren't So Bird-Brained," *New Scientist* (19 Aug 2008), http://www.newscientist.com/article/dn14552-mirror-test-shows-magpies-arent-so-birdbrained.html?DCMP=ILC-hmts&nsref=news4_ head_dn14552/.

50. P. Rincon, "Crows and Jays Top Bird IQ Scale," *BBC News* (22 February 2005), http://news.bbc.co.uk/2/hi/sci/tech/428696 5.stm/.

51. "Crows Are as Intelligent as CHILDREN: Study Reveals Birds Are as Clever as a Seven-Year-Old Human," *Daily Mail* (26 March 2014), http://www.dailymail.co.uk/sciencetech/article-2590046/Crows-intelligent-CHILDREN-Study-reveals-birds-intelligence-seven-year-old.html/.

52. L. Greenemeier, "The Secret Lives of Tool-Wielding Crows," *Scientific American* (4 October 2007), http://www. scientificamerican.com/article/the-secret-lives-of-tool/.

53. L. Castro & E. Wasserman, "Crows Understand Analogies," *Scientific American* (10 February 2015), http://www.scientificamerican.com/article/crows-understand-analogies/.

54. R. McKie, "Clever Raven Proves That It's Not Birdbrain," *The Guardian* (29 April 2007), http://www.theguardian.com/science/2007/apr/29/theobserversuknewspages.uknews1/.

55. A.A. Smirnova, O.F. Lazareva, & Z.A. Zorina, "Use of Numbers by Crows: Investigation by Matching and Oddity Learning," *Journal of Experimental Analysis of Behaviour* 73 (2000): 163–176.

56. L. Watson, "Who's a Clever Boy Then! Parrot Shown to Have Same Intelligence Level as Four-Year-Old Child," *Daily Mail* (13 March 2013); I.M. Pepperberg, "Grey Parrot Numerical Competence: A Review," *Animal Cognition* 9, no. 4 (2006): 377–391.

57. Pepperberg, 2006, Ibid.

58. U. Khan, "Pigeons 'Intelligence' Compared to a Three-Year-Old Child," *The Telegraph* (13 June 2008), http://www.telegraph.co.uk/news/newstopics/howaboutthat/2125306/Pigeons-intelligence-compared-to-a-three-year-old-child.html/.

59. S. Agnew, "Pigeons Are Smarter Than You'd Think," *Futurity* (16 February 2015), http://www.futurity.org/pigeons-intelligence-856552/.

60. F. MacRae, "Can Chickens REALLY Be Cleverer Than a Toddler? Students Suggest Animals Can Master Numeracy and Basic Engineering," *Daily Mail* (18 June 2013), http://www.dailymail.co.uk/sciencetech/article-234419 8/Chickens-smarter-human-toddlers-Studies-suggest-animals-master-numeracy-basic-engineering.html/.

61. R. Grillo, "Chicken Behavior: An Overview of Recent Science," *freefromharm.org* (7 February 2014), http://freefromharm.org/ chicken-behavior-an-overview-of-recent-science/.

62. B. Friedrich, "The Cruelest of All Factor Farm Products: Eggs from Caged Hens," *Huffington Post* (14 January 2013), http://www.huffingtonpost.com/bruce-friedrich/eggs-from-caged-hens_b_2458525.html/.

63. Forschungsverbund Berlin e.V. (FVB), "Do Fish Feel Pain? Not as Humans Do, Study Suggests," *ScienceDaily* (8 August 2013), http://www.sciencedaily.com/releases/2013/08/130808123 719.htm/.

64. ARC Centre of Excellence in Coral Reef Studies, "I've Got Your Back: Fish Really Do Look After Their Mates," *ScienceDaily* (25 September 2015), http://www.sciencedaily.com/releases/2015/09/15092508 5344.htm/.

65. M. Bekoff, "Who Lives, Who Dies, and Why? How Speciesism Undermines Compassionate Conservation and Social Justice," in *The*

Politics of Species: Reshaping Our Relationships with Other Animals, ed. R. Corbey and A. Lanjouw, 15-26 (Cambridge: Cambridge University Press, 2013).

66. S. Griffiths, "Is This Why Grey Squirrels Are So Common? Hidden Hazelnut Puzzle Reveals Intelligence and Adaptability of Crafty Rodents," *Daily Mail* (6 July 2015), http://www.dailymail.co.uk/sciencetech/article-3151182/Is-grey-squirrels-common-Hidden-hazel nut-puzzle-reveals-intelligence-adapt ability-crafty-rodents.html/.

67. J. Viegas, "IQ Test Suggest Pigs Are Smart as Dogs, Chimps," *News Discovery* (11 June 2015), http://news. discovery. com/animals/iq-tests-suggest-pigs-are-smart-as-dogs-chimps-150611.htm/.

68. "Prairie Dogs' Language Decoded by Scientists," *CBC News* (21 June 2013), http://www.cbc.ca/news/technology/prairie-dogs-language-decoded-by-scientists-1.132 2230/.

69. University of Maryland Center for Environmental Science, "Prairie Dogs Disperse When All Close Kin Have Dis-appeared," *ScienceDaily* (7 March 2013), http://www. science daily.com/releases/2013/03/130307145444.htm/.

70. F. De Waal, "The Brains of the Animal Kingdom," *The Wall Street Journal* (22 March 2013), http://online.wsj.com/news/articles/SB10001424127887323869604578370574285382756; S. Killingsworth, "Why Not Eat Octopus?" *The New Yorker* (3 October 2014), http://www.newyorker.com/tech/elements/eating-octopus/.

71. S. Montgomery, *The Soul of an Octopus: A Surprising Exploration into the Wonder of Consciousness* (New York: Artia Books/Simon & Schuster, 2015).

72. D.M. Braun, "The Slightly Disturbing Science of Squid," *National Geographic* (12 April 2011), http://voices.national geographic. com/2011/04/12/squid-octopus-ceph alopod-facts-video/.

73. J. Dunayer, "The Rights of Sentient Beings: Moving Beyond Old and New Speciesism," in *The Politics of Species: Reshaping Our Relationships with Other Animals*, ed. R. Corbey & A. Lanjouw, 27-39 (Cambridge: Cambridge University Press, 2013).

74. B. Switek, "Debate Continues: Did Your Seafood Feel Pain?" *National Geographic* (4 February 2013), http://news.nationalgeographic. com/news/2013/13/130208-seafood-pain-debate-crabs-fish-science/.

75. M. Lihoreau, L. Chittka, & N.E. Raine, "Travel Optimization by Foraging Bumblebees Through Readjustments of Traplines After

Discovery of New Feeding Locations," *The American Naturalist* 176, no. 6 (2010): 744-757.

76. Swiss Federal Ethics Committee for Non-Human Biotechnology, *The Dignity of Living Beings with Regard to Plants: Moral Consideration of Plants for Their Own Sake* (April 2008), http://www.ekah.admin.ch/en/documentation/publications/index.html); C.K. Yoon, "Loyal to Its Roots," *The New York Times* (10 June 2008); Research at the International Laboratory of Plant Neurobiology (LINV) in Italy; N. Martinelli, "Smarty Plants: Inside the World's Only Plant-Intelligence Lab," *The New Yorker* (30 October 2007); F. Koechlin, "The Dignity of Plants," *Plant Signaling & Behavior* 4, no. 1 (2009): 78-79; J. Christmas, "Plants Recognize Their Siblings, Biologists Discover," *Daily News*, http://dailynews.mcmasters.ca/article/plants-recognize-their-siblings-biologists-discover/.

77. Helmholtz Centre For Environmental Research-UFZ, "Complex Plant Behavior? In Fight Against Parasites, Barberry Sacrifices Seeds Depending on Survival Chance," *ScienceDaily* (4 March 2014), http://www.sciencedaily.com/releases/2014/03/140304071204.htm/.

78. Plataforma SINC, "Plasticity of Plants Helps Them Adapt to Climate Change," *ScienceDaily* (17 March 2011), http://www.sciencedaily.com/releases/2011/03/110316084909.htm/.

79. Penn State, "Plant Sniffs Out Danger to Prepare Defenses Against Pesky Insect," *ScienceDaily* (17 December 2012), http://www.sciencedaily.com/releases/2012/12/121217140747.htm/.

80. Wageningen University and Research Centre, "Plants Cry for Help When an Attack Can Be Expected," *ScienceDaily* (6 September 2012), http://www.sciencedaily.com/releases/2012/09/120906084306.htm/

81. Salk Institute, "How Plants Grow to Escape Shade: Findings Could Lead to High-Yield Crops," *ScienceDaily* (16 April 2012), http://www.sciencedaily.com/releases/2012/04/120416101030.htm/.

82. Swiss Federal Ethics Committee for Non-Human Biotechnology, *The Dignity of Living Beings with Regard to Plants,* op.cit.

83. M. Margil & B. Price, "Pittsburgh Bans Natural Gas Drilling," *Yes! Magazine* (16 November 2010), http://www.yesmagazine.org/people-power/pittsburgh-bans-natural-gas-drilling); A. Goodman with D. Moynihan, "Get the Frack Out of Our Water: Shale-Shocked Citizens Fight Back," *Democracy Now!* (20 September 2012), http://www.democracynow.org/blog/2012/9/20/shale_shocked_citizens_fight_back/.

84. S.M. Wise, "Nonhuman Rights to Personhood," *Pace Environmental Law Review* 30, no. 3 (2013): 1278-1290.

References

Anderson, Kristin J. *Benign Bigotry: The Psychology of Subtle Prejudice.* Cambridge: Cambridge University Press, 2010.

_____. *Modern Misogyny: Anti-Feminism in a Post-Feminist Era.* New York: Oxford University Press, 2015.

Baird, Robert M. and Stuart E. Rosenbaum (eds). *Hatred, Bigotry, and Prejudice: Definitions, Causes, and Solutions.* Amherst: Prometheus Books, 1999.

Banaji, Mahzarin R. and Anthony G. Greenwald. *Blindspot: Hidden Biases of Good People.* New York: Delecorte Press, 2013.

Beattie, Geoffrey. *Our Racist Heart: An Exploration of Unconscious Prejudice in Everyday Life.* New York: Routledge, 2013.

Boteach, Shmuley. *Hating Women: America's Hostile Campaign Against the Fairer Sex.* New York: HarperCollins, 2005.

Bronner, Stephen Eric, *The Bigot: Why Prejudice Persists.* New Haven: Yale University Press, 2004.

Corbey, Raymond and Annette Lanjouw (eds.). *The Politics of Species: Reshaping Our Relationships with Other Animals.* Cambridge: Cambridge University Press, 2013.

DeConick, April D. *Holy Misogyny: Why the Sex and Gender Conflicts in the Early Church Still Matter.* New York: Continuum, 2011.

Dixon, John and Mark Levine (eds.). *Beyond Prejudice: Extending the Social Psychology of Conflict, Inequality and Social Change.* Cambridge: Cambridge University Press, 2012.

Doidge, Norman. *The Brain That Changes Itself.* New York: Penguin Books, 2007.

Douglas, Susan J. *Enlightened Sexism: The Seductive Message That Feminism's Work Is Done*. New York: Times Books, 2010

Dovidio, John, Peter Glick, and Laurie Rudman. *On the Nature of Prejudice*. Malden: Blackwell Publishing, 2005.

Dworkin, Andrea. *Pornography: Men Possessing Women*. New York: Dutton, 1989.

Eisler, Riane T. *The Chalice and the Blade: Our History, Our Future*. New York: Harper & Row, 1989.

Gervais, Sarah J. (ed.). *Objectification and (De)Humanization: 60th Nebraska Symposium on Motivation*. New York: Springer, 2013.

Gilligan, Carol. *In a Different Voice: Psychological Theory and Women's Development*. Cambridge, MA: Harvard University Press, 1982.

Gladwell, Malcolm. *Blink: The Power of Thinking Without Thinking*. New York: Little, Brown and Company, 2005.

Gullette, Margaret M. *Agewise: Fighting the New Ageism in America*. Chicago: University of Chicago Press, 2011

Henley, Nancy M. *Body Politics: Power, Sex, and Nonverbal Communication*. Englewood Cliffs: Prentice-Hall, 1977.

Heyd, Thomas (ed.). *Recognizing the Autonomy of Nature*. New York: Columbia University Press, 2005.

Holland, Jack. *Misogyny: The World's Oldest Prejudice*. New York: Carroll & Graf, 2006.

Hooks, Bell. *Feminism Is for Everybody: Passionate Politics*. Cambridge, MA: South End Press, 2000.

Hüther, Gerald. *The Compassionate Brain: How Empathy Creates Intelligence*. Boston: Shambhala Publications, 2006.

Joshi, Sunand T. (ed.). *In Her Place: A Documentary History of Prejudice Against Women*. Amhearst: Prometheus Books, 2006.

Kang, Jerry. *Implicit Bias: A Primer*. National Center for State Courts, August 2009.

Kantor, Martin. *Homophobia: The State of Sexual Bigotry Today*. Westport: Praeger, 2009.

Laszlo, Ervin. *Quantum Shift in the Global Brain: How the New Scientific Reality Can Change Us and Our World*. Rochester: Inner Traditions, 2008.

Lehrer, Jonah. *How We Decide*. New York: Houghton Mifflin Harcourt, 2009.

Lipton, Bruce. *The Biology of Belief: Unleashing the Power of Consciousness, Matter, & Miracles*. Santa Rosa, CA: Mountain of Love, 2005.

Lipton, Bruce, and Steve Bhaerman, *Spontaneous Evolution: Our Positive Future*. Hay House: 2009.

Lovelock, James. *The Ages of Gaia: A Biography of Our Living Earth*. New York: Norton, 1988.

MacKinnon, Catharine A. *Only Words*. Cambridge: Harvard University Press, 1993.

Mamet, David. *The Wicked Son: Anti-Semitism, Self-Hatred, and the Jews*. New York: Schocken Books, 2006

Marsh, Jason, Rodolfo Mendoza-Denton, and Jeremy A. Smith, *Are We Born Racist? New Insights from Neuroscience and Positive Psychology*. Boston: Beacon Press, 2010.

Margulis, Lynn. *The Symbiotic Planet: A New Look at Evolution*. London: Phoenix, 1998.

Margulis, Lynn and Dorion Sagan. *Microcosmos: Four Billion Years of Microbial Evolution*. Berkely: University of California Press, 1997.

Miles, Rosalind. *Who Cooked the Last Supper? The Women's History of the World*. New York: Three Rivers Press, 2001.

Nelson, Todd D. (ed). *Ageism: Stereotyping and Prejudice Against Older People*. Cambridge: MIT Press, 2004

Olweean, Steve S. "Psychological Concepts of 'The Other': Embracing the Compass of the Self," 113-128. In Chris E. Stout (ed.) *The Psychology of Terrorism: A Public Understanding*, Greenwood, 2002.

Pert, Candace. *Molecules of Emotion: The Science Behind Mind-Body Medicine*. New York: Scribner, 1997.

Plous, Scott (ed.). *Understanding Prejudice and Discrimination*. New York: McGraw-Hill, 2003.

Plumwood, Val. *Feminism and the Mastery of Nature*. London: Routledge, 1993.

_____. *Environmental Culture: The Ecological Crisis of Reason*. London: Routledge, 2002.

_____. "Toward a Progressive Naturalism." In *Recognizing the Autonomy of Nature*, edited by Thomas J. Heyd, 25-53. New York: Columbia University Press, 2005.

Riddle, Dorothy I. *Service-Led Growth: The Role of the Service Sector in World Development*. New York: Praeger, 1986.

_____. *Positive Harmlessness in Practice*. Bloomington: AuthorHouse, 2010.

_____. *Principles of Abundance for the Cosmic Citizen*. Bloomington: AuthorHouse, 2010.

Sternberg, Robert J. (ed.). *The Psychology of Hate*. Washington, DC: American Psychological Association, 2005.

Swimme, Brian. *The Hidden Heart of the Cosmos: Humanity and the New Story*. Maryknoll, NY: Orbis Books, 1996.

Talbot, Michael, *The Holographic Universe*. New York: Harper Perenniel, 1991.

Walby, Sylvia. *The Future of Feminism*. Cambridge: Polity Press, 2011.

Waring, Marilyn. *If Women Counted: A New Feminist Economics*. San Francisco: Harper & Row, 1988.

Watts, Charlotte and Cathy Zimmerman, "Violence Against Women: Global Scope and Magnitude," Lancet 359 (2002): 1232-1237.

Wise, Steven M. *Drawing the Line: Science and the Case for Animal Rights* New York: Basic Books, 2003.

Index

List of Exercises

Printed in the United States
By Bookmasters